Amateur Media

The rise of Web 2.0 has pushed the amateur to the forefront of public discourse, public policy and media scholarship. Typically non-salaried, non-specialist and untrained in media production, amateur producers are now seen as key drivers of the creative economy. But how do the activities of citizen journalists, fan fiction writers and bedroom musicians connect with longer traditions of extra-institutional media production?

This edited collection provides a much-needed interdisciplinary contextualisation of amateur media before and after Web 2.0. Surveying the institutional, economic and legal construction of the amateur media producer via a series of case studies, it features contributions from experts in the fields of law, economics and media studies. Each section of the book contains a detailed case study on a selected topic, followed by two further pieces providing additional analysis and commentary. Using an extraordinary array of case studies and examples, from YouTube to online games, from subtitling communities to reality TV, the book is neither a celebration of amateur production nor a denunciation of the demise of professional media industries. Rather, this book presents a critical dialogue across law and the humanities, exploring the dynamic tensions and interdependencies between amateur and professional creative production. This book will appeal to both academics and students of intellectual property and media law, as well as to scholars and students of economics, media, cultural and internet studies.

Dan Hunter is a Professor of Law and Director of the Institute for Information Law & Policy at New York Law School. He is author of *Oxford Introduction to US Law: Intellectual Property*,(Oxford University Press, 2011).

Ramon Lobato is a postdoctoral fellow with the ARC Centre of Excellence for Creative Industries and Innovation at the Swinburne Institute for Social Research, Swinburne University of Technology, Melbourne. He is the author of *Shadow Economies of Cinema: Mapping Informal Film Distribution*,(British Film Institute/Palgrave, 2012).

Megan Richardson is a Professor of Law and Joint Director of the Centre for Media and Communications Law at the University of Melbourne. She is co-author, with Julian Thomas, of *Fashioning Intellectual Property: Exhibition, Advertising and the Press, 1789–1918*, (Cambridge University Press, 2012).

Julian Thomas is Professor of Media and Communications and Director, Swinburne Institute for Social Research, Swinburne University of Technology, Melbourne. He is co-author, with Megan Richardson, of *Fashioning Intellectual Property: Exhibition, Advertising and the Press, 1789–1918*, (Cambridge University Press, 2012).

Amateur Media

Social, cultural and legal perspectives

Edited by
Dan Hunter, Ramon Lobato,
Megan Richardson and Julian Thomas

Routledge
Taylor & Francis Group

LONDON AND NEW YORK

First published 2012
This version published 2014
by Routledge
2 Park Square, Milton Park, Abingdon, Oxon, OX14 4RN

Simultaneously published in the USA and Canada
by Routledge
711 Third Avenue, New York, NY 10017

Routledge is an imprint of the Taylor & Francis Group, an informa business

British Library Cataloguing in Publication Data
A catalogue record for this book is available from the British Library

Library of Congress Cataloging-in-Publication Data
Amateur media : social, culturual and legal perspectives / edited by Dan Hunter ...
[et al.].
    p. cm.
    Includes bibliographical references.
    1. Social media–Law and legislation. 2. User-generated content. 3. Internet–Law
and legislation. I. Hunter, Dan, 1966-
    K564.C6A835 2012
    302.23'1–dc23
                2011052495

ISBN: 978-0-415-78265-4 (hbk)
ISBN: 978-0-415-70907-1 (pbk)
ISBN: 978-0-203-11202-1 (ebk)

Typeset in Garamond
by Taylor & Francis Books

MIX
Paper from
responsible sources
FSC
www.fsc.org   FSC® C013056

Printed and bound in Great Britain by
TJ International Ltd, Padstow, Cornwall

Contents

Notes on contributors

Lisa Austin is an Associate Professor in the Faculty of Law at the University of Toronto, where she is affiliated with the Centre for Innovation Law and Policy. She holds a bachelor's degree from McMaster, and a law and doctoral degree in philosophy from the University of Toronto. Prior to joining the faculty, she served as law clerk to Mr. Justice Frank Iacobucci of the Supreme Court of Canada, and she was called to the Bar of Ontario in 2006. Her research and teaching interests include privacy law and property law.

Kathy Bowrey is a Professor and formerly Associate Dean – Research (2008–11) in the Faculty of Law at the University of New South Wales, Sydney. She was previously Associate Dean – Research (2006–7) at the Faculty of Law, University of Technology, Sydney. Her expertise primarily relates to intellectual property, media and information technology regulation, reflecting a broad range of interests pertaining to socio-legal history, media and cultural studies and legal theory. She also researches on western laws affecting indigenous cultural and intellectual property.

Jean Burgess is a Senior Research Fellow in the Creative Industries Faculty and Deputy Director of the ARC Centre of Excellence for Creative Industries & Innovation, based at Queensland University of Technology, Brisbane. She is a co-author of the first research monograph on YouTube – *YouTube: Online Video and Participatory Culture* (Polity Press, 2009), also translated into Polish, Portuguese and Italian; and co-editor of *Studying Mobile Media: Cultural Technologies, Mobile Communication, and the iPhone* (Routledge, 2012). Her current research focuses on methodological innovation in the context of the changing media ecology, especially the practical and ethical aspects of the 'computational turn' in media and communication studies.

Melissa de Zwart is an Associate Professor at the Adelaide Law School, the University of Adelaide, and a Member of the Commonwealth Attorney-General's Classification Review Board. Prior to joining academia, she was Legal Manager at CSIRO, advising upon protection and commercialisation of intellectual property. She has provided advice to the EU, UK government and the OECD on legal issues affecting virtual worlds and online games, and was a key contributor to the ENISA report *Virtual Worlds, Real Money: Security and Privacy in Massively-Multiplayer Online Games and Social and Corporate Virtual Worlds*. Her key areas of research interest include copyright, social networking and online communities.

Lawson Fletcher is a postgraduate student at the Institute for Social Research, Swinburne University, Melbourne, whose research centres on the aesthetics and textures of cultural technologies, drawing on media theory, material culture and sound studies. His doctoral thesis examines the domestic afterlives of older media in the context of obsolescence and nostalgia.

Jake Goldenfein is a PhD student at the Melbourne Law School's Centre for Media and Communications Law and works as a research assistant in intellectual property, cyberlaw and media theory at the Melbourne Law School, New York Law School and Swinburne University's Institute for Social Research. His current research explores the relationship between legal and sociological concepts of resistance to surveillance, and law's role in formalising those oppositional ideologies.

Eva Hemmungs Wirtén is a Professor in Library and Information Science (also Associate Professor – 'Docent' in Swedish – in Comparative Litera-ture) at Uppsala University, Sweden. Her research is focused on the history, theory and philosophy of intellectual property and the public domain. She is the author of *No Trespassing: Authorship, Intellectual Property Rights, and the Boundaries of Globalization* (2004) and *Terms of Use: Negotiating the Jungle of the Intellectual Commons* (2008), both University of Toronto Press. In 2011 she published a small volume on translation and copyright entitled *Cosmopolitan Copyright: Law and Language in the Translation Zone* (Uppsala Universitet). Her new book project will be on the intellectual properties of Marie Curie and is funded by HERA (Humanities in the European Research Area).

David Hesmondhalgh is a Professor of Media and Music Industries at the University of Leeds, where he is Head of the Institute of Communications Studies and Director of the Media Industries Research Centre. His books include *Creative Labour: Media Work in Three Cultural Industries* (co-written with Sarah Baker, Routledge, 2011), *The Cultural Industries* (3rd edition, Sage, 2012) and *The Media and Social Theory* (co-edited with Jason Toynbee, Routledge, 2008). He is currently leading a UK Arts and Humanities Research Council-funded project on Cultural Policy in Europe, and writing a book on music.

Steven Hetcher is a Professor at Vanderbilt University Law School, Nashville, Tennessee. His research explores fundamental theoretical issues that arise as courts and scholars attempt to develop a coherent jurisprudence of the emerging information economy. In particular, he focuses on copyright and privacy issues that are increasingly important to individuals as their online presence becomes a dominant part of their daily lives. His recent scholarship has included bottom-up explorations of specific issues, including Facebook's privacy-related practices and the Google Book Settlement, as well as top-down theoretical analyses, such as a defence of the rejection of strict liability in copyright infringement doctrine and the defence of a right of anonymous online participation.

Dan Hunter is a Professor and Director, Institute for Information Law & Policy at New York Law School. He is an expert in internet law, intellectual property, and artificial intelligence and cognitive science models of law. He regularly publishes on issues dealing with the intersection of computers and law, including papers dealing with the regulation of virtual worlds, the use of artificial intelligence in law and high-technology aspects of intellectual property. His research has appeared in journals such as the *California Law Review, Texas Law Review, William & Mary Law Review* and *Journal of Legal Education*. He is the author of *The Oxford Introductions to US Law: Intellectual Property*,(Oxford University Press, 2011).

Greg Lastowka is a Professor of Law at Rutgers School of Law, Camden, New Jersey, and a co-director of the Rutgers Institute for Information Policy & Law. His research focuses primarily on the intersection of intellectual property and new technologies. He has published many book chapters, articles and essays exploring the application of legal doctrines such as copyright, trade mark and computer trespass law to technologies such as search engines, websites, video games and email. He is the author of *Virtual Justice* (Yale University Press, 2010), which explores the legal issues raised by virtual worlds, video games and other forms of social software. The book is available as a free PDF download offered under a Creative Commons licence at http://bit.ly/virtualjustice.

Ramon Lobato is a postdoctoral research fellow with the ARC Centre for Excellence in Creative Industries and Innovation at the Swinburne Institute for Social Research, Melbourne. His research explores the interactions between formal and informal media systems. He is the author of *Shadow Economies of Cinema: Mapping Informal Film Distribution* (British Film Institute/Palgrave, 2012) and essays in *Media International Australia, International Journal of Cultural Studies, Continuum, International Journal of Communication, Camera Obscura* and *New Review of Film and Television Studies*.

Christian McCrea is Program Director for Games at RMIT University, Melbourne. He researches digital histories, aesthetics and audiences, and changing play cultures. Among his published chapters and articles are those on Starcraft and e-sports cultures, horror videogames and the pleasure of difficulty, portable game consoles and Pokémon. His current research project considers the place of game design in the broader changes to the digital content industries, and how formal training in game design is altering the fabric of contemporary culture.

Brian Murchison is the Charles S. Rowe Professor of Law at Washington and Lee School of Law, where he has served as Acting Dean and as Director of the Frances Lewis Law Center, the school's research arm. His under-graduate and law degrees are from Yale University. He has written on the changing nature of First Amendment values, due process in the regulatory state and statutory interpretation. He was co-founder and supervising attorney of a legal clinic representing coal miners in federal disability claims. He teaches torts, mass media law and administrative process.

John Quiggin is an Australian economist and a Professor at the University of Queensland. He has frequently been awarded and recognised for his research, including twice receiving Federation Fellowships from the Aus-tralian Research Council. His most recent book is *Zombie Economics: How Dead Ideas Still Walk Among Us* (Princeton University Press, 2010). He is a Fellow of the Econometric Society and in 2011 received the Distinguished Fellow Award of the Economic Society of Australia. Professor Quiggin writes a blog and is a regular contributor to Crooked Timber. He is a research fellow at the Centre for Policy Development, an Australian public interest think tank.

Megan Richardson is a Professor of Law and Joint Director of the Centre for Media and Communications Law at the University of Melbourne. Primarily an intellectual property and privacy lawyer, she has previously co-edited several collections of essays including (with Andrew Kenyon) *New Dimen-sions in Privacy Law* (Cambridge University Press 2006) and (with Andrew Kenyon and Sam Ricketson) *Landmarks in Australian Intellectual Property Law* (Cambridge University Press, 2009). Her co-authored book with Julian Thomas, *Fashioning Intellectual Property: Exhibition, Advertising and the Press, 1789–1918,*(Cambridge University Press, 2012).

David Tan is an Assistant Professor at the National University of Singapore Law Faculty. He is also a fine-art fashion photographer, having published the coffee-table book *Visions of Beauty* (2000) in association with Versace, and *Tainted Perfection* (2003) in collaboration with Cartier in Singapore. He was formerly with the Singapore Administrative Service, serving as Director of Sports at Ministry of Community Development, Youth & Sports and Director of International Talent at Ministry of Manpower. In the area of law, he has published in a diverse range of journals including the *Cardozo Arts & Entertainment Law Journal, Yale Journal of International Law, Harvard Journal of Sports & Entertainment Law* and *Media & Arts Law Review.*

Julian Thomas is Director of the Swinburne Institute for Social Research, and Professor of Media and Communications at Swinburne University of

Technology, Melbourne. His research interests are in information policy and the history of new communications technologies. His co-authored book with Megan Richardson, *Fashioning Intellectual Property: Exhibition, Advertising and the Press*, (Cambridge University Press, 2012). He is a member of the Consumer Consultative Forum of the Australian Media and Communications Authority, and is a programme leader in the Australian Research Council Centre of Excellence in Creative Industries and Innovation (CCI).

Marc Trabsky is a PhD student at the Melbourne Law School. He teaches in the Melbourne Law School and the School of Social and Political Science at the University of Melbourne. He completed a BA/LLB (Hons) at the University of Melbourne and a MPhil in the Department of Gender and Cultural Studies at the University of Sydney. His articles have been published in *Law in Context* and *Griffith Law Review*.

Kimberlee Weatherall is an Associate Professor at the University of Sydney Law School. She specialises in intellectual property law with particular focus on copyright in a digital context, interdisciplinary empirical research into intellectual property use and enforcement, and the interaction between intellectual property and international law. Her publications include 'Patent Infringement in Australia: Results from a Survey' in *Federal Law Review* (with Beth Webster), 'ACTA as a New Kind of International Law-making' in *American University Journal of International Law* and 'Of Copyright Bureaucracies and Incoherence: Stepping Back from Australia's Recent Copyright Reforms' in *Melbourne University Law Review*.

Preface

Amateur [a. Fr. *Amateur* ad. L. amātōr-em, n. of agent f. amā-re to love]

1. One who loves or is fond *of*; one who has a taste for anything.
2. One who cultivates anything as a pastime, as distinguished from one who prosecutes it professionally; hence, sometimes used disparagingly, as = dabbler, or superficial student or worker.
3. Hence *attrib.* almost *adj.* Done by amateurs.

A New English Dictionary on Historical Principles, 1888[1]

Here, in the *New English Dictionary*, is a familiar division in our thinking about the amateur and their ethos. First, there is the positive sense of an attachment or commitment to a pastime of some kind, without a commercial motivation. Then there is the negative sense of a lack of skill or knowledge. The preparation of the dictionary itself casts another light on the problem. A much-celebrated product of epic scholarship, the *Oxford English Dictionary*, as it became known, was based on the contributions of many thousands of amateur 'readers', who sent in millions of quotations in response to advertisements in libraries and newspapers.[2] Without those amateur contributions, the dictionary would not have been possible. The *OED*, both in its content and in its remarkable production process, introduces some of the themes we explore in this book about amateur media. It illustrates the 'double language' of the amateur – a persistent ambivalence that permeates contemporary media and the scholarship around it. It reminds us how important amateur labour may be in certain creative enterprises and industries; how closely connected the worlds of the amateur and the professional often are; and it suggests how amateur activity can be encouraged and cultivated by professionals through institutional channels.

In the case of the dictionary, the work of the amateur readers was highly organised, structurally separated from the editorial process, and closely controlled: *OED* histories make a clear division between the editorial heroics of the professional lexicographers, and the almost excessive enthusiasm of the amateurs. The status of the professionals and the amateurs seem to be partly defined by the roles of their counterparts on the other side of the divide. In all these things, the *OED* is an instance of a larger pattern, a proximate, unequal and mutually reinforcing relation between the amateur and the professional. Marjorie Garber, a distinguished sociologist of the amateur, wrote that the amateur and the professional 'are always in each other's pockets', and described their endemic rivalry.[3]

Amateur activity, understood as such, has a long history and has stimulated a substantial literature. The work of sociologists such as Garber and Robart Stebbins[4] remains illuminating in helping to define and specify the distinctive features of amateur work, and the reasons why people in market economies are motivated to undertake it. In the field of communications, amateur production has generated attention and interest for many years: in television, with 'funniest home video' programmes; in cinema, with a long tradition of amateur film-making; in publishing, with self-publishing and the disparaged institution of the 'vanity press'.

The spark for this book is a recent phenomenon: the extraordinary profusion and proliferation of amateur media content made possible by the internet. From online video to reference works; from photography to commentary; and from the blogosphere to social media, the domain of what we often now call 'user-generated content' has dramatically expanded in the two decades since the opening of the internet to public use. Alexa's well-known ranking of the world's ten most popular websites does not include any traditional media businesses.[5] It lists the dominant English and Chinese language search engines and web service portals, as we would expect. Alongside those we find YouTube, Wikipedia and Blogspot, and the social media behemoths Facebook and Twitter. These sites are quite different, more so in fact than the search and services portals, but they all incorporate and depend upon amateur content – posts, text entries, photographs, videos, links and comments – to attract their remarkable volumes of user traffic.

Our frameworks for understanding contemporary amateur media and their consequences remain far less well developed than the objects of our interest. This book, therefore, is exploratory. It is not a critique (or a celebration) of amateur media, and it does not denounce the dumbing down of formerly professional domains. We are interested in how we can better understand the remarkable proliferation of amateur producers, both online and in more established media contexts. We wish to contribute to knowledge of the fluid and diverse contemporary relations between amateur media and their commercial and professional contexts and rivals. Because the amateur and professional continue to be in 'each other's pockets', the book is particularly concerned with the volatile and demonstrably productive relationships between amateur work and the commercial and professional internet and media industries. This involves not only mapping points of friction, but also looking more closely at how amateur media are defined and constituted, through law, through cultural practices, and through underlying economic and social relations. We see amateur media as a relational category, shaped through interactions with its various others.

We are interested in experimenting with useful concepts and intriguing problems. The chapters here look at many different examples and kinds of amateur media: online video, reality television, games, music journalism, subtitling communities and bloggers. These instances help us raise larger questions: What historical frameworks are useful for tracing the dynamic interfaces between amateur and professional media? How is amateur content legally, culturally and economically intertwined with the commercial and the institutional? What are the implications of the participatory web ('Web 2.0'), and its burgeoning commercial platforms, for the amateur producers who provide most of their content? How important are ideas of anonymity and privacy in amateur production? Engaging with these questions requires ideas and critique from many disciplines.

The organisation of the book follows from this logic of inquiry and exploration. Each part consists of a longer chapter setting out a particular approach to a problem or a concept. There are then two shorter chapters in response. Some of the responses engage with the longer pieces directly, some by way of an alternative example or perspective.

The chapters grew out of a workshop held at the University of Melbourne in November 2010. We wish to thank all those who took part for their questions and their comments. The project's origins lie in a research project on amateur media funded by the Australian Research Council, and we would like to thank the ARC for making this possible. We wish to acknowledge also the support of the Law School at the University of Melbourne and its Centre for Media and Communications Law, the Swinburne Institute for Social Research and the ARC Centre of Excellence for Creative Industries and Innovation, which supported and encouraged our work in this area. We are also grateful to Katie Carpenter, Commissioning Editor – Law at Routledge, who encouraged us in our plan to produce an experimental book on amateur media, as well as Stephen Gutuirrez who shepherded us through the editing process at Routledge. Finally we thank Alex Heller-Nicholas and Oscar O'Bryan for their dedicated research support and assistance in the preparation of the manuscript.

Dan Hunter
Ramon Lobato
Megan Richardson
Julian Thomas
Melbourne and New York
December 2011

Notes

1 James A. Murray (ed), *A New English Dictionary on Historical Principles: Founded Mainly on the Materials Collected by the Philological Society*, with the assistance of many scholars and men of science, Volume 1: A and B, Oxford at the Clarendon Press, 1888.
2 See Simon Winchester, *The Meaning of Everything: The Story of the Oxford English Dictionary*, Oxford: Oxford University Press, 2003.

3 Marjorie Garber, 'The Amateur Professional and the Professional Amateur' in *Academic Instincts*, Princeton, NJ: Princeton University Press, 2001, p. 1 and p. 5 especially.
4 Especially Robert Stebbins, *Amateurs: On the Margin Between Work and Leisure*, Beverly Hills, California: Sage Publications, 1979; Robert Stebbins, *Amateurs, Professionals and Serious Leisure*, Montreal: McGill-Queen's University Press, 1992.
5 See www.alexa.com/topsites (last visited 1 December 2011).

Part I

Economic histories

1 Histories of user-generated content

Between formal and informal media economies

Ramon Lobato, Julian Thomas and Dan Hunter

Introduction

Founded in 1665, the *Journal des sçavans* and the *Philosophical Transactions of the Royal Society* are early examples of what we would today call 'user-generated content' ('UGC'). The articles published in these journals took the form of letters announcing a discovery or a scientific observation.[1] But although these journals are seminal examples of scientific UGC, processes of scholarly exchange existed much earlier, usually in the form of private correspondence between scientists (which is why scholarly journals to this day sometimes still have the word 'Letters' in their name). Publication of these letters in a journal was, of course, a more efficient way of spreading the news of scientific discovery and delineating claims over first discovery, but initially it wasn't the invention of a new form; it was the evolution of older, less organised, practices of content creation. Other examples of this process are well known: newspapers and periodicals began printing letters to the editor as early as the eighteenth century;[2] more recently, the apparently casual observations that once would have passed as workplace gossip or dinner-party conversation have migrated onto the internet in the form of blogs and short messages; amusing family moments are uploaded to YouTube; lullabies that once were passed down orally through generations are recorded and sold. The dynamic at work here is one of making small-scale cultural production more visible, more regulated, more commercial and more institutional. But although recent scholarship recognises this dynamic, UGC remains a category typically defined in relation to its normative opposites: the professionally produced content that is supported and sustained by commercial media businesses or public organisations, and the purportedly docile and passive modes of consumption associated with mass analog media.[3] Contemporary UGC is often imagined as a disruptive, creative force, something spontaneously emerging from the creativity of individual users newly enabled as expressive agents by digital technologies. The analysis that derives from this is focused on the ostensibly revolutionary changes ushered in by UGC; putatively new forms of media subjectivity, such as the 'pro-am' or 'prosumer';[4] or on how 'old media' businesses respond to the UGC 'challenge'.

In this chapter, we see UGC not in opposition to 'producer media', or in hybridised forms of combination with them, but in relation to a concept that connects new media studies with wider social science: that of informality in media production, distribution and consumption. Following the anthropological and sociological literature on informal economies, we define informal media systems as those which fall largely or wholly outside the purview of state policy, regulation, taxation and measurement. The informal media economy encompasses an extremely diverse range of production activities along with an equally large range of distribution activities, from disc piracy and peer-to-peer file-sharing through to second-hand markets and the parallel importation of CDs, DVDs and games. Clearly, much UGC production and distribution occurs in the informal sector. However, as the example of the *Philosophical Transactions* reminds us, UGC appears also in formal media systems. Hence, the historical migration of scientific writing from informal letters to formal published journals is not the whole story.

We describe in this chapter how UGC moves back and forth between formality and informality over time, and how different components of particular UGC platforms and content exhibit differing degrees of formality at any one time. There are many varieties of UGC, from political blogs to fansubbing networks, which exhibit high levels of tacit or extra-institutional coordination, rationalisation and professional scrutiny, all qualities which are not usually associated with amateur media. The field of UGC is therefore not only internally heterogeneous but also engaged with, and reliant on, numerous industrial and institutional media systems and governmental forces.

The analytical framework outlined in this chapter provides a way to understand the inherent diversity of UGC and its historical and structural interfaces with other media systems. We begin with the broader frame of social-science scholarship of informal economies. We then outline a conceptual schematic – the spectrum of formality – and illustrate it with examples of UGC, including games, talkback radio and comics. The chapter concludes by considering the policy implications arising from a historically grounded understanding of UGC in relation to current debates over ownership, intellectual property and the appropriateness of certain forms of regulation.

The informality model

Informal economic activity is typically defined as that which escapes the regulatory gaze of the state, occurring outside conventional forms of measurement, governance and taxation. The concept came into widespread use after the publication of two papers in the early 1970s: an International Labour Organization report into unemployment in Kenya,[5] and a study of urban labour markets in Ghana by the anthropologist Keith Hart.[6] In different ways, and for different audiences, these papers proposed an alternative framework for analysing urban economies in the Third World, one which did not privilege formal salaried labour as the only meaningful form of productive work. The purpose of this intervention was to bring into view an array of informal activities – from hawking and street vending to urban agriculture and pawnbroking – and to understand them as income-generating activities at the core rather than the margins of the economy. The informality model subsequently gained momentum in other nations whose labour markets were poorly suited to the implicitly ethnocentric idea of 'unemployment', and has been particularly prominent in Latin American social science. Pioneering studies by Castells and Portes[7] and Sassen[8] extended the analysis to advanced economies, arguing that the informal economy is a constituent feature of neoliberal restructuring rather than the residue of a pre-industrial age.

Today, complex discussions about informality continue among anthropologists, sociologists, development economists and urbanists.[9] There is ongoing debate about the size, nature and scale of the informal economy; whether it is a sector, a dynamic, a process or a mode of production; whether it is a problem to be addressed or a capacity to be harnessed. Although it is not possible to rehearse these arguments here, we feel that the utility of the informality approach for media and communications research lies in its ability to enlarge frames of reference and to reorganise existing categories of analysis. In the same way that the 1970s' research demonstrated the shortcomings of a definition of 'employment' that was blind to the diverse ways in which people make ends meet outside salaried labour, there is a need for accounts of media industries which do not ignore informal media simply because it is not captured in the data. In other words, we must avoid conflating media economies (ecologies of exchange and production encompassing the formal and the informal) with industry sectors (visible spheres of regulated and statistically enumerated media enterprise). The history of the book is not the same thing as the history of the publishing industry, in the same way that broadcasters constitute only one part of the story of radio, and the music economy is not reducible to the record industry.

One way to represent 'diverse economies'[10] of media is to imagine a spectrum ranging from the formal to the informal. At one end of the spectrum are the consolidated and regulated industries scrutinised in political-economic and media policy analysis: entertainment conglomerates, satellite networks, publishing houses, public-service media, and so on. At the other end are innumerable small-scale, unmeasured and unevenly regulated media circuits which are barely captured in the statistics on industry output and trade and which rarely figure in media industry analysis. This is not to say, however, that informal circuits have been absent from the broader field of media and communications research, as there is a body of work in media anthropology,[11] in internet and convergence studies,[12] in studies of alternative media,[13] in diasporic media studies,[14] and elsewhere, which takes the informal mediascape seriously as a site for exchange and meaning-making. Studies such as these have revealed a great deal about the contours of informal circuits and production infrastructures and have attempted to do justice to their histories and to their cultural contexts.

The approach we propose in the next section builds on this work by exploring the interrelations between the formal and informal media sectors. As most accounts of the informal economy stress, there is a great deal of traffic between the formal and the informal. Economies, including media economies, are characterised by an intricate array of these cross-fertilisations and mutual dependencies. It is not always appropriate to view informal media as an exception, a novelty, a resistance or a leftover from a pre-industrial age, when it is in fact integrated into the mainstream in various ways. Perhaps the most important lesson of the 1970s' research was that the informal economy 'is not a marginal phenomenon for charitable social research, but a fundamental politico-economic process at the core of many societies'.[15] For this reason, informal media systems should not be analytically ghettoised but brought into the mainstream of media and communications research as objects for comparative analysis. In the following section we take the example of UGC and tease out some of these interdependencies, tracking its oscillation between the formal and the informal via a conceptual schematic in three stages.

UGC and the spectrum of formality

The first step in analysing UGC through an informal economies framework is to develop a simple schematic which can represent the range of UGC in all its diversity, while also illuminating its interfaces with other media.

Figure 1.1 illustrates the degrees of formality and informality associated with various kinds of UGC. UGC appears at different places along this continuum, not only at the informal end. For example, UGC has a venerable if delimited presence in mainstream newspapers as published letters to the editor. While clearly a form of UGC, letters to the editor are typically professionally edited, framed by expensive display advertisements, conform to a strict set of guidelines regarding length, content and style, and bear many other hallmarks of formal media. Popular magazines too have long understood the value of reader contributions: one of Australia's culturally and politically formative nineteenth-century magazines, *The Bulletin*, cherished for many years the tag line 'half Australia writes it, all Australia reads it'.[16] UGC also has an important role in highly regulated twentieth-century electronic media, notably in programming formats such as talkback radio[17] as well as in open-access and community radio and television channels.[18] More recently, websites seeking user content for the purposes of a commercial promotion – 'Invent our new flavor!', 'Caption

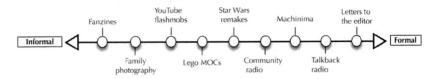

Figure 1.1 UGC across the spectrum of formality

this photo/cartoon', and so on – generate carefully managed, legally controlled transactions soliciting user involvement in highly formalised environments.

Of course, UGC also appears further towards the informal end of the spectrum, in forms that include amateur family photography, blogs and wikis. The most informal examples are produced by amateurs who produce for pleasure and allow permissive use of their content by others, typically through Creative Commons licences.[19] But even here we can see that many of these forms come with various attributes of formality, most evidently some kind of contracted licence that derives from the mode of production or the host of the content. Amateur film – made possible first by small-gauge film cameras, then by new videotape formats in the 1970s, and in the new millennium by the proliferation of cheap digital video hardware and software – may be almost entirely informal but, when distributed on services such as YouTube or Vimeo, becomes subject to formal legal governance through end-user agreements, as are blogs on commercial hosting services like Typepad or Blogger (owned by Google).

So, although we may often associate UGC with informality, UGC is not entirely at the informal end of the spectrum: historically, it appears right across the range. The same point can be made about professionally produced media, which also appears at both ends of the spectrum of formality. It circulates through social networks in unregulated, unmetered flows, as well as in controlled markets; and of course not all such circuits infringe legal rights. However, an analysis of professionally produced content is beyond the scope of our discussion. The point we wish to foreground here is that approaching UGC economies through the lens of formality and informality renders claims about UGC's antipathy to professionalism and its 'disruptive' nature problematic.[20]

Our next step is to show how the spectrum of formality can be disaggregated into a series of constituent variables.

Figure 1.2 illustrates such a disaggregation, using the example of fansubbers (fans who create subtitles for their favourite TV shows and films and distribute them freely online). The elements of formality include various forms of state governance, which we can divide further into governmental technologies, such as taxation, measurement and regulation; and political-economic attributes, such as capital intensity, and level of institutionalisation. They refer to organisational logics which structure media production and distribution activities, as opposed to participants' motivations or desires. We emphasise that this is not an exhaustive or definitive list of variables, but rather a sample of possible criteria for gauging the formality or informality of media. Note also that any one of these variables could be disaggregated further. For example, the category of regulation comprises a number of overlapping sub-categories: the regulation of content (classification, censorship), regulation of carriage (state licensing), labour regulation (unionisation of workforce), positive cultural policy (subsidy for cultural producers), negative cultural policy (public education and media literacy campaigns), self-regulation (professional organisations and associations), and so on. Our aim here is to provide a framework for comparative UGC analysis, one that can be refined and adapted to suit a variety of tasks and inputs.

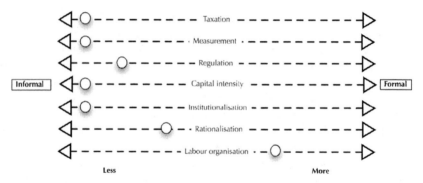

Figure 1.2 Variables of formality: the example of fansubbers

As we break the spectrum down into these component categories, any given media system or artefact will begin to take up different positions along the spectrum simultaneously. This move allows us to see similarities between what would otherwise appear to be disparate media systems. For example, the amateur subtitlers may appear at first glance to have little in common with journalists. But while fansubbers operate in an unregulated and unmonitored space, and are not paid for their labour, both groups are subject to sophisticated forms of self-management and regulation. In the field of journalism, this is realised through professional associations and vehicles for collegial recognition (ethical guidelines, prizes for outstanding practice, internal reviews) while for fansubbers the stringent eligibility criteria of the most prestigious fansub collectives perform similar gatekeeping and esteem-building functions, ensuring that subtitles are accurate and delivered in a timely fashion.[21] These systems appear similar in kind to those operating over the internet for many years in areas such as open source software and the distributed translation of technical texts. An informality framework can therefore help us to further advance the project begun by UGC discourse – that is, complicating existing notions of what counts as media production – by exposing structural analogues across otherwise disparate forms of media activity.

A further case study demonstrates the utility of this approach. If we consider 'call back' or 'talkback' radio, we find that it is highly formal when viewed from the perspective of state regulation of content and carriage. Almost all jurisdictions regulate broadcast radio stations heavily, granting and revoking licences according to formal (often formalistic) criteria enshrined in media law and policy. Because of the scarcity of spectrum in the broadcast range, licences are often auctioned, and they typically include a panoply of positive and negative regulatory obligations. The content of broadcast radio is particularly tightly regulated, and numerous examples exist of radio stations losing their licences when objectionable content is broadcast. Broadcast delays and cut-out switches are used to ensure that, in the event of a talkback caller using profane or objectionable language, the host can cut off the broadcast before transmission. According to these criteria, then, we can see that talkback radio is clearly at the formal end of the spectrum in Figure 1.1. Yet, if we take other criteria into account, the position of talkback changes. Talkback radio's callers are amateurs in at least two senses: they are unpaid, and they do not conform to the usual tenets of professionalism within radio announcing. Callers 'um', they 'ah', they ramble, they clear their throats. Their speaking voices and their language are demotic and unpolished. In this regard we can say that talkback is very informal. But looked at as a whole, talkback radio – like all forms of UGC – has certain characteristics of both formality and informality. Once we disaggregate the components of formality, as in Figure 1.2, we find that the medium is spread across the spectrum, although it clusters towards the formal end.

The historical dimension

The next stage in the analysis is to add a temporal dimension to the schematic. UGC platforms are not static over time, neither in their generalised location on the spectrum of formality (Figure 1.1) nor on any one of the component variables (Figure 1.2). Figure 1.3 illustrates this with the example of family photography.

The popularity of domestic photography has boomed for over a century with every improvement in convenience, quality and cost. What was once an expensive, occasional, studio photograph – a transaction towards the formal end of our spectrum – has become a casual, inexpensive and everyday activity,

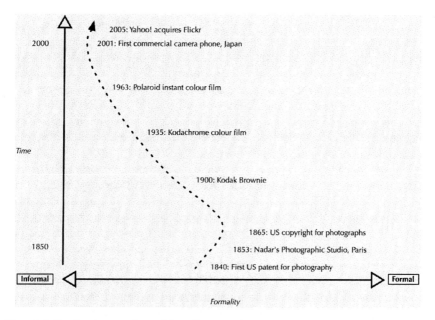

Figure 1.3 Family photography and formality, over time

more so than ever with the extraordinary global popularity of the camera phone. The twentieth-century history of photography reveals the extraordinary vitality and vigour of the informal sector. Informality, of course, has carried on into the age of the internet. But with digital content creation and networked distribution, websites such as Flickr and Picasa are making a previously private form of expression rather more public, and entangling the informality of amateur digital photography with the formality of corporate media in hitherto unprecedented ways, leading to new kinds of legal dispute. The unauthorised use of personal Flickr photos in advertising campaigns is one instance.[22] In other domains, new rules and ethical standards are considered necessary to govern where mobile-phone cameras may now be used, and how mobile-phone photography should be circulated. Facebook and sites like it take this evolution further, drawing on photography and other kinds of UGC to support and create social networks. Facebook seeks to formalise, on advantageous terms, a whole range of hitherto innocuous and obscure social transactions: users must agree to a complicated set of terms of use, and manage the famously complicated privacy and other settings.[23] A vast array of proliferating social networks rests on this formal structure.

So it is that family photography has shifted across the spectrum, beginning in the formal sector, moving towards informality and then shifting back again. This observation provides a new lens through which to view the argument between the UGC idealists and their professional media counterparts, who use examples like Wikipedia or Linux on one side and established offline media on the other to demonstrate the primacy of amateur or of commercial production, depending on their viewpoint.[24] We can see from the brief account of family photography that various types of UGC will shift back and forth across the spectrum over time, and the same is true in many respects for professional media. We see that there is no a priori distinction between either form of media production: both mainstream media and UGC demonstrate various attributes of the formal and informal. In this way, the spectrum of formality model confirms that notions of professional/mainstream media and UGC are artefacts of analysis rather than clearly defined spheres of activity; but more than this, it helps to demonstrate that these two spheres have more in common than may at first be apparent.

Consider another example: comics and comic books. Although printed illustrations and illustrated volumes have existed since the beginning of the book era, the earliest comics emerged as graphic illustrated novels in the mid-nineteenth century. What we think of as comics – the modern superhero comic book and the syndicated comic strip – were institutionalised by the Second World War, reached an apotheosis by the 1970s, and then were re-invented and subverted in narrative and form from the 1980s onwards.[25] During this period of mass production and distribution comics remained highly formalised. The format of multiple panels per page remained stable, as did the size of the pages and the nature of the publication process. As comics moved from being a mass medium to a niche commodity, the nature of its regulation and its structural contexts shifted. With the rise of the internet we saw the emergence of the webcomic, a classic informal media genre that is now increasingly situated in a grey zone between the formal and informal. One example is *Penny Arcade*, an online comic strip based around videogames (www.penny-arcade.com). Its two creators, Jerry Holkins and Mike Krahulik, moved to a web-only format for their work when they found limited physical publication venues. As with much UGC, this appears to have been motivated by expressive reasons – lacking an outlet elsewhere, the web provided a forum for their work – and like other webcomics Penny Arcade has managed to maintain its output and its focus on a remarkably narrow niche interest. For an even more striking example of webcomic success with astonishingly narrow focus, consider *xkcd* (www.xkcd.com), a 'Webcomic of Romance, Math, and Language' that is written, drawn and published by Randall Munroe, a physicist who was working at NASA's Langley Research Center, and who scanned and mounted some old sketches that he had done in his maths books. A well-known blog liked them and linked to them, and now he makes his living from the work. As with family photography, *Penny Arcade* shows potential movement back towards a more formalised mode. Starting from the purely informal, the comic is now the centrepiece of a publishing mini-empire that encompasses merchandise, an annual tradeshow (Paxprime) and charitable philanthropy (Child's Play). Evidently, this movement away from and then back towards formality cannot be adequately captured by rubrics of pro-am creativity or resistance to mainstream media. More accurately, it is a recursive trajectory along the spectrum of formality, one shared by many of the diverse activities currently glossed as UGC.

A slightly different trajectory emerges when we examine the evolution of games since the nineteenth century. Many games have moved from informal modes of development and delivery – initially developed and disseminated by word of mouth (for example, the rules of poker) or as informally circulated domestic parlour games – to highly formal consumer goods protected as intellectual property (Monopoly, Risk, Trivial Pursuit). In the video-game arena, the trajectory is different: because of the nature of the technology and the cost of development, video games began as formally structured pay-per-use attractions in commercial arcades, then moved to similarly formal licensed (and sometimes unlicensed) software for home or hand-held consoles. But now we see significant evidence of informality emerging within the videogame arena, a development that is viewed with suspicion by some professional developers and embraced by others. Examples of informal tendencies in game production and dissemination include high levels of pirated distribution; open-source game engines and emulators, such as MAME;[26] and networked games driven by high degrees of sociality rather than centrally programmed game play narratives. Highly informal features are now found in both commercial, regulated online games, and in their less regulated counterparts at the informal end of the spectrum. Even the publishers of Monopoly are now looking for ways of bringing UGC into new versions of the game.

The popular building toy Lego exhibits a related trajectory, with the evolution of a mid-twentieth-century, patented, free-form construction system, first into a series of trade mark-protected, franchised kits (1980s and later), and then into video games and movies (2000s and later). While Lego continues to successfully develop commercial digital media, the internet has also encouraged and accelerated the development of informal, user-generated Lego practices, notably through the proliferation of unlicensed, Lego 'MOC' ('My Own Creation') websites. The recent launch of a Lego virtual world can be seen as a way of reconnecting the more formal Lego digital media with the enthusiasm and creative energy of the MOC communities.

Across the spectrum of formality, then, the story of photography, comics and games is a story of 'there and back again', of recursive movements between the formal and informal. Similar trajectories may be plotted for cinema, or literature, or news media. The general trend clearly involves a disembedding of cultural practice from formal institutions, as has been made very clear in the UGC literature; but this is only part of the story. There is also a partial re-embedding in the spaces of formality through highly differentiated modes of control, governance and regulation.

Implications

We began with a reference to Keith Hart's early work on Ghana. Hart has recently reviewed the intellectual history of informality, highlighting a conceptual adaptation which we feel has some relevance here.[27] When development economists first began looking at informal trade, informality was seen as a form of backwardness which would and should be overcome. Interventions were designed around bringing informal activity into the regulated sector, establishing control over labour markets, building tax revenue to support new states and creating the knowledge base for government through statistics. Without all this, it was thought, developing countries with young, urbanising populations would face a social disaster. The disaster did not happen, and not because formalising strategies were entirely successful. At a certain point in the 1970s, it became clear that the informal was not disappearing. Rather, the relations between the formal and the informal turned out to be more complex and dynamic than had been realised.

The histories of UGC suggest the need for a similar double-take in the field of media. Here as well, informal media may not be a prototypical stage of formal media: there appears to be no necessary evolution into the formal sector. Far from being a stage of transition, informality appears to be a historical norm, if not a constant. One way of understanding the implications of this is to look at our schematic spectrum of formality in a slightly different way. Instead of imagining UGC as moving across a fixed spectrum over time, we can see certain forms of UGC as demarcating the changing boundaries of the formal and informal sectors. At different times and in different places, the informal media sector is actually larger or smaller than the formal one, and the boundary between the two may be defined by a particular media form, whether it be telegraphy in the mid-nineteenth century or email in the 1990s. In these cases, the UGC can be seen as an especially generative 'boundary object'[28] with far-reaching consequences for media economies and with continuing influence over legal and policy analysis. Boundary objects are not enclosed within either the formal or informal sectors: they occupy territory between the two, exposing points of tension, sparking frontier conflicts and becoming, in some cases, sites for accommodation and negotiation.

Take, for example, the song 'Happy Birthday', the copyright in which will subsist in the United States until 2030. Originally written by Mildred and Patty Hill in the early 1900s, the rights were eventually acquired by a division of Time-Warner. Under copyright law any public performance is subject to clearance and the payment of royalties to the rights holder, and thus the participants at millions of birthday parties are copyright infringers because they have not paid Summy-Birchard Music the appropriate royalties. Of course the song has been used informally for years without any concern on the part of the copyright holders, except where use is high profile or commercial: singing 'Happy Birthday' in a movie will inevitably be licensed. But with the advent of UGC platforms like YouTube, informal uses (and users) of the song become more visible, and a new site of tension appears at the edge of the formalised economy. UGC therefore silhouettes legal IP trade, but is at the same time produced and rendered visible by the same techno-industrial advances driving the formal media sector.[29]

The response by copyright holders is variable. Some issue notice-and-take-down actions against the individual boundary object. In the YouTube case, rights holders may use the website's own Content ID system to track the use of the contested material, engage with users, and insert advertising wherever the contested material appears. Others may seek to assert control over the entire platform as a way of regaining control over the boundary object, as the recent *Viacom v YouTube* litigation illustrates (see Chapter 4).

In analysing media and communications policy, governments and industry often presume that informal activity reflects the absence or ineffectiveness of regulatory, economic and political infrastructures. Since these players operate within formal institutions and typically maintain a deep commitment to them, the existence of the informal is seen as profoundly challenging for a host of reasons: it may represent 'market bypass'; it may affront ingrained intuitions of the legal and moral order of society; and it may flout administrative and legal authority. Standard responses are to advocate increasingly draconian law and policing, stronger international obligations, and to co-opt civil institutions to reassert moral probity.[30]

While these responses are understandable, they may also fail or over-reach. The absence of formal economies does not mean that there is no economy at all; it just means that the mechanisms of exchange lie outside the formal. Moreover, and perhaps more importantly for the analysis of media systems, the informal needs to be distinguished from the criminal. As Centeno and

Portes explain,[31] the informal and criminal spheres are connected through relationships involving cheap labour, demand for illicit goods, and so on; but they should not be conflated. Grey markets are not black markets. There exist numerous examples of informal exchange that have no illicit character whatsoever; and the conflation of the criminal with the informal merely allows us to dismiss the significance of the latter, as well as making its measurement difficult and 'irrelevant' (since, in the eyes of the formal actors, once we have 'proper' laws, this sector of the economy will be no more). We have seen this play out in numerous arenas of media and communications policy-making, and the absence of appropriate recognition of the non-criminal informal economy is implicated in the emergence of so much heated rhetoric from civil society groups who campaign against intellectual property regimes.[32] Focusing policy-makers on the informal media economies of UGC, inter alia, may lead to greater understanding of this part of the economy, and different types of policy response in recognition of the significance and potential efficiency of this form of production and exchange.

Recognising that the formal and the informal media economies co-exist and overlap, and interact in diverse ways, generates new perspectives on other long-standing arguments. Consider debates about the appropriate scope of intellectual property rights. These debates increasingly resemble the set pieces of mediaeval battles, with the forces of copyright holders arrayed on one side of the field seeking greater protection against piracy, and the copyleftists on the other side of the field arguing for user rights or decreases in statutory damages. We can describe and contextualise that tension somewhat more clearly, if not resolve it, by recognising how the internet exposes boundary objects (like 'Happy Birthday') to greater regulatory scrutiny as it enlarges the reach and scope of the informal media economy in areas like file-sharing and UGC generation and distribution, and also multiplies sites of formal–informal interface and tension.

Further, understanding these debates as frontier conflicts between the informal and the formal allows us to spot some of the traps awaiting all parties in today's copyright battles. If we see intellectual property law as one avenue among others for formal regulation, it follows that legal solutions built upon extending the scope of intellectual property are more likely to have local effects in the formal sector rather than delivering systemic solutions to the challenges of informal use. Changes to the law may modify the regulation of formal territory without expanding that territory. Consider the fair-use provisions in § 107 of the US Copyright Act of 1976. These provisions provide for exceptions to copyright infringement based upon an assessment of four factors: extent and nature of the taking, the character of the copied work, the intent of the defendant in appropriating the material and the effect of the taking on the market for the copied work. The apparent breadth of the fair-use defence is often seen by copyright sceptics outside the US as one possible countervailing reform to copyright's expansion over the last 100 years. In the context of our argument, however, it is clear that the application of the fair use defence will rarely extend to the informal sector. The defence is used mostly by those within the formal economy to prevent other formal actors from restricting re-use of their work (for instance in the areas of formally published satires or parodies). With the possible exception of the factors addressing the purpose for which the copy was made, none of the fair-use factors addresses issues within the informal media economy.

One current proposal aims directly to enlarge the territory of formal media, by compensating rights holders through a statutory royalty on internet access fees or digital media devices. An example is the Copyright Board of Canada's 29 cent levy on blank CDs, the proceeds of which are distributed to song-writers and artists through collecting societies. The idea is to make digital media goods and services subject to a new, hypothecated form of taxation. Clearly taxes of this kind do have the potential to provide a new source of revenue for content industries. But their consequences for other, established business models in the formal space are unknown, and the price of achieving some return from the informal sector may be a recognition that the internet has substantially and irreversibly diluted rights holders' capacity to control the distribution of their content.

Conclusion

Economic formality is a contingent and highly variable feature of UGC media. Innovations in technology, in business models, in policy frameworks and changing social circumstances, influence rapid movements across the formal and informal sectors. Formal industries can be informalised as a result of disruptive technologies (as when the rise of blogs appears to threaten pro-fessional journalism), or changes in legislation and enforcement (as when forms of content, such as pornography, are criminalised and driven underground), or even through deregulatory processes (as when privatisation or downsizing of broadcasters drives media professionals into informal labour markets). Informality, then, is just as much a feature of highly developed cultural economies as of emerging ones, and just as much a feature of established media industries as players within the UGC arena. Informal exchange occurs in weakly regulated states as well as highly regulated media environments, such as those in Australia, Europe and the United States. There is, therefore, no straightforward correlation between governance and informality in media cir-cuits, but there are complex and often counter-intuitive relations of mutual influence that call for further analysis. We hope that the framework outlined here, which enables the comparative study of media systems in various states of formality and informality, may be of some use in this larger project.

Acknowledgement

An earlier version of this chapter was published in (2011) 5 *International Journal of Communication* 899.

Notes

1 Harcourt Brown, 'History and the Learned Journal' (1972) 33 *Journal of the History of Ideas* 365.

2 See Karin Wahl-Jorgensen, *Journalists and the Public: Newsroom Culture, Letters to the Editor, and Democracy*, Cresskill, NJ: Hampton Press, 2007.

3 Henry Jenkins, *Fans, Bloggers, and Gamers: Exploring Participatory Culture*, New York: New York University Press, 2006; Lawrence Lessig, *Remix: Making Art and Commerce Thrive in the Hybrid Economy*, New York: Penguin, 2008.

4 See Charles Leadbeater and Paul Miller, *The Pro-Am Revolution: How Enthusiasts Are Changing Our Economy and Society*, London: Demos, 2004.

5 International Labour Office, *Employment, Incomes and Equality: A Strategy for Increasing Productive Employment in Kenya*, International Labour Office: Geneva, 1972.

6 Keith Hart, 'Informal Income Opportunities and Urban Employment in Ghana' (1973) 11(1) *Journal of Modern African Studies* 61.

7 Manuel Castells and Alejandro Portes, 'World Underneath: The Origins, Dynamics, and Effects of the Informal Economy' in Alejandro Portes, Manuel Castells and Lauren A. Benton (eds), *The Informal Economy: Studies in Advanced and Less Developed Countries*, Baltimore, MD: Johns Hopkins University Press, 1989, p. 11.

8 Saskia Sassen, 'New York City's Informal Economy' (Working paper No. 9/1988, Institute for Social Science Research, UCLA, 1 June 1988).

9 For example, Ananya Roy and Nezar AlSayyad (eds), *Urban Informality: Transnational Perspectives from the Middle East, Latin America, and South Asia*, Lanham, MD: Lexington Books, 2004; Guha-Khasnobis, Basudeb, Ravi Kanbur and Elinor Ostrom (eds), *Linking the Formal and Informal Economy: Concepts and Policies*, Oxford: Oxford University Press, 2006; Keith Hart, 'On the Informal Economy: The Political History of an Ethnographic Concept' (Working Paper No. 09-042, Centre Emile Bernheim, 2009).

10 J. K. Gibson-Graham, *The End of Capitalism (As We Knew It): A Feminist Critique of Political Economy*, Minneapolis: University of Minnesota Press, 1996.

11 See, e.g., Eric Michaels, *The Aboriginal Invention of Television in Central Australia 1982–1986*, Canberra: Australian Institute of Aboriginal Studies, 1986; Faye Ginsburg, Lia Abu-Lughod and Brian Larkin (eds), *Media Worlds: Anthropology on New Terrain*, Berkeley: University of California Press, 2002

12 See, e.g., Jenkins, *Fans, Bloggers, and Gamers*; Alex Bruns, *Blogs, Wikipedia, Second Life, and Beyond: From Production to Produsage*, New York: Peter Lang, 2008.

13 See, e.g., John Downing, *Radical Media: The Political Experience of Alternative Communication*, Boston, MA: South End Press, 1984; Chris Atton and James F. Hamilton, *Alternative Journalism*. London: Sage, 2008.

14 See, e.g., Stuart Cunningham and John Sinclair (eds), *Floating Lives: The Media and Asian Diasporas*, St Lucia: University of Queensland Press, 2000.

15 Castells and Portes, 'World Underneath', p. 15.

16 Sylvia Lawson, *The Archibald Paradox: A Strange Case of Authorship*, Melbourne: Allen Lane, 1983.

17 See Bridget Griffen-Foley, *Changing Stations: The Story of Australian Commerical Radio*, Sydney: UNSW Press, 2009.

18 See Marilyn Lashley, *Public Television: Panacea, Pork Barrel, or Public Trust?*, Westport, CT: Greenwood Press, 1992.

19 Dan Hunter and Greg Lastowka, 'Amateur-to-Amateur' (2004) 46 *William & Mary Law Review* 951.

20 Carlisle George and Jackie Scerri, 'Web 2.0 and User-Generated Content: Legal Challenges in the New Frontier' (2007) 2 *Journal of Information, Law & Technology* www2.warwick.ac.uk/fac/soc/law/elj/jilt/2007_2/.

21 Kelly Hu, 'Chinese Subtitle Groups and the Neoliberal Work Ethic' in Eyal Ben Ari and Nissim Otmazgin (eds), *Popular Culture Collaborations and Coproductions in East and Southeast Asia*, Kyoto: Kyoto University Press, forthcoming.

22 Noam Cohen, 'Use My photo? Not Without Permission', *New York Times* (online), 1 October 2007 www.nytimes.com/2007/10/01/technology/01link.html.

23 See Jennifer Hendry and Kay E. Goodall, 'Facebook and the Commercialisation of Personal Information: Some Questions of Provider-to-User Privacy' in Goodwin, Morag, Bert-Jaap Koops and Ronald Leenes (eds), *Dimensions of Technological Regulation*, Nijmegen: Wolf Legal Publishers, 2010, p. 107.

24 See, e.g., Clay Shirky, *Here Comes Everybody: The Power of Organizing Without Organizations*, New York: Penguin Press, 2008; cf. Andrew Keen, *The Cult of the Amateur: How Blogs, MySpace, YouTube, and the Rest of Today's User-Generated Media are Destroying our Economy, our Culture, and our Values*, New York: Crown Business, 2008.

25 Bradford Wright, *Comic Book Nation: The Transformation of Youth Culture in America*, Baltimore, MD: Johns Hopkins University Press, 2001.

26 Howard Wen, 'Why emulators make video-game makers quake', *Salon.com,* 4 June 1999: www.salon.com/technology/feature/1999/06/04/emulators/print.html.

27 Hart, 'On the Informal Economy'.

28 Marilyn Strathern, *Commons and Borderlands: Working Papers on Interdisciplinarity, Accountability and the Flow of Knowledge*, Oxford: Sean Kingston Publishing, 2004.

29 See Hart, 'On the Informal Economy'.

30 Dan Hunter, 'Culture War' (2005) 83 *Texas Law Review* 1105; Toby Miller et al., *Global Hollywood 2*, London: British Film Institute, 2005; William Patry, *Moral Panics and the Copyright Wars*, Oxford: Oxford University Press, 2009.

31 Miguel A. Centeno and Alejandro Portes, 'Out of the Shadows' in Alejandro Portes, Manuel Castells and Lauren A. Benton (eds), *The Informal Economy: Studies in Advanced and Less Developed Countries*, Baltimore, MD: Johns Hopkins University Press, 1989, p. 23.

32 Fred Von Lohmann, 'Unintended Consequences: Twelve Years Under the DMCA' (Report, Electronic Frontier Foundation, February 2010): www.eff.org/files/eff-unintended-consequences-12-years.pdf.

2 Competing myths of informal economies

Megan Richardson and Jake Goldenfein

Roland Barthes once said that 'myth has the task of giving an historical intention a natural justification, and making contingency appear eternal.'[1] There is a certain myth associated with informal economies that posits these as productive and even natural in the same way as other enterprises, except that they fall outside the law. The fascinating, subtle and complex chapter by Lobato, Thomas and Hunter put forward a number of examples in constructing this myth. Law in this history develops, in turn, its own myth as an oppressive regulator to be avoided and circumvented if possible – or overlooked or ignored as in the 'Happy Birthday' example. Our purpose is not to contest this account directly but rather to suggest it is not the only possible account. Thus we point to some historical examples that can be used to construct an alternative myth of informal economies – showing law in a more benign light, as offering a degree of accommodation to economies which are 'informal' in the sense that they are not based around formalised institutional structures and may draw to a substantial extent on amateur contributions. In the end, we suggest that neither myth gives a complete account since both are, in fact, contingent on the role that law selects for itself. As lawyers, we argue that the task for legal policy-makers is to insist on a role for law in regulating informal economies for productive purposes rather than simply supporting the status quo.

Crowd-sourcing: the whistle-blowing example

WikiLeaks' publication of leaked government dispatches is one example not discussed by Lobato, Thomas and Hunter. At least to date, the majority of action against WikiLeaks (the organisation) has been extra-legal,[2] and law so far has only 'indirectly' affected WikiLeaks through its application to Julian Assange and Bradley Manning. However, the longer support offered by the law to activities that may loosely be described as 'whistle-blowing' can be found in the English doctrine of breach of confidence and its iniquity defence. That defence extends from the proposition that there can be no confidentiality in an iniquity or injustice. From its first pronouncement in the mid-nineteenth-century case of *Gartside v Outram*,[3] where it was applied to a former factor of a wool-broking firm spreading stories of the firm's fraudulent activities, the defence was seen as a welcome shaper of social norms – with *The Economist*, for instance, stating that: '[w]hen a merchant knows that every servant under him will be under no obligation to conceal his misdeeds if he be inclined to be fraudulent ... there will be more caution and honesty than at present among those respectable classes of people.'[4] Neither should it surprise that the press would approve of the development. The press is one of the main beneficiaries of open access, and it provides in turn an important conduit for individuals to speak out to the public domain on matters of public interest. By the later twentieth century, the iniquity defence had expanded in the United Kingdom (and to a lesser extent in Australia) into a full public-interest defence to breach of confidence bringing under its domain the publication of information where the benefits of free speech outweighed those of preserving secrecy. The defence is, as Lord Goff noted in the *Spycatcher* case of the late 1980s, currently the most important 'limiting principle' to the action of breach of confidence.[5] This balancing of speech and secrecy that animates confidence (and privacy rights – being strongly connected to confidence in the UK and Australia) is thus institutionalised in the laws governing what the media may publish, similar to First Amendment free speech doctrine in the US

However, the public-interest defence does not confer complete immunity and some judicial decisions have been controversial – for instance, *Schering Chemicals Ltd v Falkman Ltd*[6] in 1982, where Thames Television was stopped from broadcasting a television documentary about a pharmaceutical company's role in producing and marketing a hormone pregnancy test (Primodos) now suspected of causing deformities in children born to mothers who had taken it while pregnant; and *Francome v Mirror Group Ltd*[7] in 1984, where the *Mirror* was prevented from publishing transcripts of telephone conversations of a well-known jockey whom the media suspected of race-fixing. On the other hand, the factual matrices in these cases contributed to courts finding against there being a public interest in publication. For instance, Schering was seeking to manage the publicity surrounding the adverse effects of its product rather than prevent its coming out (and for that reason had confidentially briefed the second defendant, a public relations consultant), and was facing a class action for harms allegedly suffered from the drug. It was thus concerned to avoid publicity that might be construed as a contempt of court in that action. Moreover, it was questioned whether the defendants were particularly concerned with objective reporting of the 'Primodos affair' or were rather more concerned to make and air their documentary.[8] Similarly, in the *Francome* case, the fact that the *Mirror* was a tabloid newspaper whose business model was the widest possible publication of scandalous and salacious material meant the court was wary of its public-interest argument. The transcripts were illegally obtained by an undisclosed party using a 'bug' placed on the plaintiff's home telephone line, and there was no attempt to sequester the information that might in fact point to wrongdoing on Mr Francome's part.

Also controversial are the government secret cases where courts have been inclined to support government interests against those of whistle-blowers, notwithstanding their insistence that governments have a higher burden to demonstrate that the overall public interest lies against making the material public. An example is the *Spycatcher* case, in which former MI5 agent Peter Wright, who had written a critical exposé of the operations of the British Secret Service during his employment, was said to be under a 'life-long' obligation of confidence; and the British newspapers which sought to publish extracts from his book were only exonerated from liability on the basis that the information was by then in the public domain having already been published in the US and available in Britain (and the *Sunday Times*, which published extracts earlier, was held liable and a full account of profits was awarded). As the historian A. W. B. Simpson points out in talking about the *Spycatcher* case, British courts, while expressing support for whistle-blowing in relation to government, have in practice tended to support government security interests over freedom of speech; and indeed (Simpson suggests) the idea of a utilitarian balance may be skewed in favour of government interests – especially where expressed in terms of public defence and security.[9] Contrariwise, judges have not always taken this line. For instance, in the Australian *Spycatcher* case, where Peter Wright and Heinemann Publishers Australia were defendants in an action brought by the UK government in an effort to stop the publication of the *Spycatcher* book, Kirby P was persuaded by the defendant's argument that 'the public interest of Australia … requires or at least justifies the disclosure of the matters in Spycatcher.'[10] In that case, publication was allowed.[11]

To summarise this brief discussion, viewed through the lens of courts – at least those prepared to take on the role of vigilantly fostering open business and government – the media may serve a useful function in predetermining where the public interest lies. The question is not simply one of amateur versus professional (although Wright at least may be classed as an amateur motivated by a desire to lay open a secret service he considered to be corrupt and incompetent). Nor is it just about formal versus informal media since, as *Schering Chemicals* and *Francome* show, commercial-driven and especially tabloid media may be highly formalised and yet may not be highly regarded by the courts as agents of the public interest. Rather, the question may be how the intermediary conducts itself in carrying out its function as an intermediary. If so, a problem with WikiLeaks may be preparedness to make information freely available no matter what the harm. How different is WikiLeaks, in that case, from the tabloid media of the 1980s? In other words, a key point about WikiLeaks may be that it exposes the danger of an intermediary that is willing to transgress formal rules and not filter those whistle-blowers who desire to see the secret information they possess published with no limitations.

Open-distribution networks: the example of peer-to-peer file-sharing

Lobato, Thomas and Hunter point out that peer-to-peer sharing of the means of entertainment is not just a feature of modern life but of ancient lineage.

They give the example of the sharing of family photographs – a practice that the inventor and manufacturer of the Kodak portable camera not only facilitated but actively encouraged with advertising slogans of 'complete the Kodak story' and 'ready with your Kodak'.[12] We can find further examples in the more recent past, bolstered by an array of post-war consumer technologies. Books, articles and sheet music were photocopied for both private and social use from the late 1960s. Mix-tapes were made for personal use and distribution in the 1970s.[13] Television programmes were video-taped within and between households, and live music concerts were surreptitiously filmed by and for fans since the techniques of home-filming were made available. Similarly, the idea of framing a business model around desires of individuals to have popular forms of entertainment available when and where they want it and particularly through the latest distribution technologies is as old as the technologies themselves. That copyright law has struggled to keep up with these revolutionary trends is shown by a series of test cases in the 1970s, 1980s and 1990s that were brought to 'clarify', or rather to extend, the application of copyright law's standards to these newer scenarios – with the legislature ready to step in if the courts are unable or unwilling to embrace the situation, or where it was thought there would be benefits in greater transparency in placing in a legislative format the relevant legal test.

Nevertheless, copyright expert Jane Ginsburg points out that American courts and legislatures have not been wholly on the side of content providers. Rather, they have sought to provide workable balances between the interests of content providers and new sources of distribution, in practice coming down on the side of providers who seek to engage with new technologies of distribution while penalising those who eschew them.[14] The *Napster* file-sharing case[15] is a good modern example.[16] In that case, the court indicated that the fair-use defence to copyright infringement would treat peer-to-peer music services more favourably if they offered a service that the record companies themselves did not realistically plan to offer in the foreseeable future.[17] The result was that record companies were propelled towards a business model that facilitated downloads of single tracks, with Apple the most successful provider to date of such commercial services. Indeed many parallels can be drawn between Napster and Apple, with both firms beginning in a rebellious spirit, eschewing traditional business models, and providing in the end a new model for the modern technology enterprise. But the clear difference was that Apple's Steve Jobs, unlike Napster's Shawn Fanning, was (willing and) able to negotiate arrangements with the record companies that actually worked. By the same token, the Napster case may have also spurred action outside formal media economies, in that its closure potentially provoked further illicit behaviour through subsequent peer-sharing technologies – demonstrating law's multiple potential roles in the informal to formal dynamic.

The issues surrounding music and film copying have been further complicated by the later *Kazaa* and *Grokster* cases (in Australia and the US respectively),[18] which have emphasised that infringement could be found against a peer-to-peer service provider which frames its business model around inciting or encouraging infringements of copyright. The peer-to-peer service provider's subversive culture of encouraging users to 'join the revolution' was emphasised in the judgment of Wilcox J in the *Kazaa* case, together with the fact that the peer-to-peer service's advertising revenue was derived from websites whose traffic was in large part provided by illegal downloads. More controversial is the language in the judgment to suggest that an intermediary may be held liable for its (in)actions if it elects not to distinguish between legal and illegal downloads when it was feasible to do so – although, as economist Renier Kraakman points out, there may be efficiencies on holding gatekeepers liable where they can exert control.[19] Such reasoning can be seen also in the Australian *iiNet* case where it was held that an internet service provider's failure to take steps after notices of infringements were given on behalf of content providers could not be equated to authorising the infringements, but it might have been if reasonable grounds were specified for suspecting infringement.[20]

Yet despite these recent developments, which seem to point in the direction of increasing protection of content providers, the point remains that those providers now increasingly operate legitimate (licensed) distribution models based on previously illegitimate and informal methods of 'sharing', simply centralised and institutionalised rather than peer sourced. In the case of music, this model was provided via Apple and was put in place after the Napster litigation, serving as a compromise between what the content providers claimed was simple infringement and technology providers claimed was an untapped market. Similarly, while we should be wary of the dangers of *post hoc ergo propter hoc* reasoning, the arguments of those who claim the licensed arrangements would not have occurred, or at least not at the same pace, without the disruptive behaviour of the distribution-technology providers, also seem quite plausible. In other words, it seems that the content providers and technology providers have together provided a better public service than either would have done of their own motion, with the informal actors undergirding a nascent formal industry. We also see law's role in both stigmatising an informal actor but also shaping those actions as to fit within the institutional boundaries of formality.

Social innovation: collaborative artistic productions

Primarily, Lobato, Thomas and Hunter are concerned with social innovation and how this occurs. As they point out, this may take place not only within informal economies but also within formal ones (for instance, collaborative publications in scientific journals). Yet there is the question why social innovation seems to be more a feature of informal than formal economies. We wonder whether even formal economies may have their own informal elements (and vice versa). As the economist Ronald Coase pointed out in the 1930s, with the advent of 'the firm' in the nineteenth century, society gained a single monolithic entity that apparently limited the need for markets or courts to deal with its internal arrangements.[21] But that did not mean that firms could not be organised in various ways, some formal, rigid and hierarchical and others quite informal, fluid and democratic[22] – as we now see with many modern high-technology firms. In a sense then, the formal economies built up around the idea of the firm may have masked the more informal economies that sometimes lay within.

Courts have sometimes been prepared to pierce the veil of corporate production, as in the recent Australian case of *Telstra Corporation v Phone Directories*.[23] There the issue was how the ancient pre-corporate humanistic idea of 'authorship' for copyright purposes could be applied to Telstra's corporate production of telephone directories. As it turned out, the internal arrangements were messy and not well documented. The court asked how a work could be said to be authored when there was such a fluid mix of technology and individuals involved in its production that the individual human contributions could not now be calculated. The Copyright Act's norm is one of defined individual authorship of a work and even its limited provision for 'works of joint authorship'[24] could not easily be applied where the precise contributions are unclear because they are not accurately and formally recorded – a problem further exacerbated where (as in the case of telephone-directory production) the ultimate work is done by technology.[25] When leave to appeal to the High Court was sought, Gummow J rejected the application and intimated that if the problem of apparently author-free (and thus copyright-free) works was to be resolved it would need to be done by reformist legislation.[26] This historicist approach seems to resist the idea that judges might act creatively in adapting older legislative models based mainly around individual or pre-ordered contributions to the vast array of informal collaborative scenarios we see today.

One solution is for informal economies to become more formal – for instance, to seek out techniques to record individual contributions and to provide contractual arrangements of production and ownership. Yet as Lobato, Thomas and Hunter show there will always be informal economies and these may be important drivers of creativity. Should they be left outside the law on the very fundamental questions of subsistence and ownership of intellectual property? Or should courts as well as legislatures consider ways to adapt their laws to meet the practical circumstances of communal production? In fact, Australian judges have sometimes been prepared to respond creatively to questions of informal collaborative production. In the 1976 case of *Foster v Mountford and Rigby Ltd*[27] Muirhead J in the Northern Territory Supreme Court recognised that members of an unincorporated body known as the Pitjantjara Council could represent the Pitjantjara people in an action for breach of confidence against an anthropologist who had studied the community over a period of 35 years and who was now seeking to publish his findings in the form of a book titled *Nomads of the Australian Desert*. The book included reproductions of traditional stories and drawings, the knowledge of which had been entrusted to Mountford during his fieldtrips. As Muirhead J observed, although '[t]o the lay reader, [the book] is a magnificent publication [and] to the scholar and researcher it must contain much of interest and value' nevertheless 'a number of the photographs, drawings and descriptions of persons, places and ceremonies have deep religious and cultural significance to the plaintiff Foster, and to the other plaintiffs ... [and] some of the matters hitherto secret are revealed in the book, and that this has caused dismay, concern and anger' to members of the Pitjantjara council.[28] An injunction was granted for what the anthropologist Michael Brown calls a breach of 'cultural privacy'.[29]

In the later case of *Bulun Bulun v R& t Textiles Pty Ltd*,[30] Von Doussa J was not prepared to recognise that such common-law understandings of authors' rights could extend beyond a work's publication. He further concluded that the statutory language of a 'work of joint authorship' was inadequate to recognise the particular form of collaboration involved in a traditional artwork which incorporates ideas received from the community but is executed by an individual artist exercising a degree of artistic expression. In this case, the judge said, there can be only one 'author' for purposes of the copyright statute. Nevertheless, Von Doussa J was prepared to graft a fiduciary obligation owed to the Ganalbingu people onto the artist John Bulun Bulun's authorial rights in his art work *At the Waterhole* as a way of recognising the community's special contribution to and ongoing interest in the work.[31] The outcome of the proceedings was a comprehensive settlement against an infringer who used the art work as a design on the manufacture of T-shirts for purposes of tourism. As Bulun Bulun's lawyer Colin Golvan has observed, the decision in the case 'illustrates the flexibility of the courts in adapting copyright and associated legal principles to the requirements of the age-old cultural practices' even in the absence of a specific programme of legislative reform.[32]

Might this idea of adapting fiduciary liability become a suitable model for the collaborative social innovation arrangements of the present and future? Until more sophisticated provisions for joint authorship provide new ways for formalising the relationships between collaborators it may be the next best alternative.

Implications

All this goes to show that courts, and legislatures, have choices. Sometimes law acts to exclude activities from institutional legitimacy (although at the same time it may promote adjustments that shape the activity into an acceptably formal form) and sometimes it creatively adapts text and doctrine to facilitate a nascent informal innovation. The mythology of law as oppressive regulator has a reasonable foundation drawn from the law's general preference for formality over informality, exacerbated by the legislature's tendency towards detailed regulation over more fluid standards and search for bright lines when in practice there may be none. This can make it difficult for law to adequately accommodate the entire 'spectrum' of formality demonstrated by Lobato et al.

Contrariwise, we think there are some more hopeful signs in the historical examples we have put forward that suggest that law may function not as oppressor but rather a facilitator for informal economies in an open-handed way.

Notes

1 Roland Barthes, *Mythologies* (1957) (Anette Lavers trans., London: Jonathan Cape, 1972), p. 142.
2 Yochai Benkler, 'A Free Irresponsible Press: WikiLeaks and the Battle over the Soul of the Networked Fourth Estate' (2011) 46 *Harvard Civil Rights – Civil Liberties Law Review* 311.
3 *Gartside v Outram* (1856) 26 LJ Ch. 114.
4 *The Economist*, Nov. 29, 1856, p. 1317.
5 *Attorney-General v Observer Ltd and Times Newspapers Ltd and another* [1990] 1 AC 109, Lord Goff at 281–82 (*'Spycatcher'*).
6 *Schering Chemicals Ltd v Falkman* [1982] QB 1 (*'Schering Chemicals'*).
7 *Francome v Mirror Group Newspapers Ltd* [1984] 2 All ER 408 (*'Francome'*).
8 Indeed Templeman LJ suggested that the second defendant's (Mr Elstein's) primary motivation was 'to make money out of his dealing in confidential information': *Schering* [1982] QB 1 at 40.
9 A. W. B. Simpson, 'The Judges and the Vigilant State' (1989) 4 *Denning Law Journal* 145.
10 See *Attorney-General for the United Kingdom v Heinemann Publisher Australia Pty Ltd and another* (1987) 10 NSWLR 86, Kirby P at 169–70.
11 Although ultimately (after further appeal to the High Court) this was on the basis that the case, brought by the UK Attorney-General, entailed the adjudication of a foreign public law: See *Attorney-General (UK) v Heinemann Publishers Australia Pty Ltd and Another* (1988) 165 CLR 30.
12 For instance, back-cover advertisements for the Eastman Kodak Co's Autographic Kodaks (priced at $6.50 up) on the *Saturday Evening Post* of 2 October 1920 and 21 February 1925.
13 The phenomenon was not limited to the developed world: as ethnomusicologist Peter Manuel points out, cassettes had 'a dramatic effect on the music industry and popular music throughout most of the developing world': see Peter Manuel, *Cassette Culture: Popular Music and Technology in North India*, Chicago: University of Chicago Press, 1993, pp. xiii–xiv.
14 Jane Ginsburg, 'Copyright and Control Over New Technologies of Dissemination' (2001) 101 *Columbia Law Review* 1613.
15 *A&M Records Inc v Napster Inc*, 239 F 3d 1004 (9th Cir, 2001).
16 And one that Ginsburg discusses in 'Copyright and Control Over New Technologies of Dissemination' at 1639–42.
17 *A&M Records Inc v Napster Inc*, 239 F 3d 1004, 1018–19 (9th Cir, 2001), approving the reasoning of Patel CJ at first instance at 114 F Supp 2d 896 at 913–17.
18 Universal Music Australia Pty Ltd v *Sharman License Holdings Ltd* (2005) 65 IPR 289 (*'Kazaa'*) and *Metro-Goldwyn-Mayer Studios Inc v Grokster Ltd*, 545 US 913 (2005) (*'Grokster'*); and see Arlen Duke and Megan Richardson, 'Music Markets and Bad Actors in Competition and Copyright Law' (2008) 16 *Competition and Consumer Law Journal* 203.
19 See Renier Kraakman, 'Gatekeepers: The Anatomy of a Third-Party Enforcement Strategy' (1986) 2 *Journal of Law, Economics and Organization* 53, arguing that relevant factors in assessing the efficiency of gatekeeper liability include the intermediary's ability to influence 'misconduct, and failure to do so in the absence of legal liability as well as the costs of imposing legal liability'.
20 *Roadshow Films Pty Ltd v iiNet Ltd (No 2)* (2011) 91 IPR 482. Leave to appeal to the High Court has been granted: *Roadshow Films Pty Ltd & Ors v iiNet Limited* [2011] HCATrans 210 (12 August 2011).
21 Ronald Coase, 'The Nature of the Firm' (1937) 4(16) *Economica* 38.
22 And see Paul Adler and Charles Heckscher, 'Towards Collaborative Community' in Charles Heckscher and Paul Adler (eds), *The Firm as a Collaborative Community*, Oxford and New York: Oxford University Press, 2006, p. 11.

23 *Telstra Corporation Ltd v Phone Directories Company Pty Ltd* (2010) 194 FCR 142.

24 A work of joint authorship, as defined in the Australian Act, is 'a work that has been produced by the collaboration of two or more authors and in which the contribution of each author is not separate from the contribution of the other author or the contributions of the other authors': *Copyright Act 1968* (Cth) s 10.

25 As Gordon J put it at first instance: 'the Applicants have not and cannot identify who provided the necessary authorial contribution to each Work. The Applicants concede there are numerous non-identified persons who "contributed" to each Work (including third party sources)': *Telstra Corporation Ltd v Phone Directories Co Pty Ltd* (2010) 85 IPR 571 at 575 [5].

26 See the record of the proceedings in *Telstra Corporation Limited & Anor v Phone Directories Company Pty Ltd & Ors* [2011] HCATrans 248 (2 September 2011).

27 *Foster and Others v Mountford and Rigby Ltd* (1976) 14 ALR 71.

28 Ibid., at 73–74.

29 Michael Brown, *Who Owns Native Culture?* Cambridge: Harvard University Press, 2003, ch 1.

30 (1998) 41 IPR 513.

31 See especially discussion ibid., at 531.

32 Colin Golvan, 'The Protection of *At the Waterhole* by John Bulun Bulun: Aboriginal Art and the Recognition of Private and Communal Rights' in Andrew Kenyon, Megan Richardson and Sam Ricketson (eds), *Landmarks in Australian Intellectual Property Law*, Cambridge: Cambridge University Press, 2006, p. 191 at p. 207.

3   Start with the household

John Quiggin

Ever since the emergence of the internet, those affected by its ever-growing reach have tried to make sense of the new ways of doing things made possible by this technology, and its social institutions. This process was initially undertaken by participants, who were, for the most part, professional workers in fields related to information technology.

Like most educated professionals in the late twentieth century, early adopters of the internet had at least a passing familiarity with (popularised versions of) concepts derived from the social sciences, including sociology, anthropology and economics. It was unsurprising, therefore, that they applied these concepts to produce a self-conscious theory to explain such phenomena as open-source software.

The archetypal example was Eric Raymond, who used the metaphor of gift exchange to explain the willingness of programmers to contribute to open-source projects with no direct return.[1] The idea was that, as in the potlatch ceremonies of the Pacific Northwest, those willing to offer high-value gifts to others would accrue status, which might in turn yield more tangible benefits. Raymond observed that the 'reputation one gains in the hacker culture can spill over into the real world in economically significant ways. It can get you a better job offer, or a consulting contract, or a book deal', but noted that '[t]his kind of side effect, however, is at best rare and marginal for most hackers'.[2]

Analysis of this kind was commonly utopian in tone, reflecting the sense of boundless potentiality familiar to anyone who has had the experience of encountering the internet for the first time.[3] Countervailing voices tended to the opposite extreme not merely downplaying utopian claims but either dismissing them out of hand[4] or presenting a dystopian alternative.[5] This vein of literature (particularly the debunking or dystopian version) remains prominent to this day (Keen 2008).

As the internet grew, it attracted the attention of academic social scientists, a development symbolised by the foundation of the Association of Internet Researchers in 1999. Early work of this kind was, in many ways, the opposite of that undertaken by participants in the internet. Whereas the work of Raymond and others combined a relatively superficial understanding of social science concepts with deep involvement in the actual processes of the internet, much of the early work in the emerging field of 'internet studies' involved application of standard social science methods by researchers with a limited and superficial understanding of the internet itself, aimed at readers who might be totally unfamiliar with these phenomena.

As the internet has become a central part of everyday life, the dichotomy between participants and observers has broken down. No one any longer needs to explain basic terms like 'blog' or 'social network' to their audience before proceeding to an analysis.

Yet progress in understanding the internet, and its implications, remains limited. The central problem is that of attempting to fit the various forms of social and economic activities made possible by the internet into some existing system of categorisation. No such system appears entirely adequate, but, by way of contrast, no new system has emerged to provide a better understanding.

The predominance of 'user-generated content' ('UGC') is a particularly distinctive feature of the internet. Important examples include blogs, micro-blogs such as Twitter, social networks such as Facebook, wikis and sites for sharing photos and videos. Sites of this kind co-exist with a large variety of sites presenting professionally produced content, including newspapers, music and video and a large variety of publications produced by government and non-government organisations.

In most cases, professionally produced content on the internet is an adaptation of pre-existing forms of content delivered through print or electronic media. By contrast, most UGC arises in forms that bear only a distant relationship to pre-existing forms ('blogs', for example, were originally 'weblogs' and the form owes something to traditional logs, personal journals and diaries). As a result, a recurring theme is the idea (viewed sometimes with alarm and sometimes with hope) that the newer forms of UGC associated with the internet will drive out older forms of professionally produced content.

This theme in turn lends itself to systems of classification based on binary oppositions, of which the most popular has been the 'pro-am' distinction between professionals and amateurs. The most common theme in this literature has been a return to the positive evaluation of the amateur ('one who does high-quality work for love rather than money') common in the nineteenth century, as against the generally dismissive view ('one not up to professional standards') that prevailed in the twentieth century. However, negative views of amateurism have also been prominent.[6]

Having done a good deal of work using this distinction, Dan Hunter[7] – along with co-authors Ramon Lobato and Julian Thomas – now seeks to tear it down. In their earlier chapter, Lobato, Thomas and Hunter instead propose to interpret UGC in terms of the category, commonly used in development economics, of informal economic activity. A key motivation is the desire to avoid defining the activities that produce UGC as one pole of a binary opposition with the professional sector, and instead to address UGC on its own terms. As they observe:

UGC remains a category typically defined in relation to its normative opposites, the professionally produced content that is supported and sustained by commercial media businesses or public organisations, and the purportedly docile and passive modes of consumption associated with mass analog media.

Lobato, Hunter and Thomas are right to point out the difficulties inherent in this scheme of categorisation. However, it is far from clear that the right solution is to employ an alternative category of informal activity, inevitably defined in opposition to the formal sector that dominates (measured) economic activity.

A central and mostly valid part of the pro-am analysis is that UGC is not created primarily for sale or other forms of monetisation. By contrast, the informal economy is all about money or at least about the pursuit of economic goals. Especially in developed economies, the informal sector is notable for heavy reliance on cash as a way of avoiding state control. Even where various forms of barter are involved (both in pre-monetary economies and in modern forms of informality such as internships) there is a substantial degree of economic calculation. Such calculation is typically (not invariably) absent in the UGC world.

I would argue that the natural starting point for economic analysis of UGC is not with the market economy (formal or informal) but with the economics of household production. Although it is not valued in measures such as gross domestic product,[8] the production within households of goods and services, such as meals, recreation and childcare, accounts for about the same amount of labour time as market work.[9]

The boundary between household production and market interactions shifts back and forth over time. In *More Work for Mother*, Ruth Schwartz Cowan showed how household 'labour-saving devices' like washing machines and vacuum cleaners led households and more specifically housewives to take over functions that had previously been outsourced to commercial businesses like laundries or (in the middle class) performed by servants.[10]

By contrast, the general tendency of the late twentieth century (in developed countries) was towards more marketisation of services previously provided within the households or through social interactions between households. The archetypal example was the trend towards eating out or buying take-away food replacing home-cooked meals. But there was also the emergence of specialist services such as wedding planners, personal trainers and so on, performing functions that would once have been outside the market.

The internet has, mostly, acted to reverse the trend. First, households can perform directly a range of functions (booking airline tickets, for example) that would previously have been sourced from the markets. Second, and more relevant to the current context, the range of direct social interactions that are feasible has increased greatly. In particular, these social interactions can produce what is referred to (from the perspective of market providers of information and entertainment services) as UGC. I will use the acronym to refer to any information generated by individuals and households that might be of interest to others, whether or not that was the objective.

Households undertake a wide variety of intra-household activities that are productive (in a very broad sense) ranging from food production and preparation to play and conversation. Such activities lead to the production of forms of UGC, some of which may be preserved and published more broadly in the end (for example, letters). Technological developments have changed this in various ways as the chapter shows – email is probably less likely to be widely published than letters were, but blogs, tumblrs, flickrs, et cetera more so.

Household members interact socially with members of other households in various ways. These include conversations, parties, social and sporting clubs, various kinds of informal mutual aid and so on. Social interactions involve norms of reciprocity (as do intra-household interactions to varying extents) but at least in societies with a well-developed market sector, there is usually a reasonably clear distinction between friendship and business. In particular, what is usually termed the 'informal' economy falls mainly on the business side of this divide.

Sometimes individuals cross this divide turning social interactions into a job or business – for example, a home cook who starts by giving cakes as gifts and ends up owning, or finding a job in, a cupcake shop. Conversely, activities once undertaken in the market economy may go the other way – for example, crafts that are technologically obsolete may be continued in the household sector.

In most activities this kind of crossing between social and business/work interactions is the exception not the rule. Where such crossings are frequent, as with sports players, it may be formalised into a pro-am distinction. As was observed above, the general tendency of the second half of the twentieth century was a movement from amateur to professional.

By contrast, the internet allowed the rapid development of amateur activity in fields that had previously been almost exclusively professional, particularly in relation to information and entertainment, generically referred to by the owners of transmission media as 'content'. Since the most interesting information is information about yourself, information producers on both sides of this divide have naturally spent a lot of time talking about it. However, that does not mean that the pro-am divide is the most important aspect of UGC, at least from the perspective of households.

Much of what is novel in UGC has arisen from new forms of social interaction facilitated by the internet. Social groups can now bring together people whose only interaction is online, and therefore easily retrieved and published. The publication itself, rather than being an afterthought as with old letters, is often central to the social interaction.

Take the primeval form of interaction between computer users, the bulletin board, of which USENet provided the archetypal examples. As the name 'bulletin board' indicates, these began as straightforward adaptations of a long-standing form of social interaction. Users posted notes and requests for information on particular topics, normally of ephemeral interest. However, unlike a physical bulletin board, internet message boards have effectively unlimited capacity, memory and readership. As a result, conversations could be conducted at length, and published to readers who lacked the desire or capacity to participate actively in the conversation. This process gave rise to a set of overlapping social groups associated with different lists and topics.

Much of this process leading to the production of UGC does not fit either a pro-am or a formal–informal distinction. Even the household–market distinction is problematic, because the content commonly arises from social interactions between members of different households. Rather, it may best be viewed as an output produced by civil society, or perhaps as a new form of the 'third sector', typically used to encompass non-government organisations of various kinds.

An analysis based on such a view would have to take account of the fact that UGC has, more than most of the standard candidates, the properties of a pure public good. That is (except for technical bandwidth limits that rarely bind) it is non-rival in consumption (one person reading a blog does not reduce the amount available for others) and it is non-excludable (or at least, exclusion of consumers on the basis of willingness to pay is almost never practised with respect to UGC).

There are a number of factors that may explain why UGC seems to emerge from some combination of household production and the workings of civil society. Under the technological conditions of the internet, the products of what are now ordinary social interactions can be made universally available with ease and in many cases are public by default. The absence of any easy way of capturing monetary returns, which has continually proved problematic for content producers in the market sector is much less of a problem when the product arises from large numbers of small contributions, rather than from the efforts of full-time producers.

Consideration of the role of civil society and the household sector may help to overcome some of the difficulties associated with dichotomies between professionals and amateurs or between formal and informal sectors of the economy. Nevertheless, until discussion of the internet produces its own analytical categories, rather than adapting those of a pre-internet economy, it is unlikely that these difficulties will be fully resolved.

Notes

1 Eric Raymond, 'Homesteading the Noosphere' (1998) 3(10–15) *First Monday*: www.first-monday.org/htbin/cgiwrap/bin/ojs/index.php/fm/article/view/621/542.

2 Ibid.

3 An experience no longer possible in developed societies, where everyone, even those who choose not to participate – is aware of, and more or less familiar with – the internet in its various manifestations.

4 Clifford Stoll, *Silicon Snake Oil: Second Thoughts on the Information Highway*, New York: Doubleday, 1995.

 5 Jaron Lanier, 'One-Half of a Manifesto', *Wired* (online), December 2000 www.wired.com/wired/archive/8.12/lanier.html.
 6 See, e.g., Andrew Keen, *The Cult of the Amateur: How Blogs, MySpace, YouTube, and the Rest of Today's User-Generated Media are Destroying our Economy, our Culture, and our Values*, New York: Crown Business, 2008.
 7 See, e.g., Dan Hunter and Greg Lastowka, 'Amateur-to-Amateur' (2004) 46 *William & Mary Law Review* 951; Dan Hunter and John Quiggin, 'Money Ruins Everything' (2008) 30 *Hastings Communications & Entertainment Law Journal* 203.
 8 For the very good reason that GDP is a measure of economic activity, useful in assessing the aggregate state of the market economy, not a measure of economic welfare.
 9 See the figures listed in the *Harmonised European Time Use Survey* (30 October 2007): www.h2.scb.se/tus/tus/StatMeanMact1.html.
10 Ruth Schwartz Cohen, *More Work for Mother: The Ironies of Household Technology From the Open Hearth to the Microwave*, New York: Basic Books, 1985.

Part II

Platform politics

4 Amateur creative digital content and proportional commerce

Steven Hetcher

Introduction

The goal of this chapter is to search out and explore some of the commercial aspects of amateur culture. In the Digital Millennium Copyright Act (DMCA), US copyright law refers to amateur internet 'users' in an explicit manner. The DMCA s 512(c) safe harbour is titled 'Information Residing in Systems at Direction of Users'.[1] The term 'users' here of course is referring to the users of the various internet service providers ('ISPs') for which the four safe harbours of the DMCA are intended. Similar legislation has been passed in a variety of countries, showing the robustness of the DMCA's general approach to regulating potential indirect infringement suits against ISPs.[2] ISPs have a few related features that have garnered them significant legal attention. On the one hand, they are widely perceived to be the backbone of the internet and worthy of special protection for that reason. On the other hand, they are currently implicated in much colourably infringing activity, and have deep pockets and relatively fixed locations and assets, which has garnered them the attention of plaintiffs' attorneys.

The rise of amateur creative digital content ('ACDC') has been characterised in high-minded terms, such as with the claim that it promotes democratic values by means of creating a more participatory culture.[3] It has been lauded as well for promoting new forms of culture not possible, or less likely, when motivation is purely commercial. Rebecca Tushnet argues, for instance, that large numbers of creators have been freed from the tyranny of seeking to achieve some degree of commercial success.[4] Appreciating these laudable features of ACDC is not, however, at variance with equally appreciating the essential role played by the commercial sphere in making much of this content available. Perhaps most revealing in this connection, consider the fact that two of the most significant commercial internet behemoths – Facebook and YouTube – are also two of the largest ACDC sites. From this fact it is hard not to conclude that, as oxymoronic as it may sound, amateur work may be most bountifully produced in a supportive commercial milieu. While litigants with a stake in the issue may seek to characterise all content on such sites as commercial, from a more objective, ordinary language perspective, typical creators who upload their works are no less amateurs than those college athletes whose games are commercially telecast.

Nevertheless, top user-generated content ('UGC') sites have been, and continue to be, largely advertising-based at their core. No fan of ACDC can be blind to the fact that the greatest quantities of ACDC, and some of the most culturally important as well, appear now to be arising in commercial contexts. Consider the following list of top 15 UGC sites:[5]

1   YouTube
2   Wikipedia
3   Twitter
4   craigslist
5   WordPress
6   Flickr
7   IMDB
8   Photobucket
9   Blogger
10 Tumblr
11 eHow
12 Yelp
13 TypePad
14 HubPages
15 Digg

Note the predominance of commercial sites on the list. What is changing, and significantly, are the types and diversity of content and the growing complexity and diversity of relationships whereby content plays a role in a business model. Perhaps the important practical question, then, is whether this substantial commercial connection will inexorably detract from what makes amateur content attractive in the first place.[6]

Compared to other commercial ACDC-related sites, YouTube and Facebook have something very important in common – each has somehow managed to crack the secret code when it comes to getting people to provide content to the site. Facebook should be seen as the largest ACDC site in the world with 750 million users, that is, contributors of original content, and yet, the site is typically not characterised as an ACDC site.[7] Note, for example, that the list provided above of the 15 most popular UGC sites does not include Facebook.[8] Surely this is not because the other sites have more users or more amateur content or more anything but rather that Facebook was not viewed as in the category of a UGC site. This is not so surprising as Facebook is most often described as a 'social media' site or 'social network'. These monikers play up Facebook's usefulness as a communications platform. But the copyright connection is there as well, as much of the content provided by users is copyrightable. Indeed, Facebook treats it as such, by telling users that they own their content.[9] For copyright purposes, then, Facebook is a hugely important ACDC site, and one that has achieved great financial success, with its share value at over $65 billion in the private market.[10]

Another important similarity between Facebook and YouTube can be seen in terms of how they developed. Each site was able to grow to a large size without the pressure to monetise the site too quickly. Facebook was able to afford this luxury, as it was easily able to attract significant private capital investment, due mainly to its wild initial success in attracting users.[11] YouTube could afford this luxury as its corporate parent, Google, is extremely successful financially.[12] These companies each dominate in an industry that is significantly affected by network effects. By delaying monetising, these companies were able to grow in size in a friendlier environment. Once they achieved scale, it became much harder for potential competitors to enter the market, and they could then seek to monetise.

Led by these two sites, ACDC is exploding and moreover is having an increasingly significant social impact.[13] These considerations alone make it crucial to better understand the various connections between ACDC and the commercial domain. Most straightforward, a better understanding of this connection may grease the wheels of commerce in terms of facilitating greater production of ACDC.[14] On the other hand, commercial concerns may shape amateur culture in a direction that is internally profit maximising but that may throw off negative externalities of various sorts that in sum outweigh the private benefits. For instance, significant negative externalities have been alleged with regard to Facebook vis-à-vis the issue of privacy. Indeed, while Mark Zuckerberg may have made the cover of *Time* magazine by the end of 2010 as the 'Person of the Year', his company made the cover of the same magazine earlier in the year due to its increasingly visible notoriety as a threat to privacy.[15] While privacy concerns have been the pervasive threat that Facebook is perceived to create, elsewhere I have argued that it is colourably characterised as a massive infringer of copyright as well.[16] These considerations notwithstanding, the main focus here will be on YouTube because it relies on a more legally problematic business model, but one that also promises extraordinary contributions to the social storehouse of creative works. Moreover, an important case that goes to the core business model of YouTube was recently decided. This case, *Viacom International Inc v YouTube Inc*,[17] constitutes an important contribution to the common law interpretation of the DMCA that is slowly emerging in the wake of the statute's enactment in 1998.[18] Presumably, other copyright regimes that have adopted DMCA-like legislation creating ISP safe harbours of one sort or another may find the case of interest as well. In the US context, the case is seminal inasmuch as the very existence of YouTube turns on the outcome.

Frequently left out of academic discussions of ACDC is the often intimate connection it has with the world of online commerce. This phenomenon is poignantly on display in the treatment that both Henry Jenkins and Lawrence Lessig give to teen role model Heather Lawver in their writings.[19] Indeed much of what is precious and good about ACDC is distilled in the story of

Lawver, who, as a teenager started a fan site, 'The Daily Prophet', for amateur creators of Harry Potter fan fiction to post their works, critique and comment on one another's works and in general commune on all things Harry Potter. In addition, she helped foster and support Harry Potter fan sites run by teens around the world and organised political resistance when Warner Brothers sought to shut them down.[20] A significant element contributing to the charm of her story and the significance of her activities is undeniably due to their non-commercial nature, not to mention her youthful pluck.[21]

The inspiring story of Lawver notwithstanding, it costs money to maintain collaboration projects such as 'The Daily Prophet'. This is only too clear to users of Wikipedia who are currently greeted upon each visit to the site by an image of founder Jimmy Wales, cup in hand, asking for donations.[22] Regarding Heather Lawver, Jenkins notes in passing that her efforts were not without financial cost.[23] A Google search of the term 'Daily Prophet' now yields a page populated with links to commercial sites replete with flashing banner ads and the usual indicia of the commercial internet. Lawver's original site is not to be found. Sadly, one learns from her Facebook page that she has closed down the site and now suffers serious illness. Sad in a different way, her Facebook page contains ads such as the one for the new Harry Potter attraction at Disney World.

The non-commercial, voluntary nature of new forms of digital content has been a theme explored in detail by a number of writers such as Benkler, Lessig and Clay Shirky. Benkler's key examples – open-source software and Wikipedia – arise in non-commercial contexts.[24] Similarly, Shirky finds inspiration in Wikipedia and extrapolates broadly from there.[25] These writers treat these developments in utopian terms as the cutting edge of a new age of valuable social creation, especially noteworthy due to its production without the need for corporate backing. For Benkler, there is an overt political dimension to these new forms of 'peer production', for, as he notes, they call into question the core assumption of traditional economic thinking: *homo economicus*, man the narrowly self-interested, rational actor.[26]

Following on the insights of Benkler, Jenkins and Shirkey, Lessig raises the question as to whether amateur collaborative efforts can remain stable in a commercial context. In Part II of his recent book *Remix*, Lessig provides an extended discussion of websites that seek to fuse the amateur and the commercial, referring to these as 'hybrid' sites.[27] Lessig views the core concern as one of motivation to contribute. He speaks of 'me' and 'thee' motivations.[28] He raises the issue as to whether hybrid sites can be stable or instead are inherently prone to lose participants, as amateur contributors, acting from 'thee' motives, come to feel that they are being taken advantage of by sites that profit from their users' largesse.[29] It can be concluded then that while there is an undeniable attraction to amateur content, aggregations of such content into larger wholes – Benkler's so-called 'peer productions' or Lessig's hybrids – seem beset with instability due to the problem of maintaining altruistic motivations to participate as the project became larger and more impersonal.

Some commentators will not find this lack of scalability to be unfortunate, as ACDC has attracted critics as well. Andrew Keen was the first to provide an extended critique of Web 2.0 developments in his derisively but also aptly entitled book *The Cult of the Amateur*, in which he writes:

> Today's technology hooks all those monkeys up with all those typewriters. Except in our Web 2.0 world, the typewriters aren't quite typewriters, but rather networked personal computers, and the monkeys aren't quite monkeys, but rather internet users. And instead of creating masterpieces, these millions and millions of exuberant monkeys—many with no more talent in the creative arts than our primate cousins—are creating an endless digital forest of mediocrity.[30]

Keen argues that much amateur content is derivative and low quality, and, moreover, is detrimental to the survival of established content industries such as newspapers and the film industry:

> [T]he very traditional institutions that have helped to foster and create our news, our music, our literature, our television shows, and our movies are under assault as well. Newspapers and news-magazines, one of the most reliable sources of information about the world we live in, are flailing, thanks to the proliferation of free blogs and sites like Craigslist that offer free classifieds, undermining paid ad placements.[31]

Despite his intimations to the contrary, Keen was a relative outsider to Silicon Valley digerati power circles and his words were generally dismissed as those of a failed Web 2.0 entrepreneur spewing sour grapes.[32] Lessig is uncharacteristically harsh in his appraisal:

> [W]hat is puzzling about this book is that it purports to be a book attacking the sloppiness, error and ignorance of the internet, yet it itself is shot through with sloppiness, error and ignorance. It tells us that without institutions, and standards, to signal what we can trust (like the institution (Doubleday) that decided to print his book), we won't know what's true and what's false. But the book itself is riddled with falsity – from simple errors of fact, to gross misreadings of arguments, to the most basic errors of economics ... The lesson he teaches is one we should all learn – to read and think critically, whether reading the product of the 'monkeys' (as Keen likens contributors to the internet to be) or books published by presses such as Doubleday.[33]

More recently, Jaron Lanier has made similar criticisms: 'Anonymous blog comments, vapid video pranks, and lightweight mashups may seem trivial and harmless, but as a whole, this widespread practice of fragmentary, impersonal communication has demeaned interpersonal interaction.'[34] However, due to his Silicon Valley insider status, his remarks have not invoked the same sort of disdain.[35]

My point in raising these considerations regarding ACDC is not to serve as a prelude to a fuller consideration of the issues but instead provide support for my claim that the issues raised by Benkler and Lessig, on the one hand, and Keen and Lanier, on the other hand, do not apply to the sorts of amateur content found on dominant commercial sites like Facebook and YouTube. Consider, for example, Lessig's distinction between 'me' and 'thee' motivations. It is simply inapplicable because for sites like Facebook or YouTube, by and large, users upload content because it serves their purposes – they do not understand themselves to be engaged in altruistic activities. Moreover, even those contributors who might reasonably view themselves as acting for a greater good such as uploaders from Tahrir Square in Cairo in March 2011, will view their altruism as focused on YouTube's viewers.[36] YouTube itself is likely to be viewed for what it is, which is a vehicle by which such altruists may spread their message widely and costlessly. In other words, YouTube is likely to be implicitly viewed as providing value for the economic benefit it receives from hosting such content. Similarly with Facebook, it is not a matter of 'me' and 'thee' motivation. Instead, people upload content because they benefit from doing so by taking part in a social activity they enjoy. Increasingly, users may seek to brand themselves with a good image by means of what they post to their Facebook account.[37] Either way, their motivation is personal benefit.[38]

With regard to the criticism that UGC is killing off the industries it feeds on, this claim falls flat as applied to Facebook or YouTube. Facebook has furthered the creation of content that is subjectively valuable to smaller groups who are interconnected. Thus, rather than replacing a traditional business model for content production, Facebook has created a new type of content all together. A similar claim can be made for YouTube. Increasingly, people create content specifically to upload it on YouTube.

Thus, we arrive at some basic facts. Amateur-created content is valuable in part due to its amateurness, and yet this may be an unstable existence if the content will tend not to persist in an available state. One very obvious means of providing this is through commercial support, that is, if ACDC can somehow be rolled into a legal business model. YouTube is a site that hosts large amounts of commercial content and non-commercial content of broad interest.[39] Many videos on YouTube have been viewed millions of times. Videos 'go viral'. People go to the site to view content made by strangers. YouTube is not unlike traditional television in this respect. It is not surprising, then, that YouTube's very name and corporate logo are meant to suggest TV.

YouTube is different from either traditional television or Facebook in a manner that goes to the heart of its legal status, and that is the fact that much unauthorised commercial content appears on YouTube. By contrast, while Facebook may have its legal problems, they are by and large not copyright problems. As touched on earlier, Facebook has repeatedly been attacked by the public-interest privacy advocacy community over various of its business initiatives.[40] Facebook has, however, avoided major copyright lawsuits. This is quite remarkable given the juxtaposition of two facts: first, that its users own the content that they post, and second, that Facebook exhibits nearly unfettered de facto control over this content and profits handsomely from doing so. By contrast, YouTube has a much more problematic situation when it comes to using the creative content of others. Users of the site upload mainstream commercial content such as TV shows and songs in huge quantities. This had led YouTube to be sued by Viacom and other commercial content companies in a high-stakes lawsuit of a sort that Facebook has not had to face.[41] The remainder of the discussion will focus on the YouTube lawsuit, its significance for the § 512(c) safe harbour, and, in turn, the significance of both for amateur culture.

Emerging common law safe harbours for user-uploaded content

Commercial and non-commercial content are intermingled on YouTube in a way that they are not with Facebook. YouTube works this way because it was coded to allow for the intermingling of all content – and thus foreseen, even if not intended, is the mixing of amateur and commercial content. This feature has created significant legal jeopardy for YouTube's business model. This threat is not merely theoretical but came to fruition in *Viacom v YouTube*, which was recently decided in YouTube's favour, but is on appeal.[42] With hindsight, one might view this outcome as inevitable, but it was not viewed as such before the decision, neither, for that matter, is the outcome on appeal certain. Viacom claims tens of thousands of acts of wilful infringement and hence the potential damages claim is large.[43] This is due to the potential for statutory damages, for, as YouTube is at pains to observe, Viacom has alleged little by way of actual harm.[44] A loss would mean the potential shut-down of YouTube. Such an outcome would be a huge blow to the cause of cultural productivity, given the extent to which YouTube has become an important repository of diverse content. On the other hand, if YouTube ultimately prevails this would secure a global platform for ACDC and also serve to spur its production, which YouTube does by making the cost of mass distribution of video content free. Whatever the outcome is on final appeal, the following remarks will be relevant, as I will argue that careful analysis uncovers a proportionality principle at work, such that regardless of the outcome of the case, a larger principle has been set in motion that is like a slow tide moving in the direction of YouTube and sites like it. These sites, if commercial, will be the direct beneficiaries, but other beneficiaries will include the millions of creators, uploaders, downloaders and consumers who are YouTube's users.

Importantly, the Viacom opinion makes more room for ACDC sites that also contain significant amounts of commercial content. The Court interpreted § 512(c) of the DMCA to require a high level of knowledge on the part of the ISP before it will be disqualified from the safe harbour. The court noted:

'General knowledge that infringement is "ubiquitous" does not impose a duty on the service provider to monitor or search its service for infringements.'[45] Viacom had argued that Google had the requisite knowledge.[46] If true, this could create a duty on Google's part, even without an official notice of infringement by the owner. The court noted: 'Subsection (c) (1) (A) (ii) can best be described as a "red flag" test. ... [I]f the service provider becomes aware of a "red flag" from which infringing activity is apparent, it will lose the limitation of liability if it takes no action.'[47]

The court also noted, however, that 'The tenor of the foregoing provisions is that the phrases "actual knowledge that the material or an activity" is infringing, and "facts or circumstances" indicating infringing activity, describe knowledge of specific and identifiable infringements of particular individual items'.[48] The court found that YouTube did not have the specific knowledge of this sort, and further, when it was given notice, it responded appropriately pursuant to the Notice and Takedown provisions of the DMCA.[49]

This interpretation of the red flag test and the knowledge requirement are far from inevitable, however, as can be seen by how some other courts have treated 'actual knowledge' in earlier cases involving secondary infringement liability.[50] While Congress ostensibly created the § 512(c) safe harbours to function distinctly from the case law that had emerged to that point on secondary liability, nevertheless, the DMCA safe harbour provisions are aptly viewed as a codification of preceding case law running from Sony through Netcom. What the DMCA did was to, in effect, say that an ISP in situations analogous to that of the ISP in Netcom would have a safe harbour from contributory infringement, so long as the ISP does not have knowledge of infringement. If it acquires such knowledge, it must follow the Notice and Takedown provisions as set out in the statute. So, in that sense, the § 512(c) safe harbour has a knowledge standard; namely, the defendant cannot have actual knowledge of specific acts of infringement without acting.

Even if one does not have knowledge of this sort, however, one will still not qualify for the safe harbour unless one also does not satisfy the elements for vicarious liability, inasmuch as the elements for vicarious liability are built into the safe harbour requirements.[51] In particular, there must be no direct financial benefit combined with no right and ability to control. It is not far fetched to think a court could find these elements.[52] Finding direct financial benefit is possible as there is a line of cases to cite for the proposition that commercial content acts as a draw to a site.[53] Thus, the question comes down to whether YouTube has a right and ability to control its users' uploading of infringing material. Not unreasonably, Viacom argued that of course YouTube has such a right and ability, as it regularly exercises this prerogative with other types of content when it has an interest to do so, such as with pornographic content.[54]

Instead of writing on a blank slate regarding what the right and ability to control should amount to online, the *Viacom* court followed the approach that courts have taken in recent cases such as those involving file-sharing. In particular, the court adopted the doctrine that a putative indirect infringer cannot be said to have the right and ability to control unless the defendant knew about the infringement. Here, courts have applied an objective knowledge standard; that is, whether the defendant knew or should have known about the infringement.[55] The *Viacom* court notes that it is implausible to think that YouTube should have known that some specific work owned by plaintiff and uploaded to YouTube is an unauthorised use. The court writes:

> [T]he infringing works in suit may be a small fraction of millions of works posted by others on the service's platform, whose provider cannot by inspection determine whether the use has been licensed by the owner, or whether its posting is a 'fair use' of the material, or even whether its copyright owner or licensee objects to its posting.[56]

This general line of thinking is familiar as it is an approach that goes back to *Sony* and the 'Sony Doctrine', which is the doctrine that constructive knowledge of infringement will not be imputed when a technology has both infringing and non-infringing uses.[57] The logic is that it would unduly constrain the development of new technologies if they could be taken off the market on the basis of potential infringing uses, which would have the effect of leaving them unavailable for non-infringing uses as well. The canonical language is that the technology must be actually or potentially capable of commercially significant, non-infringing uses.[58] The court in *Sony* did not give a precise specification for what would count as 'substantial' or 'commercially significant'.

Post-*Sony*, a number of leading cases have provided an interpretive gloss to this key text. In *Aimster*, for example, Judge Posner argues that the court must have had some sort of cost/benefit principle in mind.[59] He argues that it cannot be enough that there is a mere abstract possibility of such uses.[60] Under the facts in *Aimster*, Posner J argues that this was all that defendant Aimster was presenting.[61] Aimster's reply was that this was all it could give as all the files that were shared by its users were encrypted.[62] Posner J's response was that Aimster did so intentionally so that it could remain ignorant of any infringement, thus putting itself in a position to claim a lack of the actual knowledge of user-infringing behaviour on its site.[63] Likening the situation to the criminal law, Posner J concluded that this amounted to 'wilful blindness' and that wilful blindness can be tantamount to knowledge.[64] Instead of imputing knowledge, however, ever resourceful, Posner J shifted the burden to defendant Aimster to show substantial non-infringing use, which of course Aimster was in no position to do, given the encryption it had implemented. Posner J hoisted Aimster on its own petard.[65] The most important development to come out of this case is Posner J's idea that what is at issue in the Sony test is a cost/benefit conception of when courts should be willing to allow a finding of constructive knowledge in staple article of commerce-type situations:

The Court's action in striking the cost–benefit tradeoff in favor of Sony came to seem prescient when it later turned out that the principal use of video recorders was to allow people to watch at home movies that they bought or rented rather than to tape television programs ... An enormous new market thus opened for the movie industry, which by the way gives point to the Court's emphasis on potential as well as actual noninfringing uses. But the balancing of costs and benefits is necessary only in a case in which substantial noninfringing uses, present or prospective, are demonstrated.[66]

Although in most things a firebrand, here, paying heed to form, Posner J notes that surely this was what the Supreme Court had in mind in *Sony*.[67]

Interestingly, Justice Ginsburg picked up on Posner J's suggested interpretation in a footnote in her concurrence in *Grokster*.[68] She did not endorse the approach, per se, so much as note it as an alternative to the interpretation of the Sony rule put forward by Justice Breyer. Clearly Posner J's approach is more suited to her position, however, as she emphasises that the evidence of non-infringement in *Grokster* was very insubstantial and not sufficient to pass the *Sony* test.[69] Without referring to their actions as such, each of these Justices in effect performs a sort of proportionality test, comparing the amount of infringing versus non-infringing uses of Grokster's software by users. For his part, Breyer J notes that the percentage of non-infringing uses in *Grokster* is on a par with that in *Sony*.[70] Ginsburg J disagrees, noting that there is no fair use in *Grokster* whereas this was a crucial consideration in *Sony*.[71]

I will refer to the Posner J/Ginsburg J approach as the 'proportionality principle', which I claim courts de facto engage in as a crucial aspect in determining whether or not there is actual knowledge of specific infringing uses on the part of defendants. Breyer J sees Ginsburg J's approach as likely to have the impact of making it more difficult for ISPs such as Grokster to satisfy the *Sony* test, which Breyer J sees as failing to provide sufficient support for new technologies.[72] Ginsburg J contends that her approach gives the right amount of support for new technologies. In particular, it does not over-support them by allowing those that have not been shown to have substantial actual or potential commercially significant, non-infringing uses.[73] The point of going through this discussion is that it is my contention that it is this sort of de facto proportionality test the *Viacom* court has in mind in its discussion of why YouTube cannot be said to have actual knowledge of specific infringing works on its site. Contrary to the facts of a case like *Aimster* or even *Grokster*, YouTube contains a good deal of non-infringing uses.[74]

And, indeed, non-infringing uses continue to grow at a dramatic pace as YouTube continues to entrench itself as the go-to site for all things video. For example, on the day I write this sentence, the *New York Times* reported in its coverage of the Coachella music festival – one of the largest and most prestigious – that the whole festival was streamed on YouTube.[75] These past few months in the Middle East have been rocked by civil unrest in a number of countries. Video of these potentially world historic activities could be viewed each day almost in real time on YouTube. The social value of these videos speaks for itself.

By contrast, in the file-sharing cases, defendants had to work hard to come up with sufficient examples of the sorts of non-infringing uses that would, in combination, pass the *Sony* test. Defendants and their advocates were forced to rely, at least in part, on the bare possibility of future non-infringing uses. While this move is perhaps germane under the language of *Sony*, nevertheless Posner J is right that if the test is to remain true to the economist's approach, these possible outcomes must be discounted by the likelihood of their occurring. Considered as such, bare possibilities may carry little utility value.

With YouTube and the analogous test for the right proportion of infringing versus non-infringing uses, the utility calculation or cost/benefit analysis, even if only taking account of actual non-infringing uses, appears to over-whelmingly favour defendants, as the world has never before seen the likes of YouTube in terms of availability of non-infringing content. The amount of commercially significant, non-infringing content available on YouTube is simply extraordinary. Moreover, the proportion of this content to infringing content is growing. As this proportion grows, the statistical chance that any particular upload is infringing shrinks.[76] Thus, the proportionality principle implicit in courts' jurisprudence of indirect infringement by ISPs will increasingly work in YouTube's favour as time passes. This means that over time Google will increasingly be in a position to build a business model around this content rather than commercial content à la Napster, Grokster, et cetera.

We should celebrate Google for building YouTube. The company took on significant legal risk in doing so. The result is a richer, more powerful engine of amateur cultural output than anyone could have imagined. The owners of commercial content such as Viacom will be the first to point out that this has come at a cost, namely, to their dominion over their property. But the relevant policy question is not whether owners as a class were forced to carry some of the burden under the DMCA, but whether the overall social benefit compensates for this loss to owners.

The reason the cost/benefit argument is so strong in YouTube's favour is that, as noted earlier, there is little tangible harm to owners. This is in important contrast to the peer-to-peer cases, in which the uses were, to a significant degree, superseding ones. This trade-off would be the traditional manner in which to conceptualise the gains and losses. But there is another important contributor to social welfare that YouTube allows. It changes the default such that for millions of pieces of content, the default is that they are there on the site available to be searched and viewed unless the owner takes an action. Note how important this is for the practical availability of orphan works and ephemeral works.[77] Because the default has been shifted, these works will be available, once uploaded, unless the owner requests that they be taken down. Since this is unlikely to happen for these sorts of works in particular (given their orphan and or ephemeral status), the practical implication is that a whole world of video content that would generally be unavailable becomes available to anyone in the world for free simply by performing a search on YouTube. For the Viacoms of the world, this outcome does indeed create the additional expense of monitoring YouTube. But from the perspective of a proportionality approach, this is simply one cost to be factored in. This default seems to be the one that will make more creative culture available to more people. Moreover, the model is not subject to drawing from its seed corn, as YouTube does not directly compete with owners in the manner of Grokster, Aimster or Napster.

Conclusion

The goal of this chapter has been to search out and explore some of the core commercial aspects of amateur creative culture. We have seen that in a YouTube/Facebook world, a dramatically higher percentage of 'user information' for § 512(c) purposes would be available as ACDC. Copyright is about promoting creative content so it seems obvious that the more ACDC is at stake, the more important YouTube is to copyright law. This productive side of the DMCA is ignored in the literature in comparison to discussion of the extent to which the DMCA promotes the interests of the ISPs at the expense of commercial content owners. While it is true that it was the ISPs that lobbied for the safe harbours and do benefit from them, it is true as well that when ISPs such as YouTube benefit, so, too, do the users. For those involved in the production and consumption of ACDC, then, the goals of copyright are promoted. In *Lenz v Universal Music Corp*, ACDC is supported as the cost of commercial owners policing their content has gone up, thereby decreasing the incentive and expected benefit from doing so.[78] In *Viacom*, the existence of YouTube as a commercial entity was at stake. The court's discussion is also strongly in favour of users as well, who can continue to use YouTube on a mass scale. These decisions pave the way for sites that can more openly combine commercial and non-commercial uses. This will serve as a tailwind for future innovators in that, under *Viacom*, unauthorised commercial content can be an element of a business model so long as the conditions under YouTube are met. This creates a broader scope for innovation. This is potentially a huge boost to amateur culture. Time will tell what the spirit of creative ingenuity will produce, given this broader commercially laden field for amateur content to emerge.

Thus, a dozen years into the DMCA, we can get a better sense of how it is working and the important impact it is having on shaping the content world and in particular the world of amateur content. The DMCA is often characterised as the result of a deal between the two main lobbying interests, the content owner and the ISPs. The question of most interest from a policy perspective of course is how the public interest is faring in this deal. It appears that the public interest is being well served. This is of interest in the US but also more broadly, for, as noted earlier, other countries have adopted similar provisions.[79] The sorts of benefits and costs that occur in the US would appear to be the same as would occur elsewhere. Namely, commercial content owners will claim that they have lost rights, while users of sites such as YouTube will benefit and society will benefit to a greater extent. The original impetus for the DMCA was to make sure the internet was not sued out of existence. This goal has been achieved and much more. If *Viacom* stands, the DMCA can be seen as making possible a site such as YouTube that has encouraged creativity on a scale greater than anyone might have hoped.[80] The so-called Library of Alexandria has long been a goal of copyright theorists.[81] YouTube appears to be a beginning. The internet as a whole cannot be such a library; it is too much a clutter. Libraries need organisation in order to support optimal collection archiving and retrieval. Better than anyone else, YouTube provides the functionality and thus, better than anyone else, provides amateur creative digital content.

Acknowledgements

I wish to thank my research assistants, Kathryn Baker, Lee Holmes, Lauren Phillips and Shane Valenzi, and my administrative assistant, Susan Button, for their assistance. I wish to thank the many colleagues who commented on the ideas in this chapter in various fora.

Notes

1 17 USCA § 512 (West, Westlaw approved 29 June 2011).

2 See for example, Jane C. Ginsburg, 'Separating the Sony Sheep from the Grokster Goats: Reckoning the Future Business Plans of Copyright-Dependent Technology Entrepreneurs' (2008) 50 *Arizona Law Review* 577, 602 (the European Union); Karen Dearne, 'US Gets Its Way on Copyright Law', *The Australian* (Sydney) 30 November 2004, available at WLNR 12409795 (Australia); Marcia Ellis, Jean Zheng and Paul Weiss, 'Safe Harbour Protection in China: How China's New Regulations Protect the Information Dissemination Rights of Digital Networks' (2006–7) December/January *China Law & Practice*, available at WLNR 25657965 (China).

3 Henry Jenkins et al., 'Confronting the Challenges of Participatory Culture: Media Education for the 21st Century' (Report, John D. and Catherine T. MacArthur Foundation, 2009) p. xi, available at http://mitpress.mit.edu/books/full_pdfs/Confronting_the_Challenges.pdf; see also Carrie James et al., 'Young People, Ethics, and the New Digital Media' (2010) 2(2) *Contemporary Readings in Law and Social Justice* 215, 216.

4 Rebecca Tushnet, 'User-Generated Discontent: Transformation in Practice' (2008) 31 *Columbia Journal of Law & Arts* 497, 506, 513.

5 *Top 15 Most Popular Web 2.0 Websites July 2011* (last updated 15 October 2011) eBiz MBA: www.ebizmba.com/articles/web-2.0-websites.

6 Indeed, the conventional account of the fall of MySpace is that it got greedy in terms of aggressive monetisation after it was acquired by NewsCorp: see Felix Gillette, 'The Rise and Inglorious Fall of MySpace', *Businessweek* (online), 22 June 2011: www.businessweek.com/magazine/content/11_27/b4235053917570.htm.

7 Not surprisingly, given Facebook's success, social networking sites are all the rage in Silicon Valley, with Facebook's top people leaving to form them. One journalist notes: 'Facebook, the most successful start-up of the last decade, is only six years old, and an initial public offering is still a way off. But a number of Facebook's early employees are giving up their

stable jobs, free food and laundry service to build their own [UGC] businesses': Vernie G. Kopytoff, 'Facebook's Initial Crew Moving On', *New York Times* (online) 3 November 2010: www.nytimes.com/2010/11/03/technology/03facebook.html.

8   More odd, however, in *Remix*, Lawrence Lessig fails to identify Facebook as one of his hybrids that combines the amateur and the commercial: Lawrence Lessig, *Remix: Making Art and Commerce Thrive in the Hybrid Economy*, New York: Penguin, 2008, pp. 177–224.

9   Facebook, *Statement of Rights and Responsibilities* (as updated at 26 April 2011) Facebook: www.facebook.com/terms.php ('You own all of the content and information you post on Facebook, and you can control how it is shared through your privacy and application settings'). It is worth noting that even Facebook cannot decree that users own information.

10   Yuliya Fedorinova, 'Facebook Stakeholder Usmanov Says Web Asset Returns Peaked' (15 April 2011) *Bloomberg*: www.bloomberg.com/news/2011-04-15/facebook-stakeholder-usmanov-says-web-investment-returns-may-have-peaked.html ('When Usmanov and Milner bought 1.96 percent of Facebook in 2009, the deal valued the company at as much as $10 billion. Today, research firm Nyppex LLC values the world's most-used social networking site at $65 billion').

11   Network effects make the site more 'sticky', that is, harder to leave; the reason to be on Facebook is that all one's friends are on Facebook.

12   YouTube had an additional reason to delay monetisation, and this was due to the legal jeopardy it faced regarding the large amount of unauthorised commercial content owned by media giants such as Viacom located on its site. In YouTube's case, it was safer not to try to maximise profit on this initiative, as it would work to their potential disadvantage in their lawsuit.

13   See, e.g., John F. Burns and Miguel Helft, 'YouTube Withdraws Muslim Cleric's Videos', *New York Times* (online) 4 November 2010: www.nytimes.com/2010/11/04/world/04britain.html; Adam Rawnsley, 'Taliban Steps Boldly in 2007, Invades YouTube' (13 October 2009) *Wired*: www.wired.com/dangerroom/2009/10/taliban-steps-boldy-in-2007-invades-you-tube/ (describing the Taliban's foray into embedding YouTube videos on their official site and providing links to Digg, Twitter and Reddit, among other UGC sites, at the bottom of their posts); Helen A. S. Popkin, 'Power of Twitter, Facebook in Egypt Crucial, Says U.N. Rep' (11 February 2011) *MSNBC*: http://technolog.msnbc.msn.com/_news/2011/02/11/6033340- power-of-twitter-facebook-in-egypt-crucial-says-un-rep ('American U.N. Ambassador Susan Rice recognized the "enormous impact" of Twitter and Facebook on the world's stage. "Governments are increasingly cognizant of their power", Rice said Thursday morning during a town hall meeting at Twitter headquarters in San Francisco. Much of the 50-minute town hall [meeting], however, focused on the role of Twitter and Facebook in organising protests in Egypt. "The power of this technology, the power of social network-ing to channel and champion public sentiment, has been more evident in the past few weeks than ever before", Rice said.').

14   See generally, Lessig, *Remix* (setting out 'hybrid' models of amateur and commercial colla-boration that may serve as successful business models).

15   Lev Grossman, 'Person of the Year 2010: Mark Zuckerberg' (15 December 2010) *Time Magazine* (online): www.time.com/time/specials/packages/article/0,28804,2036683_2037183_2037185,00.html; Dan Fletcher, 'How Facebook is Redefining Privacy' (20 May 2010) *Time Magazine* (online): www.time.com/time/magazine/article/0,9171,1990798,00.html.

16   Steven Hetcher, 'User-Generated Content and the Future of Copyright: Part Two-Agreements between Users and Mega-Sites' (2008) 24 *Santa Clara Computer & High Tech Law Journal* 829.

17   718 F Supp 2d 514 (SD NY, 2010) ('*Viacom*').

18   *Digital Millennium Copyright Act*, Pub L No 105–304, 1998 HR 2281 (Westlaw) (codified in scattered sections of 17 USC).

19   Lessig, *Remix*, at pp. 205–21; Henry Jenkins, *Convergence Culture: Where Old and New Media Collide*, New York: New York University Press, 2006, pp. 175–216.

20   Lessig, *Remix*, at pp. 206–8.

21 Jenkins discusses the voluntary nature of the proofreaders at other amateur sites in the same glowing terms. See Jenkins, 'Confronting the Challenges of Participatory Culture', at pp. 1–3.

22 The difference in the amount of money Wikipedia claims it needs to operate and the amount of money it actually spends is a matter of some controversy: see Gregory Kohs, 'Jimmy Wales Rattles the Tin Cup', examiner.com, 8 October 2010: www.examiner.com/wiki-edits-in-national/jimmy-wales-rattles-the-tin-cup.

23 Jenkins, 'Confronting the Challenges of Participatory Culture', at pp. 2–3. There have been attempts to avoid over-commercialisation. For example, the website *Jatalla* started in 2006 to much fanfare. The site's home page noted: 'Support user-generated, ad-free, behavior-tracking free search.' The site promised relevance rankings produced only by users (not webcrawlers or page analysis algorithms). While still there, the site clearly appears to have failed, judging by the dearth of content available on it: https://jatalla.com/beta/.

24 Yochai Benkler, *The Wealth of Networks: How Social Production Transforms Markets and Freedom*, New Haven, CT: Yale University Press, 2007, pp. 5–6.

25 Clay Shirky, *Here Comes Everybody: The Power of Organizing Without Organizations*, New York: Penguin, 2008, pp. 109–13.

26 See generally, Benkler, *The Wealth of Networks*.

27 Lessig, *Remix*, at pp. 177–249.

28 Ibid., at pp. 151–54.

29 Ibid., at pp. 231–43.

30 Andrew Keen, *The Cult of the Amateur: How Today's Internet is Killing Our Culture*, New York: Doubleday, 2007, pp. 2–3.

31 Ibid., at pp. 7–8.

32 See, e.g., Jeff Jarvis, 'Snobs.com' on BuzzMachine (18 February 2006): www.buzzmachine.com/2006/02/18/snobscom/; Michiko Kakutani, 'Books of the Times: The Cult of the Amateur', New York Times (online), 29 June 2007: www.nytimes.com/2007/06/29/books/29book.html.

33 Lawrence Lessig, 'Keen's "The Cult of the Amateur": BRILLIANT!' on *Lessig 2.0* (31 May 2007): http://lessig.org/blog/2007/05/keens_the_cult_of_the_amateur.html.

34 Jaron Lanier, *You Are Not a Gadget: A Manifesto*, New York: Alfred A. Knopf, 2010, p. 4.

35 See Michiko Kaktani, 'A Rebel in Cyberspace, Fighting Collectivism', New York Times (online) 14 January 2010: www.nytimes.com/2010/01/15/books/15book.html, and compare with her criticism of Keen in 'Books of the Times: Cult of the Amateur'.

36 Multiple deadly raids in Tahrir Square were captured on video and posted to YouTube by protesters. See, e.g., Robert Mackey, 'Video Shows Deadly Raid on Cairo's Tahrir Square', New York Times (online) 9 April 2011: http://thelede.blogs.nytimes.com/2011/04/09/video-shows-deadly-raid-on-cairos-tahrir-square/.

37 See, e.g., Joy Peluchette and Katherine Karl, 'Examining Students' Intended Image on Facebook: "What Were They Thinking?!" (2010) 85 *Journal of Education for Business* 30, 33, 35.

38 It is true that for most sites there is a basic problem of how to get amateurs to contribute content. But focusing on the problem of waning altruism is not the core issue for most sites. Most sites (internet entrepreneurs) struggle to get content simply because they struggle to attract the attention of potential uploaders in an increasingly crowded market.

39 Steve Knopper, 'Digital Music's Unlikely King', *Rolling Stone*, 31 March 2011, p. 17: 'iTunes and Pandora might get more attention, but the biggest player in digital music isn't even a music service. It's YouTube, which over the past six years has helped break pop superstars from Lady Gaga to Justin Bieber as fans clicked on music-related videos hundreds of billions (yes, billions!) of times, according to digital-music analyst BigChampagne.'

40 The media has focused on the privacy problems of Facebook in seeking to monetise its content. See for example, Louise Story, 'Apologetic, Facebook Changes Ad Program', New York Times (online) 6 December 2007: www.nytimes.com/2007/12/06/technology/06facebook.html.

41 *Viacom*, 718 F Supp 2d 514 (SD NY, 2010).

42 Amanda Bronstad, 'Viacom v. YouTube' Appeal May Decide Future of Web (14 December 2010) *The National Law Journal*: www.law.com/jsp/nlj/PubArticleNLJ.jsp?id=1202476144090.

43 Michael Bazeley, 'Students File Brief in High-Profile Viacom-YouTube Copyright Case' (8 April 2011) Berkeley Law: www.law.berkeley.edu/10886.htm ('Media giant Viacom, which owns brands such as MTV Networks, BET Networks and Paramount Pictures, has been seeking $1 billion in damages from Google-owned YouTube').

44 Abigail Phillips, 'Viacom Round-Up: Still Complaining about YouTube even as They Profit from It' (17 December 2010) *Electronic Frontier Foundation* www.eff.org/deeplinks/2010/12/viacom-round-still-complaining-about-youtube-even; however, contrast this with 'Brief for Consumer Electronics Association as Amicus Curiae Supporting Appellees', at 5–6, *Viacom International v YouTube Inc*, No. 10–3270 (2nd cir).

45 *Viacom*, 718 F Supp 2d 514, 525.

46 Ibid., at 516.

47 Ibid., at 520.

48 Ibid., at 523.

49 Ibid., at 523–24.

50 *A&M Records Inc v Napster Inc*, 239 F 3d 1004, 1021 (9th Cir, 2001) ('[S]ufficient knowledge exists to impose contributory liability when linked to demonstrated infringing use of the Napster system').

51 17 USCA § 512(c)(1)(B) (West, Westlaw approved 29 June 2011): 'A service provider shall not be liable for monetary relief, or, except as provided in subsection (j), for injunctive or other equitable relief, for infringement of copyright by reason of the storage at the direction of a user of material that resides on a system or network controlled or operated by or for the service provider, if the service provider … does not receive a financial benefit directly attributable to the infringing activity, in a case in which the service provider has the right and ability to control such activity … ' The traditional elements of vicarious liability are found in many cases. See, e.g., *Shapiro, Bernstein & Co v H.L. Green Co*, 316 F 2d 304, 307 (2nd Cir, 1963).

52 For example, *Perfect 10 Inc v Visa International Service Association*, 494 F 3d 798, 810–25 (9th Cir, 2007) (Kozinski J dissenting): arguing credit card companies are vicariously liable for copyright and trade mark infringement and various state law claims because they acted as a financial bridge between buyers and sellers of pirated works, and therefore profited from the infringement in circumstances where they had the ability to control (by preventing the transaction).

53 See *Ellison v Robertson*, 357 F 3d 1072, 1078 (9th Cir, 2004) (citing *A&M Records Inc v Napster Inc*, 239 F 3d 1004, 1023 (9th Cir, 2001) (quoting *Fonovisa Inc v Cherry Auction Inc*, 76 F 3d 259, 263–64 (9th Cir 1996))).

54 Complaint at 14, *Viacom* 718 F Supp 2d 514 (SD NY, 2010), 2007 WL 775611.

55 *Viacom*, 718 F Supp 2d 514, 520–21 ('[I]n deciding whether those facts or circumstances constitute a "red flag" – in other words, whether infringing activity would have been apparent to a reasonable person operating under the same or similar circumstances – an objective standard should be used').

56 *Viacom*, 718 F Supp 2d 514, 524.

57 *Sony Corporation of America v Universal City Studios Inc*, 464 US 417, 418 ('*Sony*').

58 Ibid., 442.

59 *In re Aimster Copyright Litigation*, 334 F 3d 643, 649 (7th Cir, 2003) ('What is true is that when a supplier is offering a product or service that has noninfringing as well as infringing uses, some estimate of the respective magnitudes of these uses is necessary for a finding of contributory infringement').

60 Ibid., 651.

61 Ibid., 652 ('The evidence that we have summarized does not exclude the *possibility* of substantial noninfringing uses of the Aimster system, but the evidence is sufficient … to shift the burden of production to Aimster to demonstrate that its service has substantial noninfringing uses').

62 Ibid., 650.

63 Ibid., 651 ('[A] service provider that would otherwise be a contributory infringer does not obtain immunity by using encryption to shield itself from actual knowledge of the unlawful purposes for which the service is being used').

64 Ibid., 650 ('Willful blindness is knowledge, in copyright law … as it is in the law generally').

65 Ibid., 652–53.

66 Ibid., 649–50.

67 Ibid.

68 *Metro-Goldwyn-Mayer Studios Inc v Grokster Ltd*, 545 US 913, 942–44 (2005) (Ginsburg J, concurring) (quoting *Sony*, 464 US 417, 442) ('"The staple article of commerce doctrine" applied to copyright, the Court stated, "must strike a balance between a copyright holder's legitimate demand for effective – not merely symbolic – protection of the statutory monopoly, and the rights of others freely to engage in substantially unrelated areas of commerce"').

69 Ibid., 948.

70 Ibid., 952–53 (Breyer J, concurring).

71 Ibid., 945–47 (Ginsburg J, concurring).

72 Ibid., 955 (Breyer J, concurring).

73 Ibid., 944, n. 1 (Ginsberg J, concurring) (citations omitted).

74 Defendants' Answer and Demand for Jury Trial at 11, *Viacom*, 718 F Supp 2d 514 (SD NY, 2010) (No. 1:07-cv-02103), 2007 WL 1724620; Defendants' Answer to First Amended Complaint and Demand for Jury Trial, *Viacom*, 718 F Supp 2d 514 (SD NY, 2010) (No. 1:07-cv-02103), 2007 WL 2260018.

75 Ben Ratliff, 'At Coachella, Every Note is Writ Large', *New York Times* (online) 18 April 2011: www.nytimes.com/2011/04/19/arts/music/kanye-west-and-arcade-fire-at-coachella-festival-review.html.

76 A thoroughgoing approach to a cost/benefit proportionality principle would look not only at the percentage of infringing uses compared to non-infringing uses but also the harms that arise from the infringements.

77 For a definition of 'orphan work', see Christian L. Castle and Amy E. Mitchell, *Unhand that Orphan* (2009) 27 *Entertainment and Sports Lawyer* 1, 21 ('An "orphan work" is generally thought to be a work of copyright for which the author cannot be found after a good-faith search of relevant documents').

78 A second recent case which has been decided in a manner friendly to ACDC is *Lenz v Universal Music Corp*, 572 F Supp 2d 1150 (ND Cal, 2008). The case involved a YouTube user who uploaded a video of her toddler dancing to a Prince song that can be heard playing on the video in the background. Thus, the facts could hardly seem more in stark contrast to *Viacom v YouTube*, a battle between corporate giants and their law firms. But the facts of *Lenz* are more complex than suggested by the above factual thumb-nail sketch. To begin, this was not a typical infringement suit by an owner against an unauthorised user. Instead, Universal had effected a Notice and Takedown against the video under the procedure set out in the DMCA. The Electronic Frontier Foundation took the case, clearly spotting a perfect factual setting to attempt to create some favourable law with regard to the interpretation of the DMCA. The result is a coup of sorts for the EFF, the Stephanie Lenzes of the world and indeed for amateur users. The reason is that the court held that owners had the burden to allege lack of fair use or other authorisation of their uses: at 1154. This will stop owners from using blanket notices such as the one used in *Lenz*. The requirement of specificity will raise the cost of bringing a Notice and Takedown and hence lower the number of them, which in turn will promote amateur creative digital culture by lowering costs and increasing the benefits from participating.

79 For example, Australia's Digital Agenda Amendments brought Australian copyright protection into the twenty-first century by amending the Copyright Act of 1968. See Dale Clapperton and Stephen Corones, 'Locking in Customers, Locking Out Competitors: Anti-Circumvention

Laws in Australia and Their Potential Effect on Competition in High Technology Markets' (2006) 30 *Melbourne University Law Review* 657, 665.

80 At the time of writing, *Viacom* has been appealed and heard, but judgment has not yet been handed down: see Grant McCool, 'Appeals Court Zeroes in on Viacom-YouTube Dispute', *Reuters* (online) 18 October 2011: www.reuters.com/article/2011/10/18/us-viacom-google-idUSTRE79H8EK20111018.

81 See Rick Falkvinge, 'The Library of Alexandria 2.0' (12 March 2011) *Falkvinge & Co. on Infopolicy*: http://falkvinge.net/2011/03/12/the-library-of-alexandria-2-0/: Catherine Fredenburgh, 'Copyright Law and the New Library of Alexandria' (30 March 2006) *Law 360*: www.law360.com/ip/articles/5911/copyright-law-and-the-new-library-of-alexandria/.

5   YouTube and the formalisation of amateur media

Jean Burgess

Founded in February 2005 by three former PayPal employees, launched publicly later that year, and acquired by Google in 2006, YouTube has been around for little more than half a decade. Today it is the dominant platform for online video worldwide,[1] having experienced rapid growth in both audience share and in the amount of content uploaded – in 2011 the company announced that the site enjoyed three billion views per day and 48 hours of video footage uploaded per minute.[2] Since quite early on in the life of the platform, YouTube has been a prominent location for the 'copyright wars' – most visibly in the billion-dollar lawsuit brought by Viacom against Google in 2007, discussed in Steven Hetcher's chapter;[3] less visibly in the introduction of automated content matching often resulting in summary takedowns of apparently infringing videos, as well as the location-based filtering that results from the unevenness of content-licensing deals across national jurisdictions.[4] At the same time, YouTube has seen a flurry of experimentation with a range of monetisation strategies and business models – both on the part of the platform itself and that of the content creators who seek to exploit it.

As Joshua Green and I have discussed elsewhere,[5] at the beginning YouTube was relatively *underdetermined* as a cultural space. In 2005 it was a minimalist platform – little more than a web-based widget for video-sharing – whose purpose had yet to be defined, asking to be populated with just about anything people chose to share (with the exception of certain kinds of sexually explicit or excessively violent material).[6] As a result, it was close to an unregulated free-for-all where clips of *Family Guy*, news footage and favourite music videos ripped from television swirled around with homemade cat videos, footage of stupid stunts and amateur bedroom musical performances in a relatively flat architecture with little curation or quality control. As YouTube scaled up both as a platform and as a company, its business model and the consequences for its copyright regulation strategies have co-evolved, and so too the boundaries between amateur and professional media have shifted and blurred in particular ways.[7] As YouTube, Inc moves to more profitably arrange and stabilise the historically contentious relations among rights holders, uploaders, advertisers and audiences, some forms of amateur video production have become institutionalised and professionalised, while others have been further marginalised and driven underground or to other, more forgiving, platforms.

Despite its ongoing formalisation and legitimation as part of the contemporary media industry (and the recent disappearance of the 'Broadcast Yourself' slogan from the logo), the idea of YouTube as an open platform for amateur expression is buried deep in the DNA of the brand. An often-repeated origin myth has co-founders Chad Hurley and Steve Chen coming up with the idea for a video-sharing website after finding it difficult to upload and share their own dinner-party videos;[8] and famously, the first video uploaded to the site was a very short piece entitled 'Me at the Zoo', which featured the third co-founder Jawed Karim standing in front of the elephants' enclosure at the San Diego Zoo and making what could be interpreted as oblique comparisons between the size of the elephants' trunks and the size of other dangling appendages.[9] More than five years later, YouTube is still bubbling over with mundane home videos and other amateur content; and every now and then one of these videos hits the big time as the next big viral video or the source of yet another internet meme. One such home video, 'Charlie Bit My Finger', which captures a highly amusing but otherwise unremarkable interaction between two young brothers, still sits alongside mainstream stars like Lady Gaga and internet sensations like Justin Bieber in the most viewed videos of all time, with close to 400 million views as at November 2011.[10]

In his chapter in this volume, Steven Hetcher points to the interdependency of the non-commercial (in many cases, literally 'household') sphere of amateur content creation with the commerciality of the platforms, like YouTube, upon which this content is hosted and its audiences are produced. But it is not only the case that commercial platforms like YouTube are bringing into the sphere of the market modes of cultural participation that might formerly have been considered 'non-market' (domestic, everyday) activity. As it has matured as a commercial platform built on both amateur and professional content and supported by advertising, YouTube has been the site of another development – the professionalisation and formalisation of amateur media production. This shift is occurring through the inclusion of 'home-grown' YouTube producers in the revenue-sharing Partner Program, seeing the rise of the 'entrepreneurial vlogger',[11] as well as the new commercial cultural intermediaries that specialise in first marketising and then professionalising 'amateur' YouTube activity.

The YouTube Partner Program, which shares advertising revenue with content creators, was at first only accessible to 'big media' content providers, but soon opened up to a small group of particularly successful YouTubers (mostly videobloggers), and has become more inclusive over time. Famously, several producers of one-off viral videos (like the camera-wielding Dad behind 'Charlie Bit My Finger') or, more interestingly, long-running 'programs' of content mostly built around the videoblog genre (like Australian comic videoblogger Natalie Tran, aka *CommunityChannel*) have reportedly achieved six-figure incomes from revenue directly associated with the monetisation of their amateur content;[12] and YouTube-to-mainstream crossover celebrity Justin Bieber largely owes his career to the audiences built via the platform, and was reportedly 'discovered' there.[13] Indeed, it was the amateurs who first made a go of generating loyal audiences from their content on YouTube – addressing and collaborating with fellow YouTube users, responding to audience comments, referring to up-to-date developments in popular web culture by riffing off current YouTube memes, and so on.[14] In fact, just as it was in 2007, it is still the case in 2011 that the majority of the most-subscribed YouTube channels are, if not purely amateur, then at least primarily videoblog-style home-grown YouTube acts.[15]

In addition to pushing forward into mainstream digital media through premium television content, movie rentals and live-streaming of major sporting events, YouTube is increasingly promoting this kind of pro-am enterprise as a way forward for the platform. Such initiatives span the range between coordinated participation and high-end curation (as in the YouTube Symphony Orchestra project) through to professionalisation of amateur video production. In early 2011 YouTube announced the acquisition of Next New Networks, the small production company behind the 'Autotune the News' program and its spinoffs, and now specialising in turning other amateur YouTube talent into professional acts; in effect operating similarly to independent record labels in the music industry.[16] In an analysis of YouTube videos discussing the Partner Program, Peter Jakobsson has argued that the Partner Program in itself as well as initiatives like this has led to the encouragement of a competitive 'entrepreneurial desire' among the amateur YouTubers,[17] a dynamic that has been controversial in the wider YouTube community but that was already evident among those videobloggers who enjoyed early success on the platform,[18] and an example of the 'situated creativity'[19] that is necessary for the establishment of loyal subscribers and stable audiences in what is an extremely volatile media environment.

One particularly high-profile recent initiative is the YouTube Creators hub,[20] a dedicated area of the YouTube website which features video tutorials, detailed policy information and an extensive guide for creators called the 'YouTube Playbook'. Organised around the traditional steps in the media value chain (production, publication, and marketing), the guide details the aesthetic and formal qualities of successful YouTube videos, provides tips on metadata and search optimisation, and – crucially – discusses the highly specific strategies that are necessary to build loyal audiences on YouTube. This initiative can be seen as an attempt on behalf of YouTube to reduce the ratio of non-monetisable to monetisable amateur content, given the reluctance of advertisers to place a spot alongside poor quality content and the massive amount of footage uploaded to the server that receives very few views[21] – hence the invocations to publish at regular frequent intervals, to maintain a consistent format and brand, and so on. But, at the same time, many if not most of the examples of successful YouTube channels discussed in the guide are not recognisable media brands, but home-grown YouTube channels – whether or not they are now or ever were 'really' amateurs. The Phillip DeFranco

Show, Mystery Guitar Man, Freddie W and other YouTube channels are all used as examples of YouTube-savvy programming, collaboration and audience engagement; highlighting their demonstrated understanding of YouTube as a social network and a community of fellow producers, rather than as an inert publishing platform. Of course, the choice to focus on examples like these also helps to maintain an address to 'ordinary' amateur participants, inviting us to see ourselves as potential bona fide media producers or even celebrities-in-waiting.

However, initiatives like this, especially in combination with the machine-enforced copyright policies of the site, also tend to shape the activities of aspiring YouTube stars toward non-infringing uses of copyright – whether through one-off viral videos like 'Charlie Bit My Finger' or sustained programming, like that of the entrepreneurial vloggers. Earlier phases of YouTube saw the rise and fall of a series of hugely popular UGC genres and fads that were rife with the reuse of professional media content – including home-made music videos and rapidly mashed up or wittily quoted clips from popular television shows. The innocent days where tween fans of teen idols could cut a rip of their favourite track to their favourite ripped images of the singer are, thanks to YouTube's copyright protection technologies and automated takedowns, fading fast. Likewise, the highly generative cultural dynamics of imitation, parody and spoofing that have given rise to popular YouTube memes like the endless iterations on a particularly dramatic scene from the movie *Downfall* are increasingly under threat – falling foul of copyright violations, geofiltering, or both. For example, the literal video version of the spectacularly baroque 1980s' music video for Bonnie Tyler's 'Total Eclipse of the Heart', which substitutes a new vocal track with lyrics that literally describe the action on screen, received millions of views worldwide before an unknown change in licensing resulted in audiences outside the US being confronted with the dreaded 'this video is not available in your country' message when trying to view the video. While particularly tech-savvy users continue to find work-arounds for automated copyright violation detection[22] and it is technically possible for users to mount a fair-use argument after the fact and have their videos reinstated, the automated takedown regime is likely to have a demoralising effect on uploaders and a chilling effect on content reuse as a core dynamic of amateur creativity.

So as well as promoting 'home-grown' YouTube content, these various initiatives that aim to encourage amateur participation and professionalise amateur producers also work alongside the platform's copyright protection policies to discourage creative re-uses of existing media content by amateurs, who not only have insufficient legal and financial resources to negotiate content rights themselves ahead of time, but also often have an incomplete understanding of their own rights (like fair-use or fair-dealing provisions) as well. The promise of YouTube as a platform for genuinely new modes of cultural participation, involving not only straightforward self-expression but also the repurposing of pre-existing popular culture and media content, are less than likely to flourish as YouTube continues to mature as a commercial platform. But it is precisely these ongoing tensions between the amateur and professional, non-commercial and commercial modes of cultural production, as well as creative albeit unauthorised reuses of existing content associated with YouTube's ongoing 'underdetermination' as a platform, that have given rise to new modes of cultural production and new forms of enterprise; many of which originated with amateur uses of the platform. It remains to be seen whether these generative tensions will remain in play as YouTube continues its march towards global dominance over online video.

Notes

1 For the past several years YouTube has consistently been very close to the top of various lists of the most-visited websites worldwide. According to Alexa.com, as of November 2011 it is in third spot behind Google and Facebook. See www.alexa.com/topsites.

2 For current company-produced statistics see: www.youtube.com/t/press_statistics.

3 *Viacom International Inc v YouTube Inc*, 718 F Supp 2d 514 (SD NY, 2010). The text of the complaint is available at http://online.wsj.com/public/resources/documents/ViacomYouTube Complaint3-12-07.pdf.

4 YouTube's Content ID system is described at www.youtube.com/t/contentid.

5 Jean Burgess and Joshua Green, *YouTube: Online Video and Participatory Culture*, Cambridge: Polity Press, 2009, pp. 3–5.

6 In fact there was reportedly some talk among the team at the beginning about the idea of YouTube being either the 'Flickr of Video' or a kind of video dating service – somewhat akin to the dating site HotorNot.com. See for example: David Lidsky, *The Brief but Impactful History of YouTube* (1 Febraury 2010) Fast Company: www.fastcompany.com/magazine/142/it-had-to-be-you.html.

7 For further discussion of this process of co-evolution see Stuart Cunningham, 'Emergent Innovation through the Co-evolution of Informal and Formal Media Economies' (2012) *Television and New Media* (forthcoming).

8 John Cloud, 'The Gurus of YouTube', *Time* magazine (online), 16 December 2006: www.time.com/time/printout/0,8816,1570721,00.html.

9 The 'Me at the Zoo' video (with a mere six million views as at November 2011) is still available at www.youtube.com/watch?v=jNQXAC9IVRw.

10 For current statistics on the most popular videos on the service, see http://youtube.com/charts.

11 Jean Burgess and Joshua Green, 'The Entrepreneurial Vlogger: Participatory Culture Beyond the Professional/Amateur Divide', in Pelle Snickar and Patrick Vonderau (eds) *The YouTube Reader*, Stockholm: National Library of Sweden, 2009, p. 89.

12 See Vanessa Allen, 'The Amateur YouTube Starts Making Families £100,000 from Their Hilarious Home Videos', *Mail Online*, 14 November 2011: www.dailymail.co.uk/news/article-2060939/YouTube-stars-making-families-100-000-hilarious-home-videos.html; Asher Moses, 'Our Natalie Raking in $100,000 from YouTube', *Sydney Morning Herald* (online) 20 August 2010: www.smh.com.au/digital-life/digital-life-news/our-natalie-raking-in-100000-a-year-from-youtube-20100820-133be.html.

13 Jan Hoffman, 'Justin Bieber is Living the Tween Idol Dream', *New York Times* (online) 3 December 2009: www.nytimes.com/2010/01/03/fashion/03bieber.html?pagewanted=all.

14 In our 2007–8 study, Joshua Green and I used the 'most subscribed channels' metric as a measure of ongoing audience engagement, rather than 'viral' popularity. See Jean Burgess and Joshua Green, *YouTube: Online Video and Participatory Culture*, pp. 59–60.

15 For current statistics on the most-subscribed channels of all time see http://youtube.com/charts.

16 Jason Kincaid, 'YouTube Acquires Next New Networks, Introduces "YouTube Next" Training Squad', *Techcrunch*, 7 March 2011: http://techcrunch.com/2011/03/07/youtube-acquires-next-new-networks-introduces-youtube-next-training-squad/.

17 Peter Jakobsson, 'Cooperation and Competition in Open Production' (2010) (Creative Commons special issue, December) *PLATFORM: Journal of Media and Communicatiom* 106.

18 Jean Burgess and Joshua Green, 'The Entrepreneurial Vlogger'.

19 Jason Potts et al., 'Consumer Co-Creation and Situated Creativity' (2009) 15(5) *Industry and Innovation* 459.

20 See www.youtube.com/creators/index.html.

21 It has been revealed in a blog post by YouTube software engineer that, in an unremarkable 'long tail' distribution, 30 per cent of YouTube content receives 99 per cent of the total views on the site. See Ben Whitelaw, 'Almost all YouTube Views Come from Just 30% of Views', *Telegraph* (online) 20 April 2011: www.telegraph.co.uk/technology/news/8464418/Almost-all-YouTube-views-come-from-just-30-of-films.html.

22 User dascottjr captured footage of the literal video version of 'Total Eclipse of the Heart' with a video camera and framed it within a photographic border featuring a cat that is apparently watching the video, albeit with a somewhat bemused expression. The accompanying text says: 'The cat "border" on this video is to avoid automatic detection by YouTube. Sony has blocked my "non-cat" version in most non-US countries, so I'm posting this by request. US viewers can click here to watch it cat-less.' This video can be viewed at www.youtube.com/watch?v=ovEDhFfgdOo.

6 The relationship between user-generated content and commerce

Kimberlee Weatherall

Introduction

Steven Hetcher's chapter is a useful reminder of important issues concerning the relationship between commerce and commercial practice, on the one hand, and user-generated content ('UGC'), or user-generated creativity, on the other. In this comment, I wish to draw on two themes that emerge from Hetcher's chapter, and raise a third, further question about how the rise of UGC is changing our view of the way copyright law works.

Commerce and ambivalence

The first theme that emerges clearly from Hetcher's chapter is a deep-seated ambivalence concerning the relationship between commerce and user-generated content. Hetcher points out that the literature on user creativity frequently describes such activity in 'high-minded terms' linking such creativity with democratic values and the creation of a participatory culture. Only more rarely does such commentary grapple with the highly commercial nature of intermediaries that often bring user creativity to a mass market. This gap in the literature suggests some discomfort with the relationship between user creativity, on the one hand, and commercial user content intermediaries, or 'UCIs' as I will call them, on the other hand. It is worth examining the possible causes of that discomfort, if only because it seems they may vary depending on the UCI involved.

One possible reason for ambivalence is the fear that commercial motivations of UCIs may come to dominate a given website and its content, and drive out other, non-commercial motivations, such as altruism. Such thinking might, for example, lie behind the long-standing determination of online encyclopaedia Wikipedia not to install advertising on what is one of the most visited sites on the internet. Of the many online sites based on UGC, Wikipedia is perhaps most obviously based on a kind of altruism: contributors give time and energy to provide information to others for no obvious personal reward other than, perhaps, the feeling of satisfaction that comes from contributing to the knowledge of others and of feeling part of a communal effort.[1] Commerce could also drive out motivations based on the desire to build and foster a community.[2] Wikipedia is highly dependent on a small community of enthusiastic contributors. As numerous studies have recently pointed out, contributions to Wikipedia are highly unequal: a very large proportion of contributions come from a relatively small set of contributors, whose activities within Wikipedia are governed by a detailed set of rules and norms constitutive of an identifiable community.[3]

Concerns about the potential of commerce to crowd out volunteerism and community spirit have a long history. For example, back in 1970, Titmuss famously argued that a market for blood is both imperialistic, in that it can drive out voluntary systems for blood donation, and dehumanising, in that it 'represses the expression of altruism, [and] erodes the sense of community'.[4] Titmuss was concerned more broadly that the way we establish institutions – and these days, institutions surely includes UCIs, who provide the facilities within which individuals interact and communicate – can foster altruism and community, or destroy it. Titmuss's prescription was to avoid commerce in contexts driven by altruism: in other words, there ought not be any market for blood, lest that market drive out the non-commercial, altruistic motivations of blood donors. By (admittedly imperfect) analogy, we might say that the introduction of commercial motivations on a site like Wikipedia would repress the basic altruism and community that are the engine for Wikipedia's constant construction and reconstruction. On the other hand, a concern about crowding out does not seem so readily applicable in other contexts. As Hetcher points out, the motivations of YouTube's uploading users are hardly free from self-interest. Many, no doubt, are motivated by a desire for attention, some by the hope of 'discovery' and a commercial career.[5] A fear of driving out altruism or community seems inapplicable in the YouTube context.

A second basis for fearing the 'corruption' of user-generated creativity with the commercial motivations of a UCI might be the fear that the commercial influence will change the nature of the creativity produced or, at least, the nature of the creativity that is most accessible and/or dominant. For example, the concern might be that YouTube's increasing number of deals with commercial and professional producers will cause it to downgrade the prominence of 'genuine' user creativity. There is, after all, only so much room on the 'front page'. This source of ambivalence also has a long history dating to nineteenth-century concerns about the corrupting influence of grubby commerce on art and artistic pursuits. It finds more modern echoes in those who decry the descent in the popular media to the 'lowest common denominator'. Although UGC is a long way from the art celebrated by nineteenth-century critics or today's artistic elites, the underlying belief that purely non-commercial creativity holds some special role remains applicable.

A third basis for disquiet about the intrusion of commercial concerns of intermediaries into UGC could be the fear of the potentially demotivating impact of other people making money from users' contributions. Even if personal gain is not a motivation for creativity, the spectacle of others making money from one's creativity could be a disincentive. An example might be seen in the protests that erupted in early 2011 when the owner of the *Huffington Post*, Adriana Huffington, sold the site to AOL for US$315 million. Much of the content for the *Huffington Post* came free, from bloggers and other commentators; Adriana Huffington's 'windfall' led, not surprisingly, to accusations of inappropriate profiteering.

These three possible sources of ambivalence – crowding out, corruption and unjustified windfalls – all perhaps offer some explanation for the failure of the champions of user creativity to recognise, let alone celebrate, the importance of commerce in providing platforms for the communication of the products of user creativity, despite the undoubted importance of commercial sites in providing large-scale support for user creativity and access to a mass audience.

There is some danger, however, in framing user creativity as an essentially non-commercial activity: namely, that a condition of non-commerciality will be built into the copyright law framework. UGC in some cases skirts the boundaries of permissible use of copyright material. User creations that 'mash up' others' content may not find any readily applicable copyright exception, particularly in countries, like Australia and the United Kingdom, which employ a list of specific copyright exceptions as opposed to a flexible, open-ended exception like US-style fair use.[6] Awareness of this issue has motivated governments to contemplate copyright reform to allow or support user creativity. In so doing, however, they appear to be characterising such activity (or perhaps, the limits of *legitimate* user activity) as requiring the absence of any commercial motivation. Thus a recent Canadian bill, C-11, or the 'Copyright Modernization Act', proposes a new exception for *non-commercial* user-generated content, which would apply only to circumstances in which a user was acting for solely non-commercial purposes.[7] Interestingly, it is not clear that a user who, for example, shared in the proceeds of advertising placed with their content, would qualify for such an exception. Similarly, the UK government has talked about the need to protect 'non-commercial use', a key reason being the need to protect user-generated creativity.[8] In Australia, too, it seems that copyright interests, at least, are seeking to channel the discussion over user creativity into a discussion about exceptions for non-commercial activity only: a recent discussion paper produced by the Australian Copyright Council's 'Copyright Expert Group' advocated an exception for non-commercial transformative use.[9] The latter proposal would provide no shelter for UCIs: only for individual users engaged in 'transformative' activities.[10] Such proposals treat the intrusion of commercial interests of users and intermediaries as making an activity less legitimate and less worthy of recognition and protection in copyright law.

The rhetoric surrounding UGC, and its tendency to focus on non-commercial motivations and ignore the role of commercial UCIs are not the only reasons that recent reform proposals are so limited. The international framework that governs copyright law makes it much easier to create exceptions to copyright rights for non-commercial activity. Of particular relevance here is the 'three-step test', found in article 9(2) of the Berne Convention on the Protection of

Literary and Artistic Works of 1886, and article 13 of the Agreement on Trade-Related Aspects of Intellectual Property Rights ('TRIPS'). The three-step test acts as a constraint on the exceptions a country can introduce into copyright law. The test states that exceptions must 'not conflict with a normal exploitation of the work'. This requirement focuses on the commercial impact on the copyright owner of activities allowed under any exception to copyright law. Nevertheless, many instances of UGC are so distant from markets for the original copyright work that they are unlikely to compete directly with copyright owners: it is hard to believe, therefore, that the three-step test would require any UGC exception be limited to solely non-commercial activities.

My point here is not to examine all the legal ins and outs of potential reform in this space. Rather, I wish to point out that the focus of government proposals on non-commercial activities is supported by the tendency of debates and cheerleading in this area to throw commercial links into shadow.[11] In other words, ambivalence about commerce and the motivations of UCIs, while understandable for all the reasons outlined already, also poses longer term dangers to the viability of companies that provide platforms for UGC, and hence for UGC itself.

The cabining of UGC as a purely non-commercial activity could also be seen as creating a new, less privileged class of creativity within copyright law. Most of copyright law is geared toward encouraging creativity by enabling commercial incentives to operate: we give creators and distributors exclusive rights in order to ensure that they can reap the commercial rewards of their creativity – if it proves popular – thus encouraging investment in creation and distribution. Currently mooted reforms to allow for UGC seem to assume either that no similar incentives are required to encourage creation or distribution of UGC, or that UGC is something to be allowed or tolerated (that is, ought not to be considered infringement) but not something to be actively encouraged by the legal framework. Either way, UGC is conceived as a kind of 'second class' creativity; its distribution (overwhelmingly by commercial entities) need not be encouraged or facilitated by copyright law. It need not necessarily be so. UGC could be judged according to the extent to which it is 'transformative': whether the UGC product serves some purpose or market distant from the purpose or market of original copyright material incorporated into UGC. Genuinely transformative UGC that serves a very different purpose from the original might warrant different, better protection in the copyright system than the purely derivative; so might the activities of the intermediaries who distribute transformatively creative UGC. But to have this discussion – and to build a citizenship with full rights for UGC in the copyright system – we need to acknowledge UGC's relationship with commerce more openly.

The bureaucracy of proportionality

A second theme in Hetcher's chapter is his analysis of the importance of 'proportionality' in the courts' treatment of the companies that provide technology that can be used for both infringing, and non-infringing, activities. Hetcher contends that US courts, particularly the *Viacom* first instance court,[12] have interpreted the safe harbour provisions of the Digital Millennium Copyright Act[13] ('DMCA') consistently with prior-existing copyright law, in particular, the US Supreme Court decision in *Sony*[14] as interpreted by subsequent cases,[15] to protect technology providers like UCIs in circumstances where the costs outweigh the benefits of the technology, or where, in other words, there is a kind of proportionality when infringing uses of a technology are compared to non-infringing uses. This test protects a site like YouTube, with its many non-infringing uses, but not the Napsters, Aimsters and Groksters of the world who provide the software used in shamelessly infringing peer-to-peer file-sharing. Hetcher argues that both users and UCIs themselves will benefit from this developing common law approach.

I do not disagree with Hetcher's analysis of the outcomes of these US cases, although there is no guarantee that such approaches will be adopted by other countries which have adopted the safe harbour model, whether voluntarily (as in Europe) or as a result of a free trade agreement with the US (as in Australia). Aside from this point, however, I think it is worth recognising the broader implications of an approach based on proportionality. I am concerned that such an approach encourages the 'institutionalisation' of copyright enforcement by private actors.

Some of the potential issues were explored in the US Supreme Court decision in *Grokster*.[16] In that case, the Supreme Court was asked to consider the copyright liability of an entity that provided software which was used by others to engage in copyright infringement on a mass scale by means of peer-to-peer file-sharing. While the opinion of the court found liability on the grounds that Grokster had 'induced' (facilitated and encouraged) infringement, the broader nature of copyright liability in the area was explored in two concurring opinions, each drawing support from three justices. These concurring judgments reflect in part a split over the question whether Sony required a consideration of 'proportionality' or the extent of non-infringing uses of which a technology was capable, or whether a technology need only be 'capable' of substantial non-infringing uses.[17] The judgment of Justice Ginsburg does indeed, as Hetcher outlines, seem to support a kind of proportionality approach, expressing concern that, in the instant case, the infringing uses represented the 'overwhelming' use of the technology (and hence the technology ought not receive relief from liability for copyright infringement), and referring to the earlier 7th Circuit opinion in *Aimster* which explicitly adopted such an approach.[18]

A test based on proportionality has certain attractions. It offers individualised, case-by-case justice in which the merits and impact of a particular technology can be considered. But like all such tests, is has a cost, in the form of a heightened degree of uncertainty for technology entrepreneurs. As Justice Breyer pointed out in his concurring opinion, this has implications for innovation:

Inventors and entrepreneurs (in the garage, the dorm room, the corporate lab, or the boardroom) would have to fear (and in many cases endure) costly and extensive trials when they create, produce, or distribute the sort of information technology that can be used for copyright infringement. They would often be left guessing as to how a court, upon later review of the product and its uses, would decide when necessarily rough estimates amounted to sufficient evidence. They would have no way to predict how courts would weigh the respective values of infringing and noninfringing uses; determine the efficiency and advisability of technological changes; or assess a product's potential future markets ... The additional risk and uncertainty would mean a consequent additional chill of technological development.[19]

One way that a technology entrepreneur or UCI can reduce the uncertainty generated by a proportionality test is to take pre-emptive steps to reduce infringement. As US Professor Jane Ginsburg has argued, some of the reasoning in *Grokster*, both as contained in the opinion and in the judgment of Justice Ginsburg, might suggest that a technology entrepreneur should adopt 'pro-active measures to prevent infringement from becoming a business asset'; businesses 'may find themselves liable unless they take good faith measures to forestall infringements'.[20] Economies of scale dictate that such systems are unlikely to involve individualised 'justice': rather, they are likely to become automated and hence carry some risk of 'false positives' – rejecting or removing material that is in fact not copyright infringing.

This is a development we can see already in the larger commercial UCIs. 'Notice and Takedown' is a system, sanctioned in copyright law under the safe harbours created to protect online service providers, whereby copyright owners send notices of alleged infringement to UCIs, who are under an obligation expeditiously to remove the alleged infringing material (with users having a right to respond ex post).[21] The concept of 'Notice and Takedown' sounds highly individualised, but in fact, systems for managing this process are heavily automated, on the part of both copyright owners and many UCIs. Evidence in cases to date suggests that copyright owners have outsourced the policing of copyright infringement online to companies that use automated methods to detect alleged infringements and send notices, and, as a result, UCIs may receive many thousands of notices of alleged infringement.[22] In the *Viacom* case, evidence suggested automation on the part of the UCI also: YouTube removed 100,000 allegedly infringing videos within 24 hours.[23]

Beyond this, we have evidence that larger UCIs are adopting automated, pre-emptive filtering of copyright material. YouTube for example has its ContentID system. Under this system, a copyright owner can upload a video file to a Google-held database together with identifying metadata and instructions as to how to treat such a video if uploaded by a user (monetise, track or block). Uploaded videos are checked against the database. The copyright owner is asked what they want to do – block, track or monetise. Copyright owners can create policies depending on the proportion of a claimed video that contains their work, or the absolute length of the clip used. For example, a record label might decide to block videos that contain over one minute of a given song, but leave up videos that contain less than one minute. As of December 2010, YouTube was reporting that 100 million videos had been claimed; some four million reference files were in the database. Neither is Google the only organisation applying such technology. Evidence in the US case *Io Group Inc v Veoh Networks Inc* was that Veoh Inc had adopted the technology of Audible Magic, a means for generating a digital 'fingerprint' for each video file, which enabled Veoh to terminate access to any other identical files and prevent additional identical files from ever being uploaded again by any user.[24]

We might decide that the development of these technologies, with their automated systems for the management and enforcement of copyright rights, represents an appropriate balance between the rights of copyright owners and the desire we have to promote the existence and viability of UCIs and user creativity. But in thinking about whether that balance has been struck, we should recognise such technologies for what they are: systems that build automatic management and enforcement of copyright into the fabric of the technologies we use to communicate and express creativity. Copyright enforcement in this environment has the potential to become highly bureaucratic: involving the automatic and discretionless application of rules. This may be the cost of having a medium of mass distribution with relatively open access, like the internet, but it should be recognised as a cost. We should remember, too, that not all copyright owners own music or music videos: copyright owners can be news channels or political organisations too, and systematisation of copyright infringement is not going to be used exclusively to block the rampant piratical use of the frivolously commercial. Further, the more we expect UCIs to develop and use such systems, the more we construct a legal framework that may tend to favour larger corporations with the means to develop automated systems for copyright infringement detection and removal.[25]

Opting in to copyright

The final comment I wish to make emerges not so much from Hetcher's chapter as from its subject matter: the internet safe harbours introduced in the US via the DMCA and found also in Australia in Part V Div 2AA of the Copyright Act 1968 (Cth). Hetcher's chapter emphasises one aspect of the continuity between pre-existing copyright law in the United States and the interpretation of the safe harbours; I wish to emphasise another.

The internet safe harbours protect an online service provider (as defined in the legislation) from copyright liability arising from the infringing activities of its users, unless and until the service provider is notified of the alleged infringing conduct, at which time the service provider becomes obliged to act: in the first instance, by removing the infringing material and notifying the user.[26] Thus described, the safe harbours arguably turn copyright in the online environment into what Tim Wu calls an effective 'opt-in' form of protection: the copyright owner receives protection for its right to exclude others from its copyright material only by actively policing use online and 'engaging' protection by sending a notice of infringement.[27] This effect is strengthened by the decision of the first instance *Viacom* court that general knowledge of 'widespread infringement' did not require action by YouTube: as Hetcher describes, YouTube was only required to act to remove material once specifically notified that it was infringing; generalised knowledge of possible infringement was not sufficient to create an affirmative obligation on a service provider to act.

On one level, the apparent transmogrification of copyright in the online environment from a prima facie right to exclude others to a right that receives effective protection only following formal assertion of rights by the copyright owner might be considered radical.[28] As I have pointed out elsewhere, it is less new than it looks.[29] Musical composers learned in the early twentieth century that unless they actively 'opted in' to the copyright system by enforcing their rights, their music would be performed: this led to the first rights management organisations, to administer the performing right in copyright. For years copyright owners in sound recordings 'opted out' of formal legal protection by tolerating widespread infringement by people copying their music onto their iPods and other devices. On one view, the whole internet is one big 'opt-in' system, since chances are high that a copyright owner's material will make its way online unless copyright owners actively 'opt out' of such use through active policing.

'Opt-in' copyright is also arguably the way of the future, at least in the online and digital environment. Arguing in favour of opt-in protection are the massive potential that can be realised through digitisation of existing material and its more widespread use,[30] the known problems of orphan works, the enormous number of works being made available by individuals online without any expectation of payment or exclusivity, and the potential of projects like the Google Book project to increase access to knowledge and information. Also arguing in favour of opt-in protection in copyright is the existence and real-world use of UGC. Large amounts of UGC using existing copyright material, such as fan fiction and the mash-ups on YouTube are available without protest from copyright owners, who no doubt realise the benefits of such material in fostering awareness of and attachment to, and hence markets for, copyright-protected originals. The safe harbours allow the existence of such material and enable the implementation by UCIs of the choice of the copyright owner – to tolerate such uses, or take action to prevent it. In this context, the safe harbours stand as one legislatively backed example of opt-in copyright protection in a digital age, that, to date, appear to have worked quite effectively. The safe harbours may, in other words, point to a potentially fruitful direction for future copyright reform in the digital environment.

Final comments

Hetcher's chapter is useful in highlighting the position occupied by the online service provider safe harbours in the overall copyright regime, and the way they are being understood, and brought within that regime, by US courts. This comment has sought to expand on that analysis, by offering some thoughts on the implications of Hetcher's analysis, as well as the possible dangers of ignoring the role of UCIs and the role the safe harbours might play in pointing the way to future copyright reform. As I hope to have made clear, the questions raised by UGC, its relationship with commerce, and how we reform copyright to recognise and facilitate the creation and distribution of UGC raise important questions for how we understand copyright to work in the digital environment, now and in the future. But to reach the best outcomes for copyright and UGC, we do need to get comfortable with talking about UGC's entanglements with the commercial world. The relationship between art and commerce, we should know by now, is not always an unhealthy one.

Notes

1 On motivations of Wikipedians generally, see Oded Nov, 'What Motivates Wikipedians?' (2007) 50 *Communications of the ACM* 60. Some 'personal' motivations like 'fun' and improving personal understanding are also important to Wikipedians. It is interesting to compare, here, the difference between contributors to Wikipedia, on the one hand, and open source software, on the other. In the case of open source software, at least some proportion of programmers can, and do, parlay their experience gained through voluntary contributions to open source projects into paid employment: see generally Josh Lerner and Jean Tirole, 'Some Simple Economics of Open Source' (2002) 50 *Journal of Industrial Economics* 197. According to Nov, career-based motivations rated low for Wikipedians: Nov, 'What Motivates Wikipedians?', 63.

2 It might be noted that commercial goals coexist with the building of communities in the context of open source software: Lerner and Tirole, 'Some Simple Economics of Open Source'. Indeed, open source licenses cannot discriminate between commercial and non-commercial activity. Thus commercial aspects will not *necessarily* interfere with the building of a community; clearly other factors are important.

3 Felipe Ortega, Jesus M. Gonzalez-Barahona and Gregorio Robles, 'On the Inequality of Contributions to Wikipedia' (paper presented at the 41st Annual Hawaii International Conference on System Sciences, Waikoloa, Hawaii, 2008) 304.

4 Richard Titmuss, *The Gift Relationship: From Human Blood to Social Policy,* London: George Allen & Unwin, 1970, pp. 223, 245. See also Kenneth Arrow, 'Gifts and Exchanges' (1972) 1 *Philosophy and Public Affairs* 343; Peter Singer, 'Altruism and Commerce: A Defence of Titmuss against Arrow' (1973) 2 *Philosophy and Public Affairs* 313.

5 Guosong Shao, 'Understanding the Appeal of User-Generated Media: A Uses and Gratification Perspective' (2009) 19 *Internet Research* 7.

6 The US Fair-Use defence is found in 17 USC §107. In Australia, the *Copyright Act 1968* (Cth) provides for exceptions to allow re-use of copyright material for criticism or review, reporting news, or parody or satire. Not every 'mash-up' will fall within these categories: for example, music may be used in the background of a film in a way that does not 'comment on', or satirise, that music.

7 Copyright Modernization Act, Bill C-11, 2011 (Canada) cl 22, proposed s 29.21.

8 Intellectual Property Office (UK), © *the way ahead: A Strategy for Copyright in the Digital Age,* Report (2009) 34.

9 Australian Copyright Council Expert Group, *Directions in Australian Copyright Reform* (Report produced for the Australian Copyright Council, October 2011), 2 (available at www.copy right.org.au/pdf/Copyright%20Council%20Expert%20Group%20-%20Paper%202011.pdf).

10 By contrast, the Canadian proposal does appear to provide protection to intermediaries, as the exception entitles the user to authorise an intermediary to disseminate the content: Copyright Modernization Act, Bill C-11, 2011 (Canada) cl 22, proposed s 29.21.

11 It is not my contention that the rhetoric of UGC champions is the only factor in shaping government discussions of reform. Naturally, the international framework of copyright law, and in particular, the limit on copyright exceptions imposed by the so-called 'three-step test' is also a relevant factor: see *Berne Convention for the Protection of Literary and Artistic Works*, opened for signature 9 September 1886, as last revised at Paris on 24 July 1971, 1161 UNTS 3 (entered into force 10 October 1974), article 9(2); *Agreement on Trade-Related Aspects of Intellectual Property Rights ('TRIPS')*, opened for signature 15 April 1994, 1869 UNTS 299 (entered into force 1 January 1996), article 13.

12 *Viacom International Inc v YouTube Inc*, 718 F Supp 2d 514 (SD NY, 2010) ('*Viacom*').

13 17 USC § 512.

14 *Sony Corporation of America v Universal City Studios Inc*, 464 US 417 (1984) ('*Sony*').

15 In particular, *Metro-Goldwyn-Mayer Studios Inc v Grokster Ltd*, 545 US 913 (2005) ('*Grokster*'), and *In re Aimster Copyright Litigation*, 334 F 3d 643 (7th Cir, 2003).

16 545 US 913 (2005).

17 The split between the judgments also reflects differing views by the judges as to whether the evidence on the face of the record suggested that the defendants could clearly show substantial non-infringing uses, such that a full trial was not required.

18 *In re Aimster Copyright Litigation*, 334 F 3d 643 (7th Cir, 2003), cited *Grokster*, 545 US 913, 944 (2005).

19 *Grokster*, 545 US 913, 959-60 (2005).

20 Jane C. Ginsburg, 'Separating the Sony Sheep from the Grokster Goats: Reckoning the Future Business Plans of Copyright-Dependent Technology Entrepreneurs' (2008) 50 *Arizona Law Review* 577.

21 Under the law applicable in both Australia and the US, as well as elsewhere, users have a right to receive notice that their material has been removed, and can seek its reinstatement. In such a case, copyright owners must commence copyright infringement proceedings within a defined period of time; otherwise, the material is made available once more: in the US, see 17 USC § 512, in Australia, see Copyright Regulations 1969 (Cth) regs 20Q and 20R.

22 See, for example, *Roadshow Films Pty Ltd v iiNet Ltd* (2011) 89 IPR 1, 59 [261] (indicating that iiNet received 'thousands of unreliable robot notices per week alleging infringement').

23 *Viacom*, 718 F Supp 2d 514, 524 (SDNY 2010).

24 *Io Group Inc v Veoh Networks Inc*, 586 F Supp 2d 1132 (ND Cal, 2008).

25 Obviously copyright is not the *only* driver favouring larger entities: network effects can have the same impact.

26 Further obligations may arise depending on the circumstances: for example, the safe harbours found in the US and Australia require that online service providers have and reasonably implement a policy for the termination of accounts of repeat infringers.

27 Tim Wu, 'Tolerated Use' (2008) 31 *Columbia Journal of Law and the Arts* 617. Of course, the option always remains of taking action directly against an infringing user, in which case there is no requirement of notice. Nevertheless, the more effective form of copyright protection – that which enables instant removal of the material – is dependent on affirmative action on the part of the copyright owner.

28 See, for example, Jonathan Band, 'The Google Library Project: The Copyright Debate' (policy brief prepared for the American Library Association, January 2006) p. 1, quoting Pat Schroeder, AAP President, describing an the opt-out procedure in the Google Book Project (a procedure for opting-out of the project, and hence 'opting in' to full copyright protection) as 'shift[ing] the responsibility for preventing infringement to the copyright owner rather than the user, turning every principle of copyright law on its ear'.

29 Kimberlee Weatherall, 'So Mark Me Down as a Copyright Radical' (paper presented at the 15th Biennial Copyright Symposium, Sydney, 13–14 October 2011, also forthcoming in published form in *Copyright Reporter*).

30 See, in particular, Ian Hargreaves, *Digital Opportunity: A Review of Intellectual Property and Growth* (Independent report for the Intellectual Property Office, UK, May 2011) 47 [5.23]–[5.24], proposing a copyright exception for 'non-consumptive use' – that is, uses of a work enabled by technology which do not directly trade on the underlying creative and expressive purpose of the work. The proposed exception is imagined to cover (*inter alia*) acts like search-engine caching, and text mining for the purposes of research, and the report notes that existing rights in academic articles, for example, may prevent text and data mining that could lead to new ideas for drugs and medical treatment.

Part III

Amateurs and authenticity

7 The manufacture of 'authentic' buzz and the legal relations of *MasterChef*

Kathy Bowrey

The rise of reality TV is often analysed in media studies with reference to the changing advertising and marketing practices that have accompanied media convergence and shifting audience relations in the age of social media. Consumers are encouraged to personally identify with brand identities, but at the same time in a media-saturated world we have developed resistance to overt mass media marketing strategies. Immersive situations such as reality TV programmes rely on amateur talent and unscripted scenarios to create an illusion of real life, one in which the marketer is less visible.

Reality TV creates opportunities for contestants and viewers to engage with the story and the advertising, with the authenticity of the human drama activating commodity relations. These dynamics have been discussed by media commentators in terms of the potential for exploitation of contestants and fans. However, the nature of the legal relations that support these dynamics is not well understood. My discussion centres on the highly successful reality television programme *MasterChef Australia*. The legal relations of the programme are dissected into four different concerns: ownership of the format, contestant participation, product placement and extended brand opportunities. It is argued that law is supporting corporate control over the extended narrative of the enterprise. In the process we are seeing the emergence of new ideas of property, the corporation and of the self that support and extend the value of global brands and brand relations.

Broadcast television narratives

Television broadcasting is often described as a typical form of mass media, packaging a static experience for assembled audiences. The kind of narrative or cultural content able to be consumed by mass audiences is clearly identified in programme guides and with reference to genre and convention: news, current affairs drama, documentary, game show, children's programming. With broadcasting there are distinct kinds of narrative, but not necessarily a clear attribution of authorship. In describing the author function, Foucault notes:

> The 'author-function' is tied to the legal and institutional systems that circumscribe, determine and articulate the realm of discourses; it does not operate in a uniform manner in all discourses, at all times, and in any given culture; it is not defined by the spontaneous attribution of a text to its creator, but through a series of precise and complex procedures; it does not refer, purely and simply, to an actual individual insofar as it simultaneously gives rise to a variety of egos and to a series of subjective positions that individuals of any class may come to occupy.[1]

With television there are different kinds of narrative that suggest different kinds of author. There are, for example, clear differences between authoring the script for television drama and scripting a news or current affairs programme. The difference between fictional and reality-based genres gives rise to different kinds of expectation for attribution of ownership. However, behind all broadcast content there are also clearly numerous professional creative and technical contributions and collaborations that make the transmission possible, involving both behind the scenes and front of camera efforts. This combination makes clear attribution of authorship difficult. Law accommodates this difficulty by operating at a high level of abstraction, relying upon the kind of fixation of the subject matter and creating a proliferation of rights. A number of creative and skilled contributions associated with the television programme attract a copyright. There are separate copyrights awarded to the author of a script or dramatic work (another to any underlying literary work) and another right is granted to the 'maker' of the television broadcast, that is, the party responsible for the transmission. However, this legal complexity is hidden from view. To the public, depending upon the kind of programming, the production house, presenter, writer, actors and broadcast channel may all be used as short-hand forms of attribution to identify the origin and essential identity of the cultural experience or story.

There is already a disconnect between the way in which the public associates ownership of a television programme with the sensibilities of copyright law. Legal relations are constructed in a particular way for historical reasons, in part related to the origin of copyright with literary works. However, the contrived logic to the assignation of copyright ownership is also maintained in a mass media market in order to facilitate a process of commodification that conceives of an orderly spatial and temporal separation in the roles and expertise attached to content creator/product distributor/consumer. To the extent that commercial realities are considered relevant to the legal assignation of rights, copyright at first instance attributes the creation of value to the inherent qualities of the original work of the author and, second, to the managerial skill associated with marketing and distribution in bringing the product before the public. The role of the audience in creating cultural meaning and economic value is usually not considered at all. Copyright law has particular difficulty accommodating the reality that for commercial television, the primary product being created is not the programme content per se, but the buying and selling of audiences to advertisers. This tension that underpins broadcast copyright can be seen in the difficulty of deciding whether advertisements are legally part of, or separate to, the programme content broadcast.[2]

As a business enterprise, commercial free-to-air television broadcasting[3] relies upon the pull of different kinds of programming to particular time slots to attract the sale of advertising that fractures the programme narrative with commercial 'breaks'. The suggestion remains that there is a clear separation between content and the commercials and that the strength of the particular programme will keep viewers hooked throughout the interruptions. However, marketers have long recognised the reality of consumer disinterest and resistance to pull advertising. Heavy promotion of a product in the hope that viewers and their wallets will follow in response to the degree of media exposure has led to audience strategies of avoidance: 'Advertising no longer works as well as it once did. Companies in consumer and business markets now pay more and more to reach fewer and fewer households and executive decision makers.'[4] As advertisers have learned since the 1980s: 'People don't passively ingest a marketing message, or any type of message. They greet it with an emotional response, usually unconscious, that can vary widely depending on their own experiences and predispositions.'[5] As MediaCom chief executive Jon Mandel explains, '[w]e know when people are watching a show they care about, they watch the commercials more. Unfortunately there aren't that many shows people care about.'[6]

Where the relationship between advertising information presented to audiences and the action in the story is abstract and remote, consumers will often disengage. Media savvy audiences have come to recognise advertising as associated with artifice and manipulation. Advertising is itself also now compiled, analysed and broadcast as entertainment and serious programme content, which has also assisted audiences in decoding advertising practices.

As television viewers we know we do not simply sit and passively receive media messages. Viewers multi-task, channel flip to consciously skip the advertising and use commercial breaks to seek out alternative programmes. With access to recording technologies since the VCR, it has become commonplace to fast forward through pre-recorded programming, leading to industry attempts to prevent access to ad-skipping functions. Studies suggest DVRs with fast-forward functions may not be the threat once imagined by advertisers. This may be one reason why services like TiVo, which only allow fast-forwarding through advertisements have not been targeted like RePlay TV,[7] which allowed for ad-skipping.[8] Nonetheless, perception of audience indifference to pull advertising, access to a wide array of entertainment technologies and academic literature about changing audience consumption practice has led to development of more immersive marketing strategies. These strategies provide new ways of telling stories about products, leading to changes in the television stories offered to us and providing different mechanisms for audience interaction, in order to re-engage audiences with commercial behaviour.

The authenticity of reality television

The rise of reality TV is explained in terms of commercial dynamics. Whilst not a new genre, with popular quiz formats dating from the 1950s and 1960s and an even longer radio heritage (including talkback radio and sponsored segments), there has been an acceleration in this kind of programming from the late 1980s: 'Dramatic programming is no longer the sine qua non of prime time programming ... "unscripted" programming has become a television staple in the most coveted time slots. What was perceived as a fad has become the norm.'[9] Susan Murray and Laurie Ouellette define reality television:

> as an unabashedly commercial genre united less by aesthetic rules or certainties than by the fusion of popular entertainment with a self-conscious claim to the discourse of the real. This coupling, we contend, is what has made reality TV an important generic forum for a range of institutional and cultural developments that include the merger of marketing and real life entertainment, the convergence of new media technologies with programmes and their promotion, and an acknowledgement of the manufactured artifice that coexists with truth claims.[10]

There are various sub-genres and combinations including fly-on-the-wall documentaries, undercover exposés, self-improvement, renovation, game and competition, dating and social experiment. The various 'hooks' provide viewers with a voyeuristic experience of different kinds of what Murray and Ouellette call the 'entertaining real'. However, it is also well recognised that viewers are quite sceptical when it comes to assessing how much is actually 'real' in these programmes. The authors cite studies that suggest very few viewers believe they are watching 'reality'. They go on to argue:

> Reality TV promises its audience revelatory insight into the lives of others as it withholds and subverts full access to it. What results is an unstable text that encourages viewers to test out their own notions of the real, the ordinary, and the intimate against the representation before them. Far from being the mind-numbing, deceitful, and simplistic genre that some critics claims it to be, reality TV provides a multilayered viewing experience that hinges on culturally and politically complex notions of what is real and what is not.[11]

Without the possibility of clearly decoding who controls the narrative in any one situation, a productive dramatic tension is created around the unstable text. This allows the audience to participate in the narrative to uncover a kind of emotional truth about the identity of the participants and themselves. What is on offer is really access to an individually experienced subjectivity. The 'true story' is worked out by the viewer and, to the extent that they desire more, through engagement in 'water-cooler' talk and more participatory forums – from SMS and online voting, Twitter comments that may be rebroadcast on the television screen, official and unofficial community forums. In an age that is profoundly suspicious of abstract truth and has lost faith in the idea of objectivity in communications, there is no real need to uncover a larger truth of the narrative or to settle who is the author.[12] What is on offer is the pull of engagement with an unfolding story around which there is no narrative certainty beyond a series resolution in terms of announcement of the winner, a prize, or in some cases merely the 'self-discovery' opportunity for show participants and viewers.[13]

The active dynamics of the programming send confusing signals around ownership of the content and the participation. Access is on terms set by the production values, but the involvement of amateur talent is to varying degrees unscripted. These productions falter without engaging the emotions of the audience. This requires an ongoing mediation between producers, participants and television viewers around the fabrication of different kinds of authentic experience, as defined by the parameters of the particular sub-genre. To see what kind of property or ownership is possible within this dynamic I will now focus on one particular site, *MasterChef*. However the legal relations of this reality TV cooking contest shares features in common with other reality TV sub-genres.

What is *MasterChef*?

MasterChef Australia was produced by Fremantle Media Australia for Network Ten and broadcast in 2009, loosely based on a game/cooking reality TV format first broadcast by the BBC in 1990, and reincarnated by Elizabeth Murdoch's Shine TV as *MasterChef Goes Large* in 2005. The Australian format was developed by Mark and Carl Fennessy at Fremantle Media Australia. Novel features in the Australian version included broadcasting contestant auditions, the size and scale of the kitchen setting, running the programme six nights a week and increasing exposure to the personality and emotions of the contestants. Ratings success led to further development of the franchise with 'Celebrity' and 'Junior' *MasterChef* series. The current Australian format is owned by Shine Australia, a Shine subsidiary now run by Mark and Carl Fennessy. The 2011 licence with Network Ten is for a multi-year, multi-platform arrangement that includes broadcast, online, mobile and IPTV rights.[14] The Australian format subsequently influenced further development of the UK franchise, which created some critical and audience resistance in the UK.[15]

As television programming *MasterChef* offers a number of commercial opportunities. It is a ratings-winning formula that capitalises on the uncertainty of an amateur cooking competition. The dramatic tension that unfolds provides an opportunity for large-scale immersive product placement that normalises the association of *MasterChef*, the contestants and successful home cooking with brand identities.[16] Legally there is potential for ownership of the (1) TV format, (2) contestant participation (3) product placement and (4) extended brand activity.

Ownership of TV formats

There is considerable controversy around the legal possibility of owning a TV format because of the indeterminate nature of the narrative and lack of fixation of the copyrightable expression.[17] In copyright, the broadcast right only prevents appropriation of the broadcast signal; it does not protect the narrative content per se. The process for awarding copyright to dramatic works creates obstacles for 'unscripted' content and interactive narratives. The most commonly cited Privy Council case concerning rights to the *Opportunity Knocks* format determined:

> It is stretching the original use of the word 'format' a long way to use it metaphorically to describe the features of a television series such as a talent, quiz or game show which is presented in a particular way, with repeated but unconnected use of set phrases and with the aid of particular accessories. ... This difficulty in finding an appropriate term to describe the nature of the 'work' in which the copyright subsists reflects the difficulty of the concept that a number of allegedly distinctive features of a television series can be isolated from the changing material presented in each separate performance (the acts of the performers in the talent show, the questions and answers in the quiz show etc.) and identified as an 'original dramatic work'. No case was cited to their Lordships in which copyright of the kind claimed had been established.[18]

This programming connected with audiences through offering the authentic experience of amateur talent. The centrality of live performances to *Opportunity Knocks* meant that despite recurring signature features, in essence, each show would offer a unique experience. However, the production of that experience was an ill-fit with copyright's literary expectations, where the original author of a text is the party that is credited as the authentic source of the cultural experience.

Despite UK law suggesting doubts about the capacity for copyright protection of TV formats, a global trade, largely emanating from the UK, has continued to grow alongside the rise in cross-border trade in television programming since the 1970s and 80s.[19] A UK-based industry lobby group, the Format Recognition and Protection Association (FRAPA), estimates that during the period 2006–8 total production expenditure on formats was around €9.3 billion. FRAPA provides draft contracts and a registry of agreements to regulate trade in formats. Despite likely localised difficulties in enforcement through the courts they also make the extravagant claim that:

in 2010 – the year of its 10 [sic] anniversary – FRAPA joined forces with WIPO – World Intellectual Property Organisation. FRAPA members can now call on the services of the non-profiting-making UN agency, which offers alternative dispute resolution (ADR) mechanisms for IP and related disputes.[20]

There is a symbolic performance of law here that creates an air of authority around very uncertain legal agreements. *Inter partes* recourse to WIPO ADR services attempts to route around domestic legal realities and substitute for law, a completely unaccountable, undemocratic and unenforceable process that regulates private fantasies of law.

It is interesting to consider how industry developments alongside or outside of the formal law have the potential to impact on it. There is no simple cause and effect here; however, legal interpretations do need to connect with social and economic realities to generate legitimacy. Broader changes in cultural understanding and industry practice must inform legal understandings to some indeterminate degree.

In a recent Australian case surrounding copyright infringement of a New Zealand home-renovation format *Dream Home* there was a significant loosening in the reasoning of an Australian court that paves the way for a far more ambulatory notion of the property protected in unscripted television. Tamberlin J noted: 'It is also important to take into account that copyright in a written story gives protection not simply to the words used but can take into account the expression of themes and ideas *embedded in the production* if they are sufficiently substantial.'[21] He cited with approval UK authority that this 'may well include the combination of the main themes, incidents and characters in the story'.[22] Whereas the *Opportunity Knocks* case was fixated on the problem of owning an unfinished narrative, Tamberlin J extended the protected narrative from the textual work to 'the production'. This shift creates the legal capacity to consider creation of narrative tension, worked out within the format parameters, as a form of property.

Tamberlin J went on to find no infringement of the New Zealand renovation programme *Dream Home* by the Australian production *The Block*, as the two had different 'essential features'. Marketers consider, 'There's that aha! moment that's very specific to each property. It's the moment when I've found the true emotional connection.'[23] The 'it' factor here that distinguished the two renovation programmes was defined with reference to sub-genres (one was infotainment, the other drama) and likely audience demographics (for families, for trendy couples). Different emotional attachments signalled substantially different programmes and, for advertisers, access to different audiences:

An important point of contrast between *Dream Home* and *The Block* is that Dream Home can properly be described as a 'do it yourself' infotainment family programme whereas *The Block* is focussed on dramatic conflicts, the glamour and trendiness of the couples and multi-group interactions between quite different types of personalities. In my view, the objectives and interests of audience members watching the two programmes as a whole would be different. In the case of *Dream Home*, the audience would want to learn something about renovating and the practical problems involved, including the way in which the renovation is to be carried out, whereas, in *The Block*, the characteristics of the programme are directed to an audience interested in drama and conflict in a totally different geographic and social context.[24]

This reasoning provides for a closer reconciliation between the legal definition of protectable subject matter and reading television programmes in terms of the properties of audiences and the commercial/marketing logics of reality TV. It raises the question whether the Australian 'adaptation' of the original Shine format amounts to an altogether new dramatic work under copyright law, given its extended focus on contestant and personality. Criticism of the revised UK *MasterChef* format showed it alienated at least part of the established UK audience because of the changes. Perhaps the feel of the Australian format was more akin to *The Block*, when the rusted-on audience was expecting something closer to a *Dream Home* experience.

Contestant participation

It is clear that there are no particular difficulties with recruitment of potential 'talent' for most reality TV ventures, with massive audition turn-outs now a common feature of 'pre-show' publicity and/or included in the show. This amateur participation is essentially unpaid or very poorly paid. Superficially, the willingness to participate for free suggests a similar dynamic to the network economies associated with free software, open source and creative commons licensing.[25] There is significant academic discussion of the productivity of free labour involved in social media and fandom.[26] However, this literature fails to take into account the legal underpinnings of many of these 'exchanges'. From a legal point of view what is exchanged is not necessarily labour. To the extent that it may involve 'volunteer' labour, arguably even minimum standards of employment law do not apply.[27] To the extent that participants contribute far more than text or images, it is also not really about an assignment of intellectual property.

Reality TV participants agree to provide access to the whole person, including accepting very onerous restrictions on their liberty. There is a significant loss of privacy, not just in front of camera but extended to the vetting of participants for criminal and other 'unsavoury' details that could affect reputation. There can be extreme restrictions on freedom of movement and freedom of communication throughout the course of the 'game'. A standard feature is often a participant reward in the form of a ration of hand-written letters and personal visits. These strategies serve to underline the lack of access to ubiquitous communications technologies and to broader social relationships. The contracts thus regulate not just access to the contestant but also access to other personal connections associated with them. This functions to enhance the tensions around the 'authenticity' of the individual experience. Isolation of participants from 'real-world' comforts, family, friends and other emotional support is common. Cutting oneself adrift from known relationships of trust and being forced to negotiate overtly competitive social relationships (as if such deprivations naturally lead to the emergence of the true inner self) is part of the terms of engagement. Participants and also extended family may be bound by ongoing obligations of confidentiality, well after the programme has gone to air. On the other hand, producers can disclose what might normally be considered private information about contestants as they choose, with the *American Idol* contract including the right to 'reveal and/or relate information about me of a personal, private, intimate, surprising, defamatory, disparaging, embarrassing or unfavorable nature, that may be factual *and/or fictional*'.[28]

Reality TV contracts create access to far more than the participant's labour plus other discrete components of exchange: use of name, image, privacy, reputation. What is created is a contract of servitude or voluntary enslavement. Participants consent to personal subjection according to the strictures of a production bible that the participant (or their agent/lawyer) will not ever see. It often involves accepting game variations at the whim of the production master. These are quite different legal relations to liberal notions of freedom of contract involving informed consent to the provision of labour plus other subsidiary transactions. The logic of the reality TV game format is that the servant will not be able to anticipate the conditions of personal service, nor the nature of any reward for services rendered. It is interesting to note that the conditions of confinement experienced in game also contribute to feeding participant delusion about the nature and extent of post-game commercial opportunity on offer.[29]

MasterChef has been slammed in the press and in community forums for standard clauses that lawyers advise are unnecessarily broad and oppressive. The *Junior MasterChef* contract[30] was described as:

> ' ... an extraordinary contract,' entertainment lawyer Jules Munro says. 'You have to wonder why anyone would sign it.'

Munro says the contract for the programme, which is produced by Shine Australia, includes several 'traps for stage mums and dads. For instance, any material that parents submit to [Shine] to get their kids on screen, like holiday snaps or video of your kids in the school play, then belongs to Shine to be used as they see fit:

> Parents who sign the contract are also 'authorising these people to go snooping into you and your kid's private lives, with no undertaking to keep the sensitive stuff confidential. [Shine] can hang onto it for however long they want and use it for a tremendously broad range of uses'.[31]

Others have commented on the 'unnecessary cruelty' against adult contestants:

> They are harvesting wealth while the contestants, who suffer all the indignities, make peanuts. ... It presents itself as a meritocracy but the gruelling process of elimination is riddled with inconsistencies. What drives the show's drama is the certainty that the contestants, one by one, will have to walk the plank ... [The] heartfelt dramas that *MasterChef* provides ... [are] based on the dignity of the contestants and the indignities they must endure ... with the cameras leering in to capture the blood, sweat and tears.[32]

One contestant, Mat Beyer, described the experience as: "You are in complete lock-down ... it is like prison with no sex.'[33] His girlfriend added that in prison you get more phone calls. Beyer was kicked off the programme for using a smart phone. He was then reported as being 'locked in a motel by the show's producers in a bid to gag him about being kicked off the show'.[34] It was later reported that phone records showed he had not cheated but he had the phone, anxious to keep in touch with his girlfriend and concerned about developments in a coronial inquiry into his mother's disappearance, with filming coinciding with Mother's Day.[35] His treatment was controversial with supporters arguing:

> There is a difference between creating tension in the contest than creating emotional tension in the environment. Why do you think there are so many tears? It isn't because of the contest, it is because they are put in a stupid house, with limited emotional support, and no outlets. They are treated like lab rats rather than human beings and it isn't right.[36]

It is inevitable that at least some fans will engage in public criticism of the 'questionable morality' of restrictive arrangements, so it is worth considering why owners would insist on draconian terms of service. Obviously milking the dramatic tension in these situations and the related controversy created is part of the equation here. However, there are similar problems with the restrictive terms of service and lack of genuine user rights over contributions of fans, privacy, changing architecture or experience, that affect a wide range of social media sites and online gaming environments. Common or collective IP ownership and enhanced privacy settings are so far suggested as the main legal solution to re-establish some sense of ethics or fairness to exchanges, but ownership by whom, of what exactly? What is the legal subject matter of experiential transactions? Part of the problem here is that in the artificial environment of the entertaining real, where what is at stake is amateur participation in an unfolding narrative, within an evolving situation, across an uncertain time frame, designed to build narrative tension, it is really impossible to construct a contract for defined services or property. In the legal void all that is capable of being asked for with any legal precision is the name of the party – so what is contracted for is extended to the right of access to the entire existence of the natural person. How a court would interpret or enforce any of the highly restrictive clauses is unclear. It is, however, highly likely that producers and broadcasters would go a long way to prevent any judicial scrutiny or commentary on exploitation of participants. Related news stories would rapidly circulate and significantly undercut the commercial prospects for the particular format and reality TV more generally. As such, in a practical business sense, these contracts are probably unenforceable.

These legal relations are not commonly thought of in terms of enslavement because there may be promise of a foothold for celebrity and their own personal branding opportunities – their name on a cook book, a cooking show, appearance fees, image rights, personal product ranges and so on. Conditions of entry may demand a suspension of a right to a natural identity for a time, but this is in exchange for access to the means to turn a real-life identity into a brand identity, after the show. Hearn argues: 'These highly structured reality programmes, which narrate procedures of self-branding, and the concrete personal brands produced on and through them simultaneously function as training for life under neoliberalism.'[37] The game elements suggest that it is a battle of wills in which superior personal qualities and individual strategic calculations lead to 'future success'. This self-creation fantasy turns our attention away from understanding the way existing distributions of power and economic privilege are being maintained in the affective economy. There is an interesting play here, that in an age where old ways of branding are considered as nearing exhaustion, thus leading to the more immersive forms of advertising and product placement characteristic of reality TV, that 'successful' show participants mainly win a chance to access entry into the older, failing model of marketing, at some point in the future.

Product placement

In contrast to the legal situation for contestants, it appears comparatively straightforward to contract for product placement in television: your product here, referred to as agreed, captured in product close-ups being used or consumed by talent as well as captured in incidental shots, for a defined number of seconds per episode(s). However, this form of marketing is not simply about a deal for 'placement' of intellectual property in the form of a recognisable logo or brand. The transaction involves much more than simply a contract for display of a registered trade mark that engenders consumer awareness of the usefulness or inherent characteristics of the product.

A sign or logo is not a self-contained property. This is, however, often misunderstood because they are often described this way, perhaps influenced by accounting practice. The need to quantify the value of intangible assets leads to the adoption of somewhat circular reasoning in order to abstract a nominal value for a stable of marks and associated goodwill (including registered marks no longer used, those currently used, those registered with potential for future use). This usually involves consideration of commissioned market surveys that purport to quantify the extent of current brand recognition in a general sense.[38] These metrics are also supported with reference to current product market share and to the willingness of others to pay for trade mark license opportunities. Here the logic suggests that a sign's value equates to product demand and more generally owning potential audiences, in a pull advertising context. This radically simplifies very complex communications and exchanges related to the circulation of trade marks and goodwill, and also ignores the new media environment:

> They're still an audience, but they aren't necessarily listening to you. They're listening to each other talk about you. And they're using your products, your brand names, your iconography, your slogans, your trademarks, your designs, your goodwill, all of it as if it belonged to them – which, in a way, it all does, because after all, haven't you spent decades, and trillions, to convince them of just that?[39]

A sign does not convey a fixed narrative to audiences about the product or company behind it. A reality TV product placement deal is not simply about buying access to tell that story to a particular audience/demographic. The capacity for meaning and value in these signs is not fixed, neither is the mark's value established by the act of broadcast exposure. Rather the trade mark functions within the programme as a point of mediation between corporation and consumer. It is this dynamic dimension of trade mark that makes a sign's deployment in immersive contexts so valuable:

> The brand or logo, dispersed via a variety of media forms, comes to stand as the face of a corporation, good, or service and functions as a central point of mediation between the brander and consumer. While the object of the logo or trademark was initially intended to guarantee quality, it has now become the sign of a definite type of social identity, which summons consumers into relationship with it.[40]

Legally a trade mark has always been a far more fluid property than copyright (conceptually limited with reference to fixed expressions) or patent (with reference to a written specification and claims). The property in a registered mark is bounded by reference to its particular signifying characteristics, its actual and intended use and its established reputation. Unlike other intellectual property it is not able to be fixed in time: while theoretically it is possible to maintain a registration indefinitely, a registration can also be challenged and lost on the basis of post-registration circumstances. The law has supported extensions of commercial activity and global trade for some time by developing notions of trade mark dilution and according special privileges to marks that become well known.[41] Thus, any protection conferred by registration requires evaluation of the sign's past and ongoing functional relationships with consumers, with reference to its class of registration and how the sign is understood at a particular point in time. In law, property in the mark and value are understood to arise from the ability to (consciously or otherwise) relate a characteristic product or service to a class of consumers. Trade mark law thus accepts the active and fluid dimensions of signs and understands that any sign's value and meaning depends upon the quality of the mediation it provides between brand and consumer. In enhancing the quality of that mediation reality TV neatly fits within the established logic of trade mark law. Product placement is so central to the reality TV format that *Survivor* creator/producer Mark Barnett forwent a licence fee to deliver the inaugural season, and CBS agreed to share *Survivor*'s advertising revenue and asked him to help pre-sell the sponsorship.[42]

Product placement associated with *MasterChef* is described by Network Ten as 'a perfect fit or brands looking to engage with a cross-section of Australians ... Effective and creative online integration is a key element of TEN's viewer and client offering.'[43] A case study, offered to show the ongoing effectiveness of television advertising, opines:

> Campbell's biggest challenge was to change market perceptions and to make consumers aware that Campbell's Real Stock was different to powdered stocks available ... Campbell's uncovered the insight that consumers were more willing to be creative and confident in the kitchen if they were assured of a good result. They therefore needed to provide consumers with more reasons and opportunity to cook with confidence, by showcasing the quality of Campbell's Real Stock in environments where people looked for inspiration ...
>
> Campbell's brand integration into *MasterChef* provided unique opportunities for product demonstration and for results to be showcased in an inspiring way ...
>
> The TV and online elements of the campaigns worked seamlessly together to create outstanding results for Campbell's. Usage of Campbell's Real Stock increased among its core demographic of grocery buyers 25–54 as well as across other key demographic groups.[44]

MasterChef 'foundation partner' Coles reported sales spikes of up to 1400 per cent for ingredients featured in dishes in the programme season.[45]

Whether product placement on commercial broadcasting requires regulation is a matter of ongoing discussion globally.[46] It has long been permitted on Australian and US commercial television, and restrictions were recently lifted in the UK.[47] The lack of regulation clearly puts the interests of advertisers, marketers and television production houses to the forefront. Different regulatory standards of inclusion and requirements of disclosure interfere with the free flow of global television markets and impede market penetration by global brands. Currently children's television appears to be the only context where there is some recognition of the vulnerability of audiences to these practices.[48]

Why worry about the legality of product placement? As one marketing guru puts it:

> If the conversation is dominated by consumers themselves, and they're paying scant attention to the self-interested blather of the marketer, who needs ads – offline, online or otherwise? This raises the question of what agencies are left to do.
>
> Maybe the answer is obvious: to manage, focus, exploit, maybe co-opt the open conversation.[49]

The marketing strategy remains one of manipulation – co-opting the co-operation and interaction inherent in 'free' communications between people.

The regulatory presumption is that adult viewers are sufficiently media savvy or too cynical to be readily taken in by product placement for it to be a regulatory concern. It is also true that in reality TV contexts such as *MasterChef* the placement is rather obvious and overt. It is relatively easy for consumers to identify the chains of commercial associations that run throughout these programme narratives.

The relation between sponsor and producer mediates the audience affection for a programme and its contestants into extended commercial activity. In not regulating product placement, what the state facilitates is an opportunity for global corporations to use the affective relations generated by immersive programming to assist in selling more product. However, the regulatory silence also serves to help humanise the identity of global corporations at a time where there is consumer concern about global profit motivations swamping local and national interests. Product placement in reality TV programming encourages us to forget that the global corporation is an artificial legal personality that lacks the same properties and interests of a natural person or of communities. It allows affection for the programme and contestants to smooth over what is often nascent political dissatisfaction with the values and social impact of the global economy:

> It is no accident that the discourses of branding borrow heavily from the language of radical individualism: the 'face' or 'identity' of a brand works to establish a 'relationship' with the consumer. ... As we have seen, the degree to which a brand is able to embody human attributes is dependent on the degree to which it is able to insinuate itself into the lives of consumers in profound ways.[50]

Legal permissiveness towards product placement is clearly only one small part of much more complex neoliberal politics supported by commercial media enterprises. Nonetheless, as well as encouraging self-branding, reality TV product placement helps displace unease about the political direction of society. The apparent transparency of such arrangements signals to the audience that they should identify with the sponsors that the producers and the contestants trust, and also feel reassured about the broader commercial values underpinning these transactions. Such arrangements mobilise the social glue of immersive television to reconnect consumers with faith in the economy, humanising the global (usually foreign-owned) corporation for localised consumers.

Resistance to these dynamics is possible, but 'The emergent knowledge cultures never fully escape the influence of the commodity culture any more than commodity culture can function fully outside the constraints of territoriality.'[51] It is no surprise that there has been such a global proliferation of localised versions of reality TV franchises: *Nigerian Idol*, *Survivor* clone *Extreme Azerbaijan*, *Big Brother Angola* and so on. TV format adaptations are not cultural side-shows. The programming supports the penetration of new social aspirations into alien territories, assisting in building localised co-operation that is essential to restructuring global trade.

It is not surprising that we are also now semi-regularly seeing testing of the climate for stronger assertions of the 'human rights' of corporations such as a right to privacy,[52] extended forms of the defamation action[53] and deification of trade marks, to the extent that the state should never regulate their display or circulation.[54] Our 'freedom of communication' as reality TV viewers is part of a broader process that makes it much harder to identify a dividing line between natural and corporate persons. As the economy shifts to a logic of supporting the production of consumption, the right to a branded identity is being articulated as the ultimate, universal human right shared by individuals and corporations alike.

Extended brand activity

There are a number of new services that have been developed to track the community 'buzz' generated by social media and to monetise audience engagement:

> The embrace of engagement as a new metric for understanding audience behaviour is widespread as advertisers, content providers, and measurement firms have rather suddenly become willing to acknowledge the shortcomings in the criteria that have long dominated the audience marketplace.[55]

Refined data analysis technologies such as cookies and widgets and tailored services like Google Analytics collect information about online user practices for corporate-owned sites. For social media, Napoli lists the rise of media analysis services such as Neilsen Online BuzzMetrics, BrandIntel, E-Poll Market Research, Visible technologies, Optomedia.[56] Interactive marketers manage a wide range of communications. They monitor marketing attached to an owned channel (for example the *MasterChef* website and community), associated channels (for example Campbell's Australia site that leverage the owned channel), and media where fans and customers become the channel (for example *MasterChef* chatter on Facebook, Twitter). The organisations gather together disparate sources of information and strategies to help make the brand story work more seamlessly across platforms and outlets and to prevent strategic communications from getting lost amongst the free play and 'brand vigilantism'.[57] The objective is not to establish a command-and-control dynamic. It is more subtle and designed to, where possible, productively engage the labour of consumers in telling the corporate story,[58] and where not, minimise consumer resistance to key strategic messages. Control is discussed in terms of generating 'a complete experience', 'a brand or organisation-specific social media ecosystem' or a 'brand solar system'.[59] Marketing practices commonly include deploying fake consumers (paying models and actors to use products in public spaces), scripting 'unscripted' contributions, often to be distributed by third parties,[60] viral marketing campaigns and immersive marketing puzzles that generate 'word of mouth' about a primary product (these can also offer additional product placement opportunities through participation in the game).[61]

Analysis of data generated through online engagement and of substantive contributions and chatter provide insight into levels of consumer awareness, interest and anticipation. Genuine participation, even overtly critical of a corporation or product, can assist in undercutting consumer cynicism toward marketing, whilst consumer feedback of all sorts can be integrated into refinement of the brand strategy and the process of 'brand becoming'.[62] For participants, communications may be authentic and unrelated to self-branding but their participation is increasingly liable to be appropriated and incorporated into attempts at more controlled story telling. Any free participation related to a brand potentially entails a level of co-operation with the marketing strategy of the franchise and the creation of brand capital. The digital technologies we are using create the impossibility of contributing without knowingly or unwittingly feeding into extended brand relations.

The legal relations of *MasterChef*

The *MasterChef* example shows the potential of commercial mass media to integrate a convergent media logic that draws amateur participation into an extended brand narrative. Other cultural forms – books, films, music, computer games – have different traditions and marketing dynamics. Nonetheless, the influence of the new marketing practices integral to reality TV can also be seen at play in other kinds of media experience.

For example, the hugely successful Harry Potter franchise has moved on from a command-and-control relationship that led to push back from fans to adopt a more nuanced approach. Through trial and error[63] they have been brought to accept a more relaxed attitude towards a degree of fan-active copyright infringement, fair use and non-commercial trade mark use. This activity adds value to the franchise and reinforces a sensibility of propriety that reaffirms the centrality and authority of J. K. Rowling, the 'awesome'[64] 'original author', to the fictional universe. Fan activity enlivens both the extended narrative and the marketing of that story. Interactive marketing strategies have included leverage of fan love to assist advertising the Harry Potter Florida theme park. Key credible individuals associated with popular fansites were given privileged access and breaking news about the theme park to report on their sites. Mass media reportage of these crazy fans privileged with advance tours of the theme park then circulated as human interest news stories about fans, cults and cultural curiosities. This gloss served to diffuse identification of the corporate objectives at play in the creation of the multi-platform media opportunity.[65] The recent announcement of Pottermore,[66] a free subscription-based website and repository of unpublished J. K. Rowling Harry Potter-related material incorporated a 'Magical Quill' challenge with fans fighting it out for early access – a prize that provides Sony and J. K. Rowling with free user testing. Marketed as 'giving back to fans' the Pottermore strategy also allows the author to continue to function as the authoritative and authentic voice for all things Potter as interest in the book and movie series starts to fade away. This is a sophisticated digital re-engagement of the author function to preserve her brand potential into the future.[67]

Law is supporting the shift in commercialisation of amateur labour and facilitating a greater personal identification with brands, but this has not required major law reform. Copyright law provides uncertain support to the market in TV formats, notwithstanding the push to treat these as copyright subject matter and to stretch notions of authorship to include rights for the creator of looser, interactive narratives. Reality TV contracts that seek to 'own' all aspects of a contestant's life are probably unenforceable – legally, because the breadth of the claims makes them too vague, uncertain and inequitable to withstand much scrutiny; in a business sense, because a global Goliath seeking to enforce onerous terms against an amateur television celebrity would entail major publicity risks that would endanger both programme and associated enterprises. Trade mark law facilitates licensing and product placement that helps humanise global corporations. The legal environment is increasingly accommodating of the interests of well-known brands. However, there is little groundswell of support for more regulation of this activity and arguably increased disclosure requirements would do little to forestall deeper penetration of brand identities. The extended brand opportunities that come with tracking consumer engagement and feed back into development of new marketing opportunities is largely facilitated by 'code as law'.[68] Technologies that allow free communications to be tracked for commercial purposes enable this activity, and as with product placement, it is the absence of law or regulation that creates the commercial opportunity. There is no global conspiracy that shows law being rewritten at the behest of media conglomerations and the entertainment industry to facilitate a shift away from a mass media environment. There is no need for this. But law still has a significant role to play in the commodification of affective labour.

What we are seeing in operation is a simulacrum of law – a truth that hides the fact that there is none[69] – that activates these commercial arrangements.

There seems to be a desire, even perhaps an essential requirement to participate in a performance of legality surrounding the creation of the new kinds of ownership associated with the affective economy – from drafting contracts assigning dubious forms of intangible property, to producing expectations of compliance through fanciful references to extra-legal processes; to contestant contracts requiring 'consent' to extraordinary, undefinable terms of service; to inflated suggestions of right related to trade mark ownership and enforceability. In the case of product placement, capitalising on a regulatory absence is central to the 'right' to turn audience interaction into 'brand becoming'.

Voluntary engagement in legal gestures provides broader normative support to the ideas of property, propriety and branded identity that the parties seek to entrench. What is entirely left out of this positioning is any space for broader public deliberation about the transformation of society, community and individual identity actively being pursued by global corporations. The positioning also impacts on the reach of formal law (legislation and case law), to the extent that this still houses other traditions or values, to redirect or resist the changes under way. When law fails to uphold industry expectations about quasi-legal arrangements, the institution of law becomes vulnerable to criticism that it is 'out of step' with commercial realities and is impeding economic progress.

Trends in television viewing, including the rise of reality TV, provide a window on broader changes in society. A focus on the associated legal relations also provides broader insights into the political function of neoliberal forms of law. The manufactured authenticity of reality TV is co-dependent on creating an authentic buzz around law and legality. Another way of thinking about this is that legal relations are about as real as reality TV.

Acknowledgements

This chapter is part of an ARC-funded project: Kathy Bowrey and Michael Handler, *Entertainment Rights in the Age of the Franchise: a Reappraisal of Personality Rights Under Australian Intellectual Property Laws*. Thanks to Lloyd Sharp, Michael Handler, Kate Bond, Lucas Lixinski and to Bailee Walker for her research assistance.

Notes

1 Michel Foucault, 'What is an Author?' (trans. Donald F. Bouchard and Sherry Simon) in Donald F. Bouchard (ed.), *Michel Foucault: Language, Counter-Memory, Practice*, Oxford: Basil Blackwell, 1977, pp. 130–31.
2 See *Network Ten Pty Ltd v TCN Channel Nine Pty Ltd* (2004) 218 CLR 273, 302–3 [75]–[77] (McHugh ACJ, Gummow and Hayne JJ).
3 It is recognised that public broadcasting has a different tradition and role in connecting with audiences. However, this tradition is not itself immune from all the dynamics being discussed here.
4 James Gilmore and B. Joseph Pine II, *Authenticity: What Consumers Really Want*, Boston, MA: Harvard Business School Press, 2007, p. 145.
5 Frank Rose, *The Art of Immersion*, New York: W.W. Norton & Co, 2011, p. 88.

6 Henry Jenkins, 'Buying Into American Idol: How We Are Being Sold on Reality Television', in Susan Murray and Laurie Ouellette (eds), *Reality TV: Remaking Television Culture*, New York: New York University Press, 2009, p. 344.

7 *Newmark v Turner Broadcasting Network*, 226 F Supp 2d 1215 (Cal, 2002). The litigation effectively bankrupted the company. See Electronic Frontier Foundation, *Newmark v Turner*: www.eff.org/cases/newmark-v-turner.

8 James Gallagher, 'Duke Study: TiVo Doesn't Hurt TV Advertising', *San Jose Business Journal* (online), 3 May 2010: www.bizjournals.com/sanjose/stories/2010/05/03/daily15. html; Deloitte, *DVRs Proliferate! The 30 Second Spot Doesn't Die!* (18 January 2011): www. deloitte.com/assets/Dcom-Global/Local%20Assets/Documents/TMT/Predictions%202011% 20PDFs/8855A%20TMT%20DVRs%20LB1.pdf.

9 Ted Magder, 'Television 2.0 The Business of American Television in Transition' in Murray and Ouellette (eds), *Reality TV*, p. 142.

10 Laurie Ouellette and Susan Murray, 'Introduction', in Murray and Ouellette (eds), *Reality TV*, p. 3.

11 Ibid., p. 8.

12 See June Deery, 'Reality TV as Advertainment' (2004) 2(1) *Popular Communication* 1, 4.

13 Mark Andrejevic, *Reality TV: The Work of Being Watched*, Lanham, MD: Rowman & Littlefield, 2004, Chapter 6: 'It's all about the experience', pp. 143–71.

14 Ten Corporate, 'Ten & Shine Strike MasterChef Deal' (News Release, 15 February 2011).

15 Stuart Heritage, 'Has MasterChef Lost Its X Factor?', *Guardian* (online), 17 February 2011: www.guardian.co.uk/tv-and-radio/tvandradioblog/2011/feb/17/MasterChef-the-x-factor.

16 For a discussion of the commercialisation of home cooking see Deery, 'Reality TV as Advertainment'.

17 For a study of the trade see Sukhpreet Singh and Martin Kretschmer, 'Exploiting Idols – Case Study of International TV Formats Trading in the Absence of IP Protection' in Robert Burnett and Koos Zwaan (eds), *Your Fans are Waiting: an Academic Volume on Idol*, Durham, NC: Duke University Press, forthcoming.

18 *Green v Broadcasting Corp of New Zealand* [1989] RPC 700, 702.

19 Singh and Kretschmer, 'Exploiting Idols'.

20 The Format Recognition and Protection Association, *History of FRAPA* (2011): www.frapa. org/about/history/.

21 *Nine Films & Television Pty Ltd v Ninox Television Ltd* [2005] FCA 1404 at [48] (emphasis added).

22 *Autospin (Oil Seals) Ltd v Beehive Spinning* [1995] RPC 683, 697, cited ibid.

23 Jeff Gomez quoted in Rose, *The Art of Immersion*, p. 246.

24 *Nine Films & Television Pty Ltd v Ninox Television Limited* [2005] FCA 1404 at [92].

25 See Yochai Benkler, *The Wealth of Networks: How Social Production Transforms Markets and Freedom*, New Haven, CT: Yale University Press, 2006.

26 For example Mark Andrejevic, 'Watching Television Without Pity: The Productivity of Online Fans' (2008) 9 *Television and New Media* 24; John Banks and Mark Deuze, 'Co-Creative Labour' (2009) 12 *International Journal of Cultural Studies* 419; Ryan M. Milner, 'Working for the text: Fan Labor and the New Organization' (2009) *International Journal of Cultural Studies* 491; Tiziana Terranova, 'Free Labor: Producing Culture for the Digital Economy' (2000) 18(2) *Social Text* 33.

27 For a discussion of exploitation of children and US labour law see Christopher C. Cianci, 'Entertainment or Exploitation?: Reality Television and the Inadequate Protection of Child Participants under the Law' (2009) 18 *Southern California Interdisciplinary Law Journal* 363; Courtney Glickman, 'Note and Comment: Jon & Kate Plus … Child Entertainment Labor Law Complaints' (2010) 32 *Whittier Law Review* 147.

28 Cited in Alison Hearn, '"Meat, Mask, Burden": Probing the Contours of the Branded "Self"' (2008) 8(2) *Journal of Consumer Culture* 197 citing Olsen at 209.

29 Discussed in relation to *Big Brother* in Andrejevic, 'Watching Television Without Pity', 164–65.

30 Several clauses are published online: see Reality Raver, 'Junior Masterchef – Would You Sign the Contract?' on *Reality Ravings* (1 July 2011): www.realityravings.com/2011/07/01/junior-masterchef-would-you-sign-the-contract/.

31 Tim Elliott, 'Junior MasterChef Contract Indigestible', *Sydney Morning Herald* (online), 2 July 2011: www.smh.com.au/entertainment/junior-masterchef-contract-indigestible-20110701-1gvbl.html.

32 Paul Sheehan, 'MasterChef Leaves a Bitter Aftertaste', *Sydney Morning Herald* (online), 18 July 2011: www.smh.com.au/opinion/society-and-culture/masterchef-leaves-a-bitter-aftertaste-20110717-1hjz3.html.

33 Hamish Heard, 'Mat Beyer Locked in Motel after MasterChef Axing for Using Smartphone', *Sunday Telegraph* (online) 19 June 2011: www.dailytelegraph.com.au/news/mat-locked-in-motel-after-masterchef-axing-for-using-smartphone/story-e6freuy9–1226077729712.

34 Ibid.

35 Nathan Partenza, 'Masterchef Storm: Uncle Backs Beyer', *The Border Mail* (online), 8 July 2011: www.bordermail.com.au/news/local/news/general/masterchef-storm-uncle-backs-beyer/2220130.aspx.

36 Quote attributed to gobligook, *Ten Community – MasterChef*, 2 August 2011: http://community.ten.com.au/community/members/gobligook/default.aspx.

37 Hearn, '"Meat, Mask, Burden"', 209. Arguably the extraordinary rise in the western fashion of tattooing is an indicator of the successful penetration of the logic of self-branding amongst the younger generations, notwithstanding these signs sometimes expressing counter-cultural affiliations.

38 This expertise and evidence is often treated with suspicion in other legal contexts: see *Chocolaterie Guylian NV v Registrar of Trade Marks* (2009) 180 FCR 60; *Cadbury Schweppes Pty Ltd v Darrell Lea Chocolate Shops Pty Ltd (No 8)* [2008] FCA 470; *Cadbury Schweppes Pty Ltd v Darrell Lea Chocolate Shops Pty Ltd (No 2)* [2009] FCAFC 8; *Henschke & Co v Rosemount Estates Pty Ltd* [1999] FCA 1561; [2000] FCA 1539.

39 Bob Garfield, 'Listenomics' 10 Oct 2005 76(41) *Advertising Age* 1.

40 Hearn, '"Meat, Mask, Burden"', 199.

41 See generally Robert Burrell and Michael Handler, *Australian Trade Mark Law*, South Melbourne: Oxford University Press, 2010, pp. 5–6, 350–355.

42 Ted Magder, 'Television 2.0', p .144.

43 Ten Corporate, 'Six Sponsors eat up Junior Masterchef' (News Release, 1 September 2010).

44 ThinkTV Australia, *MasterChef Integration: a Real Recipe for Success for Campbell's Real Stock*: www.thinktv.com.au/media/Case_Studies/MasterChef_and_Campbells_Case_Study.pdf.

45 Nina Hendy, 'MasterChef Helps Coles' Sales Sizzle', *Business Spectator* (online) 22 July 2010: www.businessspectator.com.au/bs.nsf/Article/MasterChef-advertising-Coles-Wesfarmers-sponsorshi-pd20100722–7L6VY?OpenDocument&emcontent_spectators.

46 Consumer protection laws and 'soft law' in the form of a media, broadcasting and advertising code of practice may have some limited role to play in a convergent media context.

47 Lesley Hitchens, 'Product Placement comes to the UK', *Communications Law and Regulation Blog* (18 July 2010): http://communicationslawreg.blogspot.com/2010/07/product-placement-comes-to-uk.html; British Broadcasting Corporation, *BBC Licence Fee Funded Television Services and Product Placement* (April 2011): www.bbc.co.uk/editorialguidelines/page/guidance-product-placement.

48 For a UK study of the use of media and marketing practices recruiting and targeting children see Ed Mayo and Agnes Nairn, *Consumer Kids: How Big Business in Grooming our Children for Profit*, London: Constable & Robinson, 2009.

49 Garfield, 'Listenomics', p. 34.

50 Hearn, '"Meat, Mask, Burden"', 209.

51 Henry Jenkins, 'The Cultural Logic of Media Convergence' (2004) 7(1) *International Journal of Cultural Studies* 33, 35.

52 Tanya Aplin, 'A Right of Privacy for Corporations?' in Paul L. C. Torremans (ed.), *Intellectual Property and Human Rights, Enhanced Edition of Copyright and Human Rights*, Alphen aan den Rijn: Kluwer Law, 2008, p. 475.

53 *McDonald's Corporation v Steel & Morris* [1997] EWHC QB 366; *Steel & Morris v United Kingdom* (2005) 41 Eur HR Rep 22; David Rolph, 'Corporations' Right to Sue for Defamation: An Australian Perspective' (2011) 22(7) *Entertainment Law Review* 195.

54 Trade Marks Amendment (Tobacco Plain Packaging) Bill 2011 (Cth); Phillip Morris Pty Ltd, *Plain Packaging of Tobacco Products* (2011): www.plain-packaging.com/Templates/Blank_TrademarkRights.aspx.

55 Philip M. Napoli, *Audience Evolution: New Technologies and the Transformation of Media Audiences*, New York: Columbia University Press, 2011, p. 95.

56 Ibid., p. 92. See also Interactive Advertising Bureau, *User Generated Content, Social Media and Advertising-An Overview* (April 2008): www.iab.net/media/file/2008_ugc_platform.pdf.

57 Albert M. Muniz and Hope Jensen Schau, 'Vigilante Marketing and Consumer-Generated Communications' (2007) 36(3) *Journal of Advertising* 35; Chrysanthos Dellarocas, 'The Digitisation of Word of Mouth: Promise and Challenges of Online Feedback Mechanisms' (2003) 49(10) *Management Science* 1407.

58 For a critical perspective see Detlev Zwick, Samuel K. Bonsu and Aron Darmody, 'Putting Consumers to Work: "Co-creation" and New Marketing Govern-mentality' (2008) 8 *Journal of Consumer Culture* 163.

59 Brian Solis, 'Why Brands are Becoming Media', *Mashable* (online) 11 February 2010: http://mashable.com/2010/02/11/social-objects/. See also Brian Solis, *Engage: The Complete Guide for Brands and Businesses to Build, Cultivate, and Measure Success in the New Web*, Hoboken, NJ: John Wiley & Sons, 2010.

60 Gilmore and Pine, *Authenticity: What Consumers Really Want*, pp. 148–9.

61 Rose, *The Art of Immersion*, pp. 13–21.

62 Elizabeth Moor, 'Branded Spaces: The Scope of "New Marketing"' (2003) 3 *Journal of Consumer Culture* 39, 53.

63 *Warner Brothers Entertainment INC & J.K. Rowling v RDR Books And Does 1–10*, 575 F Supp 2d 513 (SDNY, 2008); Martha Woodmansee, 'The Quote's the Thing: Negotiating Copyright in Scholarly Criticism – a Symposium' (paper presented at 'The Quote's the Thing: Negotiating Copyright in Scholarly Criticism' conference, Buffalo Law School, State University of New York, 2 April 2011).

64 Clay Shirky, *Cognitive Surplus: Creativity and Generosity in a Connected Age*, New York: Penguin, 2010, pp. 90–92.

65 This example is taken from Kathy Bowrey, 'The New Intellectual Property: Celebrity, Fans and the Properties of the Entertainment Franchise' (2011) 20(1) *Griffith Law Review* 188, 215–6.

66 Warner Brothers Entertainment, *Pottermore* (2011): www.pottermore.com.

67 In this regard, a copyright faith in fair use as a mechanism for restoring the balance and empowering fans seems to altogether misunderstand the dynamics of value generation and the properties of the affective economy.

68 Lawrence Lessig, *Code and Other Laws of Cyberspace*, New York: Basic Books, 1999. See also www.code-is-law.org/.

69 The original quote is: 'The simulacrum is never what hides the truth-it is truth that hides the fact that there is none. The simulacrum is true'.—Ecclesiastes from Jean Baudrillard, *Simulacra and Simulations* (trans. Sheila Gaililee) Chicago: University of Michigan Press, 1994, p. 5.

8 *Harry Potter* and the transformation wand

Fair use, canonicity and fan activity

David Tan

In 'The manufacture of "authentic" buzz and the legal relations of *MasterChef*', Kathy Bowrey argues that 'law is supporting corporate control over the extended narrative of the enterprise' and observes that 'amateur participation [may be drawn] into an extended brand narrative.' Her comment that 'the hugely successful Harry Potter franchise has moved on from a command-and-control relationship that led to push back from fans to adopt a more nuanced approach' merits further examination. Bowrey is of the view that the rights owners of Harry Potter:

> have been brought to accept a more relaxed attitude toward a degree of fan-active copyright infringement, fair use and non-commercial trade mark use. This activity adds value to the franchise and reinforces a sensibility of propriety that reaffirms the centrality and authority of J. K. Rowling, the 'awesome' 'original author', to the fictional universe.

The preservation of the 'brand potential [of the original author] into the future' necessitates the anointment of the fans of the Harry Potter as secondary authors of an extended narrative as long as the authenticity – or canonicity – of J. K. Rowling is not challenged.

In the iconic essay 'The Death of the Author', Roland Barthes argues that 'a text's unity lies not in its origin but in its destination' and that 'the birth of the reader must be at the cost of the death of the Author'.[1] Barthes' work, controversial at the time of publication with its assault on modernity and the primacy of authorial control, has nonetheless laid the groundwork for an important body of scholarship on interpretive communities. Interdisciplinary legal writings, especially in the area of intellectual property and personality rights, have also actively engaged such themes in recent years.[2] Focusing on the distinctive characteristics of fan behavior, Nathaniel Noda contends that copyright law ought to 'keep pace with changing times and practices by recognizing that an author implicitly cedes certain interpretive rights to the general public when he or she introduces a work into the stream of public discourse'.[3] Noda's thesis on the interpretive rights of the reader – or more generally the public that is the ultimate destination of an author's creative work – implicitly draws on Barthes earlier ideas.

However, Noda makes a more important point regarding the primacy of authenticity or 'canonicity' of the original author's work. The 'canon' is that which is considered 'official' or 'have actually happened within a fictional universe' created by the original author; and the 'non-canon' is that which is not, and is the space in which fan communities and fan-based activities inhabit without 'eroding the copyright holder's incentives'.[4] Canonicity is the incontestable authorial mandate which 'sets the original author's creative teleology apart from all other creative teleologies ... [and] is an implicit stamp of legitimacy that gives the original author's work primacy over every fan-based work that comes after it'.[5] According to Noda, this delineation between canon and non-canon is a preoccupation of fans,[6] and as the testimony of J. K. Rowling would reveal, perhaps this is also a concern for original authors.[7] It has been observed that fan obsession with canonicity occurs most prominently in the United States among fans of major science-fiction works like *Star Wars* and *Star Trek* – and maybe more recently with *Harry Potter* and *Twilight* – whose fans 'have created entire [online] databases to distinguish canon from non-canon'.[8] It appears that the importance that fans ascribe to the canon works preserves the author's artistic and economic integrity, and to the fans, hence arguably also to the buying public, the authentic official will always trump the fan-made unofficial. This unofficial fan fiction – which may be in literary, video or musical form, or a hybrid of text–image–music – and has been broadly defined as 'all derivative fiction and related works created by fans, whether authorized or unauthorized by the author of or current right-holder in the original work'.[9] The secondary works of fan fiction authors can cover several genres including fantasy, eroticism, comedy, drama, adventure and mystery. Furthermore, fan-based activities like fanfic (literary form) and fanvids (image and musical hybrid) are usually undertaken as a complement to, rather than in competition with, the authentic canonical work of the original author; this 'symbiotic relationship' is likely to 'augment, rather than subtract from, the [original] author's aggregate economic and creative incentives'.[10]

In the United States, if prima facie copyright infringement were found, the 'fair-use' defence as codified in § 107 of the Copyright Act 1976 can nonetheless provide a safe harbour for the defendant, especially if transformative elements may be discerned in the infringing work.[11] Under this provision, 'fair use' is decided in balancing four statutory factors: (1) the purpose and character of the use, (2) the nature of the copyrighted work, (3) the amount and substantiality of the use (in relation to the copyrighted work) and (4) the effect of the use on the potential market for or value of the copyrighted work. In *Campbell v Acuff-Rose Music*, the Supreme Court has unequivocally stated that 'the more transformative the new work, the less will be the significance of other factors, like commercialism, that may weigh against a finding of fair use'.[12] When examining fan activities, it is clear that a product of fan culture is 'transformative' and hence most likely qualifying as fair use if it 'adds something new, with a further purpose or different character, altering the [original author's work] with new expression, meaning, or message'.[13] Thus in their interpretive activities, fans may arguably, as fair use, comment on or criticise the canonical universe of the original author, create parodies of the original works or to express their own creative teleologies that draw on the primacy of the canon. Most of these activities are not only transformative, but the 'complementary nature of fan-based works keeps them from directly competing with the works of the original author'[14] and 'any success enjoyed by the fan-based work inevitably proselytizes others to the [canonical] work'.[15]

The transformation doctrine in the first factor of fair use is a difficult one to elucidate. Stating 'the purpose and character of the use, including whether such use is of a commercial nature or is for non-profit educational purposes', suggests that (a) a change in the purpose of the secondary infringing work vis-à-vis the original work (for example, from entertaining to educational) or a change in character (for example, change in context or style) is transformative; (b) such changes should be considered in the light of the commerciality of the secondary infringing work, although this examination overlaps with the fourth factor on market impact; (c) whether the secondary infringing work serves a commercial or non-profit purpose is a separate consideration from 'purpose and character of the use'. Courts do not usually observe a strict distinction between 'purpose' and 'character', preferring to assess whether the secondary work was sufficiently transformative according to the guidelines laid down by the Supreme Court in *Campbell*.

Rachel Stroude usefully classified fan fiction works into two broad categories: referential works and participatory works.[16] Referential works provide a guide or a reference, usually in the form of plot and character summaries or alphabetised lexicons to help readers or viewers navigate their way through a complex canonical universe like *Star Trek* or *Harry Potter*. As Stroude explains, '[a]s the plot thickens, more characters appear, and themes develop, the amount of information presented to audiences grow. To fulfill their own creative impulses and to aid fellow fans, some fans will compile this information into a more accessible format.'[17] Participatory works borrow the familiar characters and settings from the canonical universe and use them in new and often startling situations created by the fans. Stroude points out that 'the new work reflects the fan fiction author's own identity and insights. Inspired by their differing interpretations, readers transform a character or pursue an alternative course of events in their participatory works.'[18] Although Stroude was of the view that participatory works 'typically are labeled as derivative of original works, and thus, reserved territory for the copyright owner to explore',[19] she thought that '[m]embers of a postmodern society can simultaneously juggle a continued following of the original canon and entertain secondary variations of this canon.'[20] Case law has not examined fair use in participatory works like fanfic, fanvids or similar products of fan culture that recodes the canonical universe.[21] It has been argued that some of these fictional literary works, collectively known as 'metafiction', are 'a well-recognized, long-standing art form in which authors rewrite canonical literature to expose and reinscribe into a new work what was excluded and marginalized from traditional literature and history'[22] and ought to be adjudged transformative works. However, many of the legal disputes to date in respect of fan works concern non-fictional referential secondary works like the *Seinfeld Aptitude Test*[23] and the *Harry Potter Lexicon*.[24]

Sonia Katyal has argued that in cyberspace, the original works have become performative cultural texts that are 'ripe for commentary, recoding, transgression, and appropriation'.[25] Focusing on the genre of slash fiction, which 'involves fictional, homoerotic pairings between male characters in mainstream television programs and films',[26] Katyal demonstrates how slash fiction 'empowers the virtual community to actively rework traditional narratives between men, demonstrating how queering mainstream characters can actually deconstruct and then transcend traditional gender norms and stereotypes'.[27] Slash fiction can 'sometimes [depict] lightly coded romances between male characters and other times [depict] graphic sexual activity.'[28] In taking male characters from the canonical universe – for example Harry Potter and Draco Malfoy[29] – and reworking their personae and performances, slash-fiction writers are able to 'dissect, appropriate, and then deconstruct the various elements of male dominance'.[30] The themes in slash fan fiction 'explore the possibility of living outside of these circumscribed boundaries [of the canon]'[31] and 'challenge the productive power of the author [by offering] a host of radically new political possibilities for a given [canonical] narrative'.[32] Such reimaginations clearly add 'something new, with a further purpose or different character, altering the [original author's work] with new expression, meaning, or message'[33] and are transformative. However, Rebecca Tushnet cautions that 'it is difficult to draw clear lines between parody and other types of transformative use, including political protest'[34] but argues that fan fiction:

> involves original input, taking the borrowed characters into new situations and exploring their thoughts and feelings in ways not present in the official texts. This type of elaboration, involving the addition of much time and effort, should fall into the category of 'transformative use'.[35]

There are ample and highly persuasive arguments marshalled by commentators like Katyal and Tushnet that fan fiction – regardless of whether they are classified as parody, satire, homage or commentary – is transformative and that this transformative nature inherent in such secondary works precludes market substitution for the original canonical works. Indeed fan fiction 'often imagines rather earthshaking changes for the characters … that the "canon" cannot accept … So long as such stories are not official, they retain their appeal because the characters return unscathed in the next episode or official form.'[36] While the emphasis of non-commerciality may be 'the communal ethos of fandom',[37] fans may sometimes venture out of this safe haven to profit from works whose content have been borrowed from the canon. What is even more problematic is when one attempts to profit from non-fictional fan works that do not re-code, parody, comment or criticise the canon, but simply reorganises the canon into an alphabetised guide. Can such referential works lay claim to possessing the requisite degree of transformation that weighs in favour of fair use?

In 2000, an avid *Harry Potter* fan, Steven Vander Ark, created a fansite called the Harry Potter Lexicon (www.hp-lexicon.org) in an effort to provide fellow fans with a comprehensive alphabetised guide to navigate the canonical universe of Harry Potter.[38] The use of this website is free and unrestricted. J. K. Rowling was initially supportive of this fansite, even publicly endorsing it in 2004 with a posting on the site:

> This is such a great site that I have been known to sneak into an internet cafe while out writing and check a fact rather than go into a bookshop and buy a copy of Harry Potter (which is embarrassing). A website for the dangerously obsessive; my natural home.[39]

In 2007, RDR Books saw the potential in publishing the Lexicon as a commercial book and contacted Vander Ark. However, Vander Ark was at first reluctant as he was 'was aware of Rowling's public statements regarding her intention to write a *Harry Potter* encyclopedia upon completion of the seventh book in the series'[40] and he also firmly believed that 'any book that is a guide to [the *Harry Potter*] world would be a violation of Rowling's intellectual property rights.'[41] Such a view clearly affirms how most fans feel about maintaining the delineation between the authentic official canon and non-commercial non-canonical secondary fan works.[42] Ultimately, Vander Ark was persuaded to proceed with the publication of the Lexicon with RDR Books 'adding an atypical clause to the publishing contract providing that RDR would defend and indemnify Vander Ark in the event of any lawsuits'.[43]

J. K. Rowling sued. Rowling testified at trial that the Lexicon took 'all the highlights of [her] work, in other words [her] characters' secret history, the jokes certainly, certain exciting narrative twists, all the things that are the highlights of [her] stories'[44] – essentially appropriating her canon as Vander Ark's own. Although the New York district court held that the market for reference guides to the *Harry Potter* works is not exclusively Rowling's to exploit or license, no matter the commercial success attributable to the popularity of the original works,[45] the court found on the evidence that the Lexicon's 'actual use of the copyrighted works is not consistently transformative'.[46] Patterson J concluded that '[t]he fair-use factors, weighed together in light of the purposes of copyright law, fail to support the defense of fair use in this case.'[47]

The *Harry Potter Lexicon* decision 'seeks to navigate a fine line between original authorial control and literary activities of fans'.[48] As Megan Richardson and I have noted previously:

> the judge faced an uphill battle in countering Rowling's insistence that she was entitled to exercise control over all products which derived from

her 'nominative genius', impinging on her 'imaginary universe', concluding ultimately that the fair use defence failed simply because the Lexicon 'appropriates too much of Rowling's creative work for its purposes'.[49]

Rowling's behaviour with regard to the Lexicon compiled by her ardent fan Vander Ark demonstrates how creators often want to exercise authorial control over their works and that such a desire may originate more from an emotional connection that creators claim to have with their works than from economic concerns. On the other hand, Rowling appears to support fan-based or even commercial publications that use an A-to-Z guide that take less of her writings of the *Harry Potter* series and provide more commentary.[50] Her concern is with poorly written guides which are perceived by her to be 'profit-driven attempts to resell to the public what it already owns'[51] as such books simply lift too much of the fictional facts that make up the *Harry Potter* universe without providing additional information or commentary. Rowling admitted in court that she did not think a number of unauthorised alphabetised guides which were commercially available raised copyright concerns at all.[52]

Rowling's tolerance – and possibly acceptance – of online non-commercial websites that draw on the *Harry Potter* universe may be construed as an implicit acknowledgement of a 'participatory culture' in which 'fans and other consumers are invited to actively participate in the creation and circulation of new content'.[53] As Bowrey intimated, the recent announcement of the Pottermore website 'allows [Rowling] to continue to function as the authoritative and authentic voice for all things Potter'. The Pottermore strategy edifies Rowling's canonical universe while recognising the importance of a participatory culture in keeping the Harry Potter brand alive by inviting fans to '[s]hare and participate in the stories, [and] showcase [their] own Potter-related creativity'.[54] While many commentators are in support of protecting fanfic and fanvids from copyright infringement suits,[55] referential works – especially in the absence of commentary or criticism of the canonical universe – that may 'act as an economic substitute for the original copyrighted work'[56] appear to fall into the category of derivative works that is within the prerogative of the original author. Regardless of the theoretical approaches adopted in these analyses of fandom, community and identity construction, it is important to ultimately relocate these debates back within the doctrine of transformation as enshrined in the first factor of fair use in order for them to be useful to the courts and the resolution of legal disputes.[57] For example, Tushnet suggests that if one were to use the parody/satire division as laid down in Campbell as a guide, then courts may find that 'a legitimate transformation exists when the new work makes overt that which was present in the original text covertly ... transformative fair uses make subtext text.'[58]

In the United States, courts appear to over-protect well-known fictional characters,[59] but fan-created sequels, remixes and alternative universes 'do serve an important social and cultural purpose that [an author like] Rowling is not only unwilling but unable to meet'.[60] As Katyal argues, 'copyright law needs to equalize the authorial monopoly of the creator in favor of a more dialogic and dynamic relationship between producers and consumers in the process'.[61] A better understanding of canonicity in the context of fan activities, as well as the social need of contemporary audience and readers who want their own opportunity to participate in today's 'Rip. Mix. Burn.' culture,[62] will no doubt assist future judicial deliberations regarding what kind of transformative fan works should qualify for fair use protection.

Notes

1 Roland Barthes, 'The Death of the Author' in Image-Music-Text (Stephen Heath trans.), New York: Hill & Wang, 1977, p. 142, p. 148.

2 See, e.g., David Tan, 'Political Recoding of the Contemporary Celebrity and the First Amendment' (2011) 2 Harvard Journal of Sports & Entertainment Law 1; David Tan, 'The Fame Monster Reloaded: The Contemporary Celebrity, Cultural Studies and Passing Off' [2010] Singapore Journal of Legal Studies 151; Sonia K. Katyal, 'Semiotic Disobedience' (2006) 84 Washington University Law Review 489; Jason Bosland, 'The Culture of Trade Marks: An Alternative Cultural Theory Perspective' (2005) 10 Media & Arts Law Review 99; Megan Richardson, 'Trade Marks and Language' (2004) 26 Sydney Law Review 193; Justin Hughes, '"Recoding" Intellectual Property and Overlooked Audience Interests' (1999) 77 Texas Law Review 923; Mark A. Lemley, 'Romantic Authorship and the Rhetoric of Property' (1997) 75 Texas Law Review 873.

3 Nathaniel T. Noda, 'Copyright Retold: How Interpretive Rights Foster Creativity and Justify Fan-Based Activities' (2010) 57 Journal of Copyright Society of USA 987, 991.

4 Ibid., 993.

5 Ibid., 1001.

6 Ibid., 993. See also Rebecca Tushnet, 'Legal Fictions: Copyright, Fan Fiction, and a New Common Law,' (1997) 17 Loyola of Los Angeles Entertainment Law Journal 651, 657 ('Fans also see themselves as guardians of the texts they love, purer than the owners in some ways because they seek no profit'); Rosemary J. Coombe, 'Author/izing the Celebrity: Publicity Rights, Postmodern Politics, and Unauthorized Genders' (1992) 10 Cardozo Arts & Entertainment Law Journal 365, 388 ('Fans respect the original texts and regularly police each other for abuses of interpretative license, but they also see themselves as the legitimate guardians of these materials, which have too often been manhandled by the producers and their licensees for easy profits').

7 See below n. 38–43. See also Salinger v Colting, 641 F Supp 2d 250 (SD NY, 2009); Salinger v Colting, 607 F 3d 68 (2nd Cir, 2010).

8 Noda, 'Copyright Retold', 993.

9 Aaron Schwabach, 'The Harry Potter Lexicon and the World of Fandom: Fan Fiction, Outsider Works, and Copyright' (2009) 70 University of Pittsburgh Law Review 387, 388; Rachel L. Stroude, 'Complimentary Creation: Protecting Fan Fiction as Fair Use' (2010) 14 Marquette Intellectual Property Law Review 191, 193–94.

10 Noda, 'Copyright Retold', 994. See also Jean Burgess and Joshua Green, YouTube: Online Video and Participatory Culture, Cambridge, UK: Polity Press, 2009, p. 12 ('Studies of fan cultures proved that (some) audiences were creative, engaging in legitimate fields of cultural production in a symbiotic (and at times uneasy) relationship with the "big media" who saw themselves as the originating authors of texts, characters, and fictional worlds that fans "made over" for their own purposes'). See generally Karen Hellekson and Kristina Busse (eds), Fan Fiction and Fan Communities in the Age of the Internet (Jefferson, NC: McFarland, 2006).

11 17 USC § 107. See also Campbell v Acuff-Rose Music Inc, 510 US 569, 578 (1994) ('Campbell').

12 Campbell, 510 US 569, 579 (1994).

13 Ibid.

14 Noda, 'Copyright Retold', 1013.

15 Ibid., 1000.

16 Stroude, 'Complimentary Creation', 194–97.

17 Ibid., 194–95.

18 Ibid., 196.

19 Ibid., 209.

20 Ibid. (citing Jacqueline Lai Chung, 'Drawing Idea from Expression: Creating a Legal Space for Culturally Appropriated Literary Characters' (2007) 49 William & Mary Law Review 903, 935).

21 See generally Anupam Chander and Madhavi Sunder, 'Everyone's a Superhero: A Cultural Theory of "Mary Sue" Fan Fiction as Fair Use' (2007) 95 California Law Review 597. However, a recent case on the interpretation of the take down provisions of the Digital Millennium Copyright Act, where a mother posted a clip of her eighteen-month-old child spontaneously dancing to a Prince song on YouTube, suggests that courts are likely to be supportive of the fair use rights of amateur remixers. See Lenz v Universal Music Corp, 572 F Supp 2d 1150 (ND Cal, 2008).

22 Amy Lai, 'The Death of the Author: Reconceptualizing 60 Years Later: Coming Through The Rye as Metafiction in Salinger v. Colting' (2010) 15 Intellectual Property Law Bulletin 19, 21. See also ibid., 41 (Metafiction 'legitimately takes on the characteristics of both scholarly commentary and commercial fiction').

23 Castle Rock Entertainment Inc v Carol Publishing Group Inc, 150 F 3d 132 (2nd Cir, 1998).

24 Warner Brothers Entertainment INC & JK Rowling v RDR Books And Does 1–10, 575 F Supp 2d 513 (SDNY, 2008).

25 Sonia Katyal, 'Performance, Property, and the Slashing of Gender in Fan Fiction' (2006) 14 Journal of Gender, Social Policy and the Law 461, 467. For a thorough examination of fan fiction, see, e.g., Henry Jenkins, Textual Poachers: Television Fans and Participatory Culture, New York: Routledge, 1992; Karen Hellekon and Kristina Busse (eds), Fan Fiction and Fan Communities in the Age of the Internet: New Essays, Jefferson, NC: McFarland & Co, 2006. For a broader analysis of remix and fair use, see Steven Hetcher, 'Using Social Norms to Regulate Fan Fiction and Remix Culture' (2009) 157 University of Pennsylvania Law Review 1869, 1872 ('remix works are created by taking digital snippets from various sources and combining them to create a new work ... There is a strong argument, however, that much of this remix is fair use and hence legal').

26 Kaytal, 'Performance, Property and the Slashing of Gender in Fan Fiction', 468. See also Anne Kustritz, 'Slashing the Romance Narrative' (2003) 26 Journal of American Culture 371, 372.

27 Kaytal, 'Performance, Property and the Slashing of Gender in Fan Fiction', 469.

28 Ibid., 484–85.

29 See, e.g., Complex Love: Harry/Draco Slash Fanfiction Fanlisting (22 October 2011): http://hdslash.saranya.net/.

30 Kaytal, 'Performance, Property and the Slashing of Gender in Fan Fiction', 486.

31 Ibid., 489.

32 Ibid., 494–95.

33 Campbell, 510 US 569, 579 (1994).

34 Tushnet, 'Legal Fictions', 668.

35 Ibid., 665.

36 Ibid., 671.

37 Ibid., 685. See also Jenkins, 'Textual Poachers', 279–80 ('Fandom generates systems of distribution that reject profit and broaden access to its creative works'); Jeff Bishop and Paul Hoggett, Organizing Around Enthusiasms: Mutual Aid in Leisure, London: Comedia, 1986, p. 53 ('The values ... are radically different from those embedded within the formal economy; they are values of reciprocity and interdependence as opposed to self-interest, collectivism as opposed to individualism').

38 *Warner Brothers Entertainment Inc & JK Rowling v RDR Books and Does 1–10*, 575 F Supp 2d 513, 520 (SD NY, 2008) ('*Harry Potter Lexicon*') ('His purpose in establishing the website was to create an encyclopedia that collected and organized information from the *Harry Potter* books in one central source for fans to use for reference').

39 Ibid., 521.

40 Ibid.

41 Ibid., 522.

42 Ibid. ('Vander Ark had even stated on a public internet newsgroup that he would not publish the Lexicon "in any form except online" without permission because Rowling, not he, was "entitled to that market"'). Hetcher has also explained that amongst the fan community, there exists a social norm against commercialising fan fiction and amongst owners, a tolerance for noncommercial fan uses: Hetcher, 'Using Social Norms ... ', 1885–91.

43 *Harry Potter Lexicon*, 575 F Supp 2d 513, 520 (SD NY, 2008).

44 Ibid., 526.

45 Ibid., 550.

46 Ibid., 551.

47 Ibid.

48 Megan Richardson and David Tan, 'The Art of Retelling: Harry Potter and Copyright in a Fan-Literature Era' (2009) 14 *Media & Arts Law Review* 31, 32.

49 Ibid., 33.

50 Ibid., 81.

51 Ibid.

52 For example, David Colbert, *The Magical Worlds of Harry Potter*, New York: Berkley Publishing, 2004; George Beahm, *Fact, Fiction and Folklore in Harry Potter's World*, San Francisco, Hampton Roads Publishing, 2005; Tere Stouffer, *The Complete Idiot's Guide to the World of Harry Potter*, New York: Alpha Books, 2007.

53 Henry Jenkins, *Convergence Culture: Where Old and New Media Collide*, New York: New York University Press, 2006, p. 290; Burgess and Green, *YouTube: Online Video and Participatory Culture*, p. 10. Other copyright owners have made similar concessions. See Hetcher, 'Using Social Norms ... ', 1888 fn. 77.

54 See *About Pottermore* (2011), Pottermore: www.pottermore.com/en/about.

55 See, e.g., Dennis S. Karjala, 'Harry Potter, Tanya Grotter, and the Copyright Derivative Work' (2006) 38 *Arizona State Law Journal* 17; Katyal, 'Performance, Property, and the Slashing of Gender in Fan Fiction'; Chander and Sunder, 'Everyone's a Superhero'; Chung, 'Drawing Idea From Expression'. See also Hetcher, 'Using Social Norms ... ', 1883 ('in the context of fan fiction and remix ... it is implausible in most instances to argue that anyone is harmed. Indeed, it would be more intuitive ... to see how commercial owners would likely benefit from such activities').

56 Tushnet, 'Legal Fictions', 654.

57 See, e.g., Rebecca Tushnet, 'Copyright Law, Fan Practices, and the Rights of the Author' in Jonathan Gray, Cornel Sandvoss and C Lee Harrington (eds), *Fandom: Identities and Communities in a Mediated World*, New York: NYU Press, 2007, p. 60, p. 61.

58 Ibid. 68.

59 See, e.g., the examination of cases in Michael Todd Helfand, 'When Mickey Mouse is as Strong as Superman: The Convergence of Intellectual Property Laws to Protect Fictional, Literary and Pictorial Characters' (1992) 44 *Stanford Law Review* 623.

60 Karjala, 'Harry Potter, Tanya Grotter, and the Copyright Derivative Work', 36.

61 Katyal, 'Performance, Property, and the Slashing of Gender in Fan Fiction', 468.

62 Lawrence Lessig, 'Innovating Copyright' (2002) 20 *Cardozo Arts & Entertainment Law Journal* 611, 617; Chung, 'Drawing Idea From Expression', 917–18. Lessig, in particular, argues that '[t]here is no good reason for copyright law to regulate this [amateur] creativity. There is plenty of reason – both costs and creative – for it to leave that bit free': Lawrence Lessig, *Remix: Making Art and Commerce Thrive in the Hybrid Economy*, New York: Penguin Press, 2008, p. 255.

9   The *simulation* of 'authentic' buzz

T-Mobile and the flash-mob dance

Marc Trabsky

The manufacture of 'authentic' buzz is an advertising and marketing strategy which, as Kathy Bowrey illustrates in her chapter on the legal dimensions of *MasterChef Australia*, is increasingly deployed by corporations that produce and broadcast reality television. In a world mediated by the dissemination of signs, corporations routinely eschew 'pull advertising' for subtle forms of brand activity. Bowrey outlines the nature of these penetrating activities – product placement, covert signage, audience engagement through convergent media and the creation of immersive commercial environments – which, rather than adopting a 'command-and-control' approach, delicately embed branding into the entertainment itself.[1] The objective is to ensure that the consumer will not be able to differentiate between the advertisement of a product and their affective response to the spectacle of reality television. Undeniably corporations expect consumers to differentiate their brand from their competitors, but in response to those 'media-savvy' consumers who fast-forward commercials using a digital video recorder (DVR) or watch reality television online, they seek to ground brand differentiation in the consumer's attachment to the spectacle of television.[2]

The aim of these advertising and marketing strategies is to inundate (savvy) consumers with a panoply of signs such that they will no longer be able to locate a 'true' origin of what Jean Baudrillard describes as the simulacra of reality. This is to say they will no longer be able to determine whether the contestants on *MasterChef* truly enjoy exploiting the products they use when cooking or whether the producers have made it compulsory to use those particular products through the legal artifice of contract. For Baudrillard, Disneyland exemplifies the simulations of our televised world – where our relationship to the world is mediated through the screen – and the Disney Corporation, in its comprehensive branding activities, elongates that simulacra.[3] Disneyland does not reveal a true city beyond the ticket booth, but instead exposes the surrounding areas in Los Angeles to be simulations of the theme park. In the world of reality television, this simulacra is extended towards the entire world. As Bowrey explains, the activities employed by advertisers to foster consumer attachment to their brands are indistinguishable from the strategies used by producers to ensure audience members continue to watch their show. In fact, both practices encourage attachment by appealing to the 'authenticity' of real people sharing real emotions in a real world. Hence, in the universe of reality television, there is no longer a difference between Disneyland and Los Angeles, a theme park and a real city, fictional characters and real people. As Guy Debord writes, '[t]he spectacle presents itself simultaneously as society itself, as a part of society, and as a means of unification.'[4] In the *MasterChef* universe, television substitutes reality and characters unify with human beings.

Notwithstanding the ubiquity of the spectacle of television and the subtlety of immersive brand activity, traditional forms of 'pull advertising' have not lost their lustre. Rather corporations are increasingly seeking to combine conventional styles of advertising with novel forms of marketing. Rossella Gambetti explains that corporations are employing innovative marketing strategies to advertise their products, such as 'ambient communication', which seeks to engage consumers through 'unconventional promotional initiatives that involve people and employ urban guerrilla techniques'.[5] The appeal of such marketing strategy 'lies in its ability to intrigue, amuse, and activate consumers by artistically *decontextualizing* space … Benefits of guerrilla actions are that they reach consumers in places and times when their advertising consciousness is deactivated.'[6]

The flash-mob event,[7] as Gambetti briefly notes, when appropriated by a corporation in a public place, is an example of the use of ambient communication or guerrilla advertising. Insofar as the event jolts, amuses or astounds onlookers, it produces in the consumer an active rather than passive response to the corporation's brand.[8] It invites the consumer to affectively participate in the branding experience. However, what kind of environment is actualised when guerrilla marketing strategies are combined with the traditional 'command-and-control' approach to advertising? What are the effects of integrating unconventional marketing techniques with conventional television commercials?

In the remainder of this comment, I will discuss how a T-Mobile[9] commercial from 2009 exploits the tactics of guerrilla advertising in order to *simulate* buzz in the advertisement itself. Rather than manufacturing buzz by extending the brand narrative beyond the confines of television in online forums and other forms of convergent media,[10] T-Mobile facilitates interest in its brand by repeatedly imitating 'authentic' buzz. This artifice of authenticity is made possible by simulating the spontaneity of the spectacle of the flash mob. My comment thus contributes to Bowrey's insightful analysis of the manufacturing of authenticity in reality television by examining how the strategies deployed in that genre also operate in traditional styles of advertising. I provide an example from the pervasive world of television advertising to engage with her concept of manufactured authentic buzz. Although I refrain from discussing how the law sustains and fosters these marketing strategies, this comment offers conceptual tools for understanding the ways in which corporations decisively simulate authentic buzz in order to encourage consumer attachment to their brand.

'The T-Mobile dance'[11]

'The T-Mobile dance', which is accessible through T-Mobile's official YouTube channel (lifesforsharing) (and which was broadcast in the UK in 2009), associates the corporation with the spectacle of the flash mob. The beginning of the commercial features in pale grey at the bottom of the screen the word 'Advertisement', which although only lasting for a couple of seconds is presumably intended to avoid confusing in the mind of the consumer different genres of film-making. Even so what is clearly depicted as 'authentic' in the advertisement is the spontaneous formation of a flash dance. Despite the subtle pronouncement that this is an advertisement, we are encouraged to believe that the film-makers are merely 'documenting' a flash-mob event, where a random group of people, usually strangers, cohere punctually in a public place, and impulsively perform a strange, unusual or pointless act which lasts for under ten minutes. By imitating the 'amateur' actions of a group of flash mobbers dancing in Liverpool Street Station at 11.00am on 15 January 2009, T-Mobile does not only simulate a spontaneous flash-mob event, it also simulates authentic buzz in its mobile-phone network. The advertisement appears then as a documentary of what we are supposed to believe is widespread interest that already exists in the T-Mobile brand.

The advertisement simulates buzz in the T-Mobile brand through two complex hermeneutical mechanisms. First, the simulacra is facilitated by the cinematography of the commercial. To be more specific, by capturing onlookers using their mobile phones while viewing the flash-mob event, the advertisement implies that those people are communicating their experience of taking part in the dance – even if they are simply viewing it from afar – through the use of the T-Mobile phone network. This is to say T-Mobile establishes through the arrangement of different camera angles, editing techniques and the use of an unscripted narrative, a connection between general interest in the brand and particular curiosity in the flash-mob event. We, the consumer, are unable to differentiate between the buzz generated by the spectacle of the flash mob, the implication that onlookers are using the T-mobile network to communicate that buzz to others and the real choices that are made by onlookers who took part – perhaps unexpectedly – in the filming of the event. Hence, we may find ourselves asking when viewing this scene what is holding the attention of onlookers in the advertisement? Is it the pre-arranged, rehearsed and choreographed flash dance or the capacity to narrate one's experience of the event to another person through the use of a mobile-phone network?

The counter-argument that could be of course levelled against this exegetic breakdown of the commercial is that T-Mobile explicitly admits that they manufactured the flash-mob event. (This is similar to the argument that everyone knows (reality) television is drastically different to reality.) However, even if T-Mobile renders explicit in grey words that the clip is an 'Advertisement', the admission that it is manufacturing the flash mob only serves to further attach the spectacle of the event to that of the brand experience. For instance, T-Mobile actually filmed a 'behind the scenes' documentary to explain the process of creating the T-Mobile dance.[12] While the documentary, which was not aired on television, emphasises the notion that the dance was manufactured, choreographed and directed by people on behalf of T-Mobile, it simultaneously renders the dance all the more authentic. The director sought amateur rather than professional dancers, hid cameras in strategic places around Liverpool Street Station and made it clear that the event could only take place once. The objective of the marketing strategy then, which reveals itself in a 'behind the scenes' documentary is contradictory: T-Mobile desires to manufacture that which cannot be manufactured, to choreograph the spectacle of a spontaneous event.

The second hermeneutical mechanism that functions in the T-Mobile dance emphasises the historical context of flash mobs. The invention of the term 'flash mob' has been credited to Sean Savage, the founder of the blog 'chee-sebikini?'.[13] It differs from Howard Rheingold's concept of smart mobs[14] insofar as the later depicts organised, directional and functional events in public spaces, such as planned protests, occupy movements, promotional tours, publicity stunts and commercial advertisements. In the T-Mobile dance, however, the dichotomy between flash and smart mobs is entangled, precisely because of the confusion I have already discussed between the boundaries of the professional and the amateur. While T-Mobile employs amateur dancers and operates according to an unscripted narrative, it also actively professionalises the process of manufacturing a flash-mob event.

The ambiguity between the professional and the amateur is moreover entrenched through the *implied* use of mobile technology in the creation of the T-Mobile dance. For, as Judith Nicholson argues, mobile mass communication made the first incarnations of flash mobbing possible.[15] That is, the use of the web, email and text messaging were integral elements in the formation of the first flash events. This historical aspect of the configuration of flash mobs is appropriated by T-Mobile to suggest that the spontaneous flash dance 'documented' in its advertisement is made possible only through the use of mobile-phone technology, particularly the T-Mobile network. In other words, by underscoring the historical conditions of flash mobbing the corporation are able to link in the advertisement the spontaneity of the flash dance to the real use of the T-Mobile network. The T-Mobile dance is formed, then, we are led to believe, through the use of mobile-phone networks and, in turn, the event is communicated to others through the same use of mobile-phone networks. The circular, even closed nature of this hermeneutical process, far from confusing the consumer typifies the operation of simulacra in our televised world. For to return to Baurillard there is no origin behind or an end point to simulation. Instead what we experience in the simulacra of our reality – whether this includes the watching of reality television or conventional television advertisements – are waves of simulation, without beginning or ending.

Final remarks

The worst fears of flash mobbers, according to Nicholson, were that the spontaneous and frivolous events that were created by means of mobile mass communication would be one day co-opted by corporations.[16] She quotes a marketer who, for instance, wrote '[a]t the height of the trend ... that: "[T]he flash mob concept if applied to marketing can lead to an avalanche of ideas. ... though, the bottom line is whether we're talking the same language as the mob: fast, adventurous and fun."'[17] Despite these flagrant admissions of appropriation and co-optation, Nicholson and Walker still maintain that flash mobs were always political – I am using past tense here since most flash mobbers, including 'Bill', 'the original moberator', believe the movement ended in 2005[18] – and radically challenged conceptions of space in a capitalist system. 'The T-Mobile dance' has surely realised these fears, for not only does the corporation co-opt the tactics of the flash mob, but it does so to promote monadic consumption. The commercial does not render 'flash mobs passé in the eyes of the general public'.[19] Rather by appropriating the spectacle of a flash event the commercial suggests that the buzz in the brand is as authentic as the flash mob itself. Through the combination of conventional styles of advertising – such as the 'command and control' approach that Bowrey mentions in her chapter – and guerrilla-marketing strategies, primarily the idea of the flash-mob event, T-Mobile are able to manufacture, but more importantly simulate, authentic buzz in its brand. That the spectacle of the flash mob is appropriated by the pioneers of guerrilla advertising is hardly surprising. But what still remains controversial today is what Baudrillard highlighted many years ago; that '[t]oday what we are experiencing is the absorption of all virtual modes of expression into that of advertising.'[20] What we are experiencing today is the conflation into the simulacra of the authentic and the spectacle, the professional and the amateur, television and reality. And the consequence of this movement is, as Bowrey, writes 'the emergence of new ideas of property, the corporation and of self that support and extend the value of global brands and brand relations'.

Acknowledgement

Thanks to Jake Goldenfein for his insightful comments.

Notes

1 Ibid.
2 Ibid.
3 Jean Baudrillard, 'Simulacra and Simulations' (trans. Mark Poster) in Mark Poster (ed.), *Selected Writings*, Stanford, CA: Stanford University Press, 1988, p. 166.
4 Guy Debord, *The Society of Spectacle* (trans. Ken Knabb, Bureau of Public Secrets (online), 2005): www.bopsecrets.org/SI/debord/, p. 3.
5 Rossella C. Gambetti, 'Ambient Communication: How to Engage Consumers in Urban Touch-Points' (2010) 52(3) *California Management Review* 34, 37.

6 Ibid., 38.

7 Rebecca A. Walker provides a succinct definition of the flash-mob phenomenon in 'Badgering Big Brother: Spectacle, Surveillance, and Politics in the Flash Mob' (2011) 7(2) *Liminalities: A Journal of Performance Studies* 1, 2 ('Flash mobs are a type of performance that emerged on the streets of New York City in the spring of 2003. They are essentially choreographed group tricks. Whether created as complex communal in-jokes or a modern form of cultural critique, flash mobs act as elaborate pranks played out within the quasi-public realm of the capitalist city, exposing its heretofore unrealized methods of operation').

8 Gambetti, 'Ambient Communication', 39.

9 lifesforsharing, *The T-Mobile Dance* (16 January 2009) YouTube: www.youtube.com/watch?v=VQ3d3KigPQM. T-Mobile is a mobile communications brand in Europe, US and UK The company, which is based in Germany, offers one of UK's largest mobile and wireless network.

10 Given that I am accessing these commercials from T-Mobile's YouTube channel, 'Life's for Sharing': www.youtube.com/user/lifesforsharing – as of the writing of this comment the channel has been viewed 5,616,612 times and features 772 videos – it is clear that T-Mobile is also seeking to extend its brand narrative across forms of convergent media. However, this does not detract from the essence of my argument.

11 *The T-Mobile Dance*: www.youtube.com/watch?v=VQ3d3KigPQM>. T-Mobile organised a similar flash-mob event at Heathrow Terminal 5 on 27 October 2010: lifesforsharing, *The T-Mobile Welcome Back* (29 October 2010) YouTube: www.youtube.com/watch?v=NB3NPNM4xgo. 'The T-Mobile Welcome Back' clip differs radically from the earlier commercial. It imitates the musical genre, where characters break into song and dance routine spontaneously. The actors and actresses in this advertisement are clearly talented singers, but once again the emphasis is placed on the unrehearsed decision to break into song and the likewise impulsive decision to communicate the spectacle to others through the use of mobile technology.

12 Lifesforsharing, *Making of T-Mobile Dance* (24 January 2009) YouTube: www.youtube.com/watch?v=uVFNM8f9WnI&feature=relmfu.

13 See Judith A. Nicholson, 'FCJ-030 Flash! Mobs in the Age of Mobile Connectivity' (2005) 6 *The Fibreculture Journal*: http://six.fibreculturejournal.org.

14 Howard Rheingold, *Smart Mobs: The Next Social Revolution*, Cambridge, MA: Perseus Publishing, 2002.

15 Judith A. Nicholson, 'FCJ-030 Flash!'.

16 Ibid.

17 Ibid. Nicholson is quoting Ivy Wong, 'Ways to Showcase Your Brand in a Flash With Mob Mentality', *Media*, 19 September 2003, 15.

18 Ibid.

19 Rebecca A. Walker, 'Badgering Big Brother: Spectacle, Surveillance, and Politics in the Flash Mob' (2011) 7(2) *Liminalities: A Journal of Performance Studies* 1, 10. Walker is referring here to the dismal attempt made by the Ford Motor Company to create a flash mob in the summer of 2005 to sell its latest product: Ford Fusion.

20 Jean Baudrillard, 'Absolute Advertising, Ground-Zero Advertising' in *Simulacra and Simulation*, trans. Sheila Faria Glaser, Ann Arbor: University of Michigan Press, 1994, p. 87.

Part IV

Cultural intermediaries

10 Prestige and professionalisation at the margins of the journalistic field

The case of music writers

Ramon Lobato and Lawson Fletcher

We are all by now familiar with the claim that journalists are an endangered species in the digital age. Mass lay-offs in newsrooms, the rise of partisan political bloggers, the *Los Angeles Times* and *Newsweek* going into receivership – these are flash points in a narrative of professional decline. Advocates of amateur media can of course point to the many contributions to public debate made by citizen journalists and other non-professional writers, but there is still a pervasive nostalgia for a pre-internet era of ostensible journalistic integrity, fastidious fact-checking, and the structural separation of advertising and editorial. Such sentiments reach their apotheosis in widely read polemics like Andrew Keen's *The Cult of the Amateur*, which laments the web's 'endless digital forest of mediocrity'.[1]

One curious aspect of this narrative of decline is that it now encompasses areas of journalism that were never professional to begin with. Take for example music criticism, an activity which can only very loosely be described as a profession. Here, one sees all the same apocalyptic predictions about the dilution of standards at the hands of the amateur. Writing in the *Columbia Journalism Review*, Jacob Levenson lambasts the 'opinion-driven environment of the [music] blogosphere' and its corrosive effects on serious rock criticism, exemplified by the work of Lester Bangs (the fabled *Rolling Stone* and *Creem* scribe) and Robert Christgau (long-time critic for *The Village Voice*).[2] For Levenson, the internet has eroded the authority of the music press, instituted uncritical populism as a norm and merged cultural critique with public relations. The field of music writing becomes, in this line of argument, yet another site across which the de-professionalisation effect of digital technology plays out.

In this chapter, we want to move away from grand claims of decline vs. democratisation and take a closer look at the interactions between professional institutions and amateur cultural production. Popular music writing – encompassing criticism, reviewing and journalism – offers a rich case study in this respect.[3] Music reviews and interviews are staple features of the mainstream press, appearing widely in newspapers since the 1960s, but most of the writers who produce this content work outside the institutional norms of journalism. Almost all are freelancers, many receive no payment whatsoever and most see their work as a hobby rather than a profession. In smaller markets like Australia (the site of our study), securing an ongoing salaried position is near-impossible, even for the most talented writers. The full-time music critic, despite the currency of this concept within popular culture, barely exists as an industrial category of the creative workforce. Yet, as we argue, the practice of music writing is nonetheless regulated by 'proto-professional' norms and values, which work to give some structure to a disorganised cultural economy.

This tension between writers' precarious working conditions and the highly refined regimes of quality which govern their practice is our primary focus here. In what follows, we track some of the implicit models of professionalisation at play in the Australian music media, showing how these shape the way writers understand their work and their careers. We also consider how the relation between amateur and professional modes of production is being reshaped by online technologies. Our findings are informed by a series of interviews with music writers at various stages of their careers as well as our own experiences over the last decade as writers working in this area.[4]

The changing profile of the music writer

Music writing can best be described as a peripheral creative field, in the sense that it forms part of the creative economy and is subject to sophisticated hierarchies of prestige and value but is not typically regarded as an artistic endeavour in its own right. As cogs in the promotional apparatus of the music industry, music writers promote and contextualise other people's cultural products (records, films, tours, festivals). For this reason, they do not fit easily into the analytical frameworks that have structured most of the existing research on cultural labour, and are better understood as cultural intermediaries rather than cultural producers.[5]

In their history of rock criticism, Lindberg et al. designate the years 1967–72 as the period when amateur writing cohered into a 'field with its own criteria, discourse and "clergy"' of revered figures. This was a largely Anglo-American development, yet it came to structure the practice and culture of music criticism worldwide:

> The field of rock criticism was not only defined as regards content in this period, but also in terms of publications and geography. A few new US rock periodicals established themselves as the center of the field and other channels had to relate to the discourse developed there. From these US centers the discourse spread to most Western countries. Within a few years British rock criticism became about as important as the American, whereas elsewhere rock criticism was peripheral in the sense that it related itself to these centers and was not distributed outside of national arenas, even though these national discourses were often highly developed.[6]

This observation applies well enough to the case of Australia, which has long been a net importer rather than exporter of music writing, but the industrial structure described here is now much more diffuse. Music-related news, reviews and interviews are now found in a wide variety of outlets, including magazines, books, anthologies, academic publications, trade papers, industry newsletters and fanzines. The dedicated music press exists alongside, and in an interdependent relationship with, a vast online music mediascape (MP3 blogs, review blogs, genre-specific blogs, review aggregators, online magazines, music/lifestyle portals and social media). Music writing also appears in broadcast media, in the form of scripted reviews and other content for radio and TV. It is therefore increasingly difficult to clearly define what music writing is, where it occurs or who produces it. Aspiring writers negotiate an increasingly fragmented media environment as part of their professional practice, in which there are many more outlets for music writing than ever before, though most of these pay their writers little or nothing.

Some brief comments on the demographic characteristics of writers are also in order. Most of the writers we interviewed are in their 20s and early 30s, with a tertiary degree of some sort, frequently in the humanities or social sciences (though few believe this contributes to their abilities or success as a writer). Music writing in Australia is a male-dominated activity: we estimate that at least three-quarters of practising music writers in Australia are men, an observation which corresponds broadly with studies of the music writer workforce in other nations.[7] The reasons for this are disputed by the writers we spoke to, but it seems likely that the imbalance is exacerbated by informal, friend-to-friend commissioning practices, which reproduce a male-dominated writing culture, and the gendered spatiality of rock culture, which revolves around the pub environment. Though we did not observe deliberate policies of exclusion on the part of editors, the very high levels of social and cultural capital needed to do well in this field appear to be the result of informal networks, friendships and associations, the structure of which may exacerbate demographic imbalances that are already present in the rock and indie subcultures from which most writers emerge.

Structures of expertise and quality in music writing

Writing about popular music is, variously, a vehicle for self-expression and a way to make a living; a hobby and an art form; a mode of critique and a promotional activity. Each genre of music writing – from the 100-word CD review to the 10,000-word artist profile – can be the vehicle for public relations, advocacy or cultural commentary, depending on how it is executed. As a result, there is much debate within music writer circles as to whether the role of the writer is to report on current events, to provide objective critique, to support local music industries, to guide consumers in their choices, to champion emerging genres, or to foster elite modes of music appreciation. In the present section, we identify some of the discourses of professionalism that regulate this largely unprofessional field, focusing on three different models of expertise in music writing. While lacking the formal structures associated with many other fields of creative labour, music writing is nonetheless regulated by tacit ideologies of expertise that writers at all stages of their careers take seriously, which emerge from discrete modes of writing practice in Anglo-American music journalism and their uptake in Australia.[8] For the purposes of analysis we arrange these discourses about music writing along a spectrum, ranging from skill and craft-based accounts of writing practice through to more individualised and 'artistic' discourses.

At one end of the spectrum of professional practice is the kind of efficient, economical writing practice associated with entertainment trade papers. For the better part of a century, trade papers have provided the music industries with information on new releases and tours, technological developments, and profiles of current artists. Among the best-known trade papers are *Billboard* (US) – active since 1896 and running music reviews since the jukebox explosion in the 1930s – and the early *Melody Maker* (UK) – founded as a weekly jazz newspaper in 1926, reborn as a pop mag in the post-war period and folded into *NME* in 2000. Characteristic of this genre of music media is the capsule review, in which the essential elements of a record or live performance are summarily described. Functionalist and instrumental, this mode of music writing values currency above all else: the purpose is to communicate to the reader (often assumed to be an industry worker) what a record sounds like, what its commercial prospects are and where it fits within current scene developments.[9] Individual voice is arguably less important than a writer's ability to keep on top of the latest developments and engage the reader with clean, crisp prose. Prestige is accrued by being extremely well informed about current industry machinations and having clout with record and touring company people. A crucial element in success is flexibility, as one of our respondents (a well-known veteran freelancer) notes:

> I work on assignment now – there are things that I'd like to do and I do get to do them, but I also value the idea that you can give me virtually anything, and I can write a good story on it. It's not about what I like. I write strong, contained, concise, informative [articles] about any actor, director, musician, producer, in any genre, and not anyone can make that switch. That's a skill of the craft.

A different model of professional aspiration can be found in the tradition of 'serious' popular music criticism that emerged in the 1960s. This kind of music writing is associated with the US counter-culture, the alternative press, the New Journalism movement and above all with magazines like *Rolling Stone* and *Creem*. In contrast to the functionalist style of the trade press, the new breed of music magazines specialised in New Journalism-influenced immersion reporting in the form of long, literary pieces peppered with autobiographical elements of the writer.[10] Here we see a quite specific ideal of professional music writing, in which flair and writerly voice are privileged.

As Roy Shuker notes, the elevation of rock critics to 'star status' was a central feature of this second model.[11] By-lines began to be more prominently highlighted, appearing on magazine covers. Writing became more individualised and eccentric.[12] This tendency is typified by now-canonical writers including Christgau, Bangs and Jon Landau. Bangs – who died of an overdose in 1982 – looms especially large in the popular canon of music writing, and has become synonymous with a certain romantic model of rock criticism as vocation. While his skills as a writer were certainly formidable, Bangs' fame has as much to do with his anti-professional disposition. Consider the following quote, in which Bangs articulates his distaste for the professional music media and the entertainment industries in general:

> I think everybody's a rock critic, to the extent that you when go into a record store and you decide to buy this one over that one, you're being a rock critic. I don't have any more credentials than anyone else … I think that being a rock critic a lot of times—the impetus for me and a lot of people I knew was just that we really love rock 'n' roll and wanted to talk about it, you know? And there was this outlet. And what kind of makes me mad is a lot of times today it looks like a lot of rock critics that are writing in these magazines it's like a good way to get a start in a career in journalism or something, you know? It's not—you don't sense a real passion for the music.[13]

Through canonical figures like Bangs, the post-New Journalism model of music criticism has established a set of codes and forms for 'serious' criticism which endure to this day. As such, this genre of music writing represents a curious intersection of amateur and professional modes of production, incorporating an ethos of anti-professionalism ('everybody's a rock critic') alongside a strong code of ethics (independence, integrity, a commitment to subjective but consistent evaluative criteria) which constitutes a kind of *de facto* Hippocratic Oath for music writers.[14] From this perspective, being a good music writer is about maintaining distance from the corrupting pressures of the record industry – a very different ideology of professionalism compared to that which regulates the trade-paper tradition.

As the balance of power shifted from music magazines to online media in the 1990s and 2000s,[15] new kinds of writing practice have emerged in response to a rapidly changing landscape of music distribution. For example, the ability to sample music online via MP3 streaming and downloads has fundamentally diminished the gatekeeping, juridical role of the writer. In the internet age, the writer no longer functions as privileged intermediary, describing and interpreting music that the reader cannot hear for themselves. In response, two related strategies for reaffirming the value of music writing present themselves, both of which update the aforementioned professional models in different ways. In some cases, the writer acts as a curator or cultural filter, echoing aspects of the trade-paper function; in other cases, there is a movement towards elite and anti-professional criticism, thus extending (and deepening) the neo-romantic model of serious music writing.

The salient example here is music blogging. On the one hand, blogs have provided an autonomous space, away from the demands of the recording industry and music press, for writers to develop long-form, in-depth music criticism following the model of the critic-intellectual, where the writing itself is expected to stand alone as a worthwhile artefact. For example, UK critic Mark Fisher's well-known blog *k-punk* blends detailed aesthetic analysis with cultural theory in his discussion of contemporary genres – framing dubstep, for instance, through Derrida's notion of hauntology. On the other hand, the trade tradition has been reinvented with the emergence of regularly updated MP3 blogs which, although they organise their functions and appeal around the consumer – rather than the industry – keeping abreast of trends, still act as more or less acknowledged intermediaries between the two.[16] Incorporating concise, functional posts describing and hosting emerging artists' songs (often intentionally 'seeded' to blogs by publicity firms) as well as coverage of news and rumours for established acts, these blogs also tend to limit themselves to particular genres or scenes, purporting to act as filters selecting for their readers the best new music in a certain area. This curatorial model of hyper-current MP3 blogs echoes the norms and rhythms of trade press publishing even within the most apparently unprofessional reaches of the internet.

The history of *Pitchfork Media*, arguably the most influential review website in the rock/indie field for the past decade, reflects this cohabitation of critical and curatorial models online. Beginning in 1995 as an upstart webzine with a staff of one, *Pitchfork* is now often described as this generation's *Rolling Stone* for its ability to break new bands and canonise established ones.[17] It has also fostered its own intellectual standard of knowledgeable, in-depth criticism, positioning itself as a bastion of 'quality' music writing in an online landscape apparently littered with poorly formulated, indiscriminate blogging. *Pitchfork*'s maturation into a fully fledged indie institution, with its own dedicated following, house style and lucrative spin-off music festivals, combines the DIY, auto-didact ethos of internet culture with a savvy understanding of the industrial dynamics of an increasingly deformalised record industry.

Nonetheless, in recent years *Pitchfork* has ceded a certain power to blogs and implicitly admitted it cannot keep up with the lightning pace of new music, effectively outsourcing its more timely, workaday writing to a coterie of international bloggers for its own blog *Altered Zones*, which focuses on fast-morphing, bedroom-musician subgenres such as witch house and chillwave. Whereas its main site features extended critical reviews and features, *Altered Zones'* bloggers cleave to the same no-frills, short-form, instrumental writing that defines other MP3 blogs. The mode of professionalism valued here is similar to that of the industry reporter, in that these writers have an intimate knowledge of the scenes they report on and an ability to filter what is most worthwhile. This recent alliance with the amateur specialists of *Altered Zones* reflects the centripetal logic of crowdsourcing-as-renewal that is such a feature of internet economies. The decision to create two sites thus not only speaks to a certain relationship between established and emerging outlets, but also between different practices of music writing – the curatorial, 'post-critical'[18] model of *Altered Zones* updates the industry reporter, whereas the erudite *Pitchfork* scribe is indebted to the intellectual–critic.

These developments within rock criticism in the US and UK are of relevance not only to those nations. Rather, they have generated industrial structures and trajectories of professionalisation for writers around the world, especially in media markets which take their lead from the Anglo-American music spheres. In the following section, we consider how these discrepant traditions of professional music writing interact with local practices and industry structures in Australia.

The music media food chain: career trajectories in Australia

In Australia, imported music media exist alongside an array of domestic publications and local websites. Models of expertise associated with each of these scales of music media cross-pollinate, resulting in a diverse array of writing practices and industrial arrangements. To understand the relationship between professional and amateur modes of cultural production in this field, we must pay attention to the interplay between local and imported traditions of music media. This section will provide some context for how the Australian industry operates before moving on to consider some of the issues shaping how writing careers are established and maintained.

A key feature of the Australian market is the relative absence of national music magazines. Unlike the US and UK, where monthly glossies and weekly trade papers have played a central role in popular music culture, the Australian market is not big enough to sustain more than a few publications over the long term, and numerous dedicated music mags – *Juke, Ram, Juice, Go Set* – have come and gone over the years.[19] As a result, the tradition of long-form print music journalism is relatively weak. Australian readers look to imported magazines like *Rolling Stone, Uncut* and *The Wire*, and now to music blogs and websites, for long-form music writing, while seeking out the more fast-moving local knowledge (gig listings, touring acts, industry movements) in metropolitan 'streetpress' magazines.

These streetpress magazines are a distinctive feature of the Australian music mediascape. Weekly or bi-weekly publications like *Beat* and *Inpress* (Melbourne), *Drum Media* and *3D World* (Sydney), and *Rave* (Brisbane) have long performed the descriptive and promotional roles associated with trade papers, function-ing as rough-and-ready guides to local music scenes.[20] Distributed freely at shops and music venues, these advertiser-funded publications contain extensive gig listings along with short reviews, articles and columns. Their function is mimetic rather than agenda-setting: a successful street paper needs to reflect the priorities of the city's local record industry, the state of the live music scene and the rhythms of the international touring schedule. There is little room here for 'serious' music journalism.

Streetpress has long been the first port of call for aspiring music writers in Australia. It occupies a position at the bottom of the prestige hierarchy, as content is dictated by advertising (it is an unwritten law that purchasing advertising space leads to favourable coverage). This is reflected in the pay rates for writers: gig and CD reviews are typically unpaid, while interviews attract rates as low as A\$30, sometimes less. While well-connected writers sometimes syndicate work to multiple outlets and to magazines overseas, most find it impossible to live on streetpress wages alone. For this reason, there is a constant need for new writers and correspondingly low barriers to entry.

In the pre-internet age, the typical career trajectory for a successful Australian music writer was to start out in the streetpress then, after a few years, move into writing reviews on a freelance basis for the handful of Australian monthlies or more prestigious US/UK-based magazines. The most successful of the street-press writers graduated to become CD/gig reviewers for daily newspapers like *The Age* in Melbourne or *The Sydney Morning Herald*, with the handful of full-time music critic roles going to the 'old guard' in the field.[21] However, the internet has dramatically transformed this career structure, eroding the (already weak) base of paid employment. The story is a familiar one: in the face of stiff competition from online media, newspapers and music magazines are seeing their advertising revenues tumble and are sizing-down their workforces. Opportunities for music writers within the print sector are in steep decline.

Online music media has absorbed most of the functions of the music press and generated many new fora for reviewing and criticism, without necessarily replicating the industrial structures of the print economy. Within the major Australian music news/reviews websites, the competing traditions of music writing mapped out earlier – functionalist reportage vs. neo-romantic criticism – are reconfigured and remixed. Websites like *FasterLouder*, owned by Sydney-based new media company Sound Alliance, are comparable to streetpress magazines in terms of what they offer (listings, gig guides and short, descriptive reviews) and in what they pay (little or nothing).[22] Other music websites like *inthemix* and *Mess+Noise* are considered more professional and maintain a smaller, dedicated writing staff. The latter pays reasonably well for articles: up to A\$100 for features and A\$30 for reviews. Mainstream media companies also compete within this online space through entertainment and lifestyle portals, and often pay higher wages (lifestyle portal *The Vine*, owned by newspaper publisher Fairfax, is one example).

In comparison to these websites, which are more or less established and professional operations, the Australian music blogosphere is highly fragmented, encompassing semi-professionalised news blogs, MP3 blogs that mainly post new music with little or no contextual editorial, and smaller scale, individually run fan, genre and criticism blogs devoted to particular micro-scenes. Whilst the last might be seen as the most 'amateur' forms of music writing, the often in-depth, knowledgeable, long-form criticism that takes place on them complicates this label. So too does the increasing legitimacy of bloggers within the music industry. Key Australian bloggers are now courted by record industry and touring company promo staff, receiving all the usual enticements to offer favourable coverage: free tickets, CDs, promo items, invitations to launches, drink cards, and so on. Many scenes are now almost entirely driven by blog-hype, and certain bloggers have assumed an unprecedented level of recognition, both at the level of international scene developments and in the more localised gig/tour/club-based scenes (the blogger as local celebrity).[23] This reflects the increasing divergence between different constituent features of the 'professional', as levels of influence and prestige become separated from conditions of remuneration. Hence it becomes difficult to equate blogs with amateur media in any meaningful sense, as the blogosphere is increasingly the site for entrepreneurial, careerist activity among writers.

Living and labouring at the edges of the music industry

The technological and industrial restructuring of the music-writing field described in the previous section is understood in various ways by the writers we interviewed. Very few share the despondent sentiments of Andrew Keen or Jacob Leveson about the deprofessionalising effects of digital media. On the contrary, almost all are enthusiastic about the potential and diversity of internet-enabled music writing, and most take a pragmatic approach to the current climate. One Sydney-based writer and editor comments that '[l]ike all journalism, the web has completely pulled down the barriers between amateurs and professionals. Music journalism is not a career I'd want to be paying my mortgage on. But for the most part, it never was.' Note that this is not a cause for lament. This same writer argues that Australian music writing is now in a much healthier and more diverse state than ever before, as the 'removal of "career opportunities" has the benefit of introducing a much more experimental ethos'.

The same sentiment is echoed by other bloggers who see their work as a proudly non-commercial hobby or vocation. This is the mode of music writing closest to the traditional understanding of the amateur, a participant motivated by love not money. Many highly successful bloggers operate within this framework, rejecting a professional model of full-time employment in favour of a different, and more proudly romantic, understanding of the role of the music critic:

> My love of music and writing and wanting to share it with the world motivates me to maintain [my blog] ...

> [We] have a very deliberate and reflexive policy of never monetising the blog or turning it into a going concern. This keeps it within a kind of gift economy, and helps us build genuine trust with the artists and readers who we respect. And this is worth much more than money (provided you have a salary from elsewhere [...]).

This approach to music writing represents a curious combination of amateur and professional tendencies, reflecting a highly refined code of ethics in the absence of a formal industrial structure. It is also worth noting that many of the younger writers we spoke to have grown up in an era of online music media and harbour no real nostalgia for the magazine/newspaper system. For music writers in these categories, the free-labour conditions of music writing are a fact of life – sometimes a blessing, but certainly not a tragedy.

Between this pro-bono model and the more straightforwardly careerist aspirations of other bloggers, there is a grey zone of professional aspiration in which arguably the majority of writers are situated. This space is characterised by a partial and ambivalent relationship with salaried modes of writing employment, and a desire to combine writing work with other kinds of engagement with the creative industries. The desire is not necessarily to 'make it' as a full-time journalist but to follow a more flexible career-path through a variety of creative fields. Many bloggers, and even some magazine writers, end up parlaying their skills, knowledge and reputation as a music writer into other forms of income-generating activity. Some of our respondents started out as music writers and subsequently moved into news journalism, but keep penning gig and CD reviews as a hobby. Others have moved into adjacent fields, such as travel and lifestyle writing. As one well-known music critic, who now works as a technology writer commented:

> I often tell people I could earn ten times as much by writing about a stereo system than the music that gets played through it. I reckon it's because different kinds of journalism are buoyed by the industries they cover. The music industry is running out of money nowadays, so that means no more advertisements in magazines and so on. The consumer electronics industry, on the other hand, has buckets of money right now. Check out how many full-time, salaried technology journalists there are at the moment and then compare it to the number of music journos in the same boat.

There is also the option of using one's blog or column as a platform for other music-related pursuits which generate income, slender as it may be. One writer we interviewed runs club nights under the brand of his blog and another has established a small-scale record label. Others have made forays into public relations, writing bios and promotional material for record labels. Writing becomes one of a range of ways of engaging with a scene, and potentially making some money on the side.

This kind of flexible and pragmatic engagement with the media bears a resemblance to what Angela McRobbie described in 2002 as the characteristic form of post-UK 'Summer of Love' creative labour, in which the networked sociability and small-scale entrepreneurialism characteristic of club culture becomes a foundation of economic life in casualised workforces. The argument here is for the co-constitutive nature of casual work and creative life, hence McRobbie's claim that 'the intoxicating pleasures of leisure culture have now, for a sector of the under 35s, provided the template for managing an identity in the world of work'.[24] However, it must be stressed that none of our respondents, many of whom are well trained in cultural studies critique, saw their activities in these terms.

This brings us to the thorny question of exploitation. There is no doubt that this field exhibits many of the features of the dubious creative industries work practices critiqued by Andrew Ross and others, in which labour is given for free in the name of passion or love of music.[25] The over-supply of writers lets unscrupulous editors, their inboxes overflowing with the CVs of eager young scribes, make unreasonable demands of their staff (most frequently: unpaid work). Furthermore, the unionisation of writers in Australia is extremely low – only one of our 20 respondents was a paid-up union member – which means that collective action about issues such as pay and conditions is almost impossible. Exploitation of writers is normalised by these structural conditions.

There are a number of complicating factors we should take into account here. Critiques of creative labour sometimes assume a scenario of systematic exploitation by 'big media', in which labour is extracted from fans and non-professionals as a way for media companies to save on professionally produced content. The music media in Australia do not fit comfortably into this narrative. Unlike in the UK, where magazines such as *NME* are part of consolidated publishing businesses, most of the online and print-based music media in Australia is the province of undercapitalised small-to-medium sized businesses, many of which are not particularly profitable.[26] This is not to say that the prevailing commissioning practices are ethical, or that publishers could not afford to increase their pay rates if they so desired. But the 'free labour, big profits' narrative is not an accurate representation of how the music media work in Australia. The lack of unionisation among writers also reflects, to some degree, a lack of appropriate forms of industrial representation for casual workers at the fringes of the Australian media.

The writers we spoke to are under no illusions about the nature of the industry. All have their own ways of balancing paid employment with other kinds of personally fulfilling creative work. Many of the unpaid writers do not see their practice as an income-generating activity – and some like it that way. Others have an informal moral code which shapes their professional practice (one writer mentioned that she only does unpaid writing for small non-profit websites, but never for commercial publishers). Hence we must be alert to the agency of cultural workers such as these, even in a context of extreme precarity. As David Hesmondhalgh notes, it is important to resist an 'undifferentiated critique of free labour', while at the same time decrying those employment practices that are clearly exploitative.[27]

In this and other ways, the sub-industry of music writing provides some food for thought for research into the dynamics of cultural and creative industries. As we have shown throughout this chapter, music writing is produced under circumstances that could best be described as amateur. At the same time, such work is shaped by pervasive and powerful discourses of quality, value and professionalism. This is one of the many paradoxes that structure this industry-of-sorts. Music writing's unusual position as a secondary or intermediary field – located at the fringes of journalism, and simultaneously outside and within the music industry – distinguishes it from other related fields devoted to the production of tangible cultural commodities. The work of music writers, while generating consumable 'content', is fundamentally about the contextualisation and appreciation of other people's work. Hence music writers have a kind of split personality, suspended half way between art and public relations, cultural production and critique, the music industry and the content business.

The ongoing challenge for these writers, then, as for many other cultural intermediaries, is to reconcile creative expression and professional practice within an environment characterised by informal and precarious career structures and constant institutional and cultural change. In this chapter, we have outlined how the models of 'serious' critic and trade reporter have been deployed and updated by writers and publishers alike in trying to reconcile these demands. Although technological shifts – in this case, the 'threat' of the rising tide of mediocre amateur writing online – may be the stated impetus for certain responses to this challenge, we have endeavoured throughout this chapter to demonstrate the more long-standing, multifaceted industrial and vocational aspects at stake in this issue and the more complex traffic between (and redefinition of) categories of amateur and professional as they are played out in this particular cultural field. It is this dichotomy that can be said to contribute most to the schismatic experience of the music writer, and there remains much to be said about the fine grain of how this dynamic is resolved in practice.

Notes

1 Andrew Keen, *The Cult of the Amateur: How Blogs, MySpace, YouTube, and the Rest of Today's User-Generated Media are Destroying our Economy, our Culture, and our Values*, New York: Crown Business, 2008.

2 Jacob Levenson, 'Why John Lennon Matters: The Case for Professional Pop-Music Critics in an Amateur Age' (2009) *Columbia Journalism Review* 54, 58.

3 We do not draw a fine line between different sub-categories of music writing as we found that most writers move fluidly between these genres, depending on the publication they are writing for and the audience they are addressing. Note also that we have focused on rock, pop and indie writers, who constitute the centre of gravity for the music press and online music media in Australia, rather than on writers specialising in electronic, roots, urban or other genres.

4 Twenty music writers at various stages of their careers were surveyed in late 2010 on the extent and nature of the work they perform, their feelings about their practice and the institutions surrounding it and their personal philosophy of writing. Data were gathered primarily through questionnaires with a small number of face-to-face and telephone interviews conducted with more experienced writers.

5 The current discussion of cultural intermediaries can be traced back to the work of Pierre Bourdieu, who used the term 'new cultural intermediaries' in reference to arts and culture critics. It has since been taken up in a variety of scholarly contexts and for different

analytical purposes (for critical overviews, see David Hesmondhalgh, *The Cultural Industries*, London: Sage, 2002, pp. 53–54; Keith Negus, 'The Work of Cultural Intermediaries and the Enduring Distance between Production and Consumption' (2002) 16(4) *Cultural Studies* 501). On arts journalism as a sphere of cultural production, see Gemma Harries and Karin Wahl-Jorgensen, 'The Culture of Arts Journalists' (2007) 8(6) *Journalism* 619. On cultural labour more generally, see Tiziana Terranova, 'Free Labor: Producing Culture for the Digital Economy' (2000) 18(2) *Social Text* 33; Andrew Ross, *Nice Work If You Can Get It: Life and Labor in Precarious Times*, New York: New York University Press, 2009; David Hesmondhalgh and Sarah Baker, *Creative Labour: Media Work in Three Cultural Industries*, Abingdon and New York: Routledge, 2010.

 6 Ulf Lindberg, Gestur Gudmundsson, Morten Michelsen and Hans Weisenthaunet, *Rock Criticism from the Beginning: Amusers, Bruisers and Cool-Headed Cruisers*, New York: Peter Lang, 2005, p. 131.

 7 Robert O. Wyatt and Geoffrey P. Hull, 'The Music Critic in the American Press: A Nationwide Survey of Newspapers and Magazines' (1989) 17(3) *Mass Communication Review* 38. On gender politics in music media more generally, see Kembrew McLeod, '"One and a Half Stars": A Critique of Rock Criticism in North America' (2001) 20(1) *Popular Music* 47; Helen Davies, 'All Rock and Roll Is Homosocial: The Representation of Women in the British Rock Music Press' (2001) 20(3) *Popular Music* 301. For a UK perspective on the question of ethnic diversity in creative workforces, see Kate Oakley, 'Include Us Out: Economic Development and Social Policy in the Creative Industries' (2006) 15(4) *Cultural Trends* 255.

 8 A handful of universities, including NYU, now offer postgraduate degrees in cultural journalism and related fields. But there is little evidence that these accreditation systems have currency in the music press and online media.

 9 In Australia, as we discuss below, comparable functions are performed by streetpress magazines and event listings websites, which value a similarly economical writing style.

10 Eamonn Forde, 'From Polyglottism to Branding: On the Decline of Personality Journalism in the British Music Press' (2001) 2(1) *Journalism* 23.

11 Roy Shuker, *Understanding Popular Music*, London: Routledge, 2001, p. 85.

12 Forde, 'From Polyglottism to Branding'.

13 RockCritics.com, Everyone's a Rock Critic: The Lost Lester Bangs Interview: http://rockcriticsarchives.com/interviews/lesterbangs/lesterbangs.html.

14 This model of the music critic values currency and industry knowledge less than what Forde describes as 'polyglottism' – an idiosyncratic, subjective form of writing, involving an almost wilful anti-professionalism. See Forde, 'From Polyglottism to Branding'.

15 As has been well documented, most music magazines are struggling to survive amidst fierce competition from online media sources. Many venerable titles – including *Vibe*, *Blender*, *Melody Maker* and *No Depression* – have gone bankrupt or merged with other titles.

16 Though blogs are often discussed as if they were a new form of independent fan production circulating outside of established institutional channels, they are often fuelled by decidedly commercial motives; whilst the remuneration may be negligible, popularity, credibility and professional standing are key motivators for these writers. See Beatrice Jetto 'Music Blogs, Music Scenes, Sub-Cultural Capital: Emerging Practices in Music Blogs' (paper presented at Cybercultures: Exploring Critical Issues, Salzburg, Austria, 13 March 2010).

17 Music industry commentators refer to 'the *Pitchfork* effect', which is as much about influencing consumers directly as it is the trickle-down effect of guiding trends on other, smaller blogs. See Greg Kot, *Ripped: How the Wired Generation Revolutionized Music*, New York: Scribner, 2009, p. 121.

18 Simon Reynolds, 'Leave Chillwave Alone', The Village Voice (online), 19 January 2011: www.villagevoice.com/2011-01-19/music/leave-chillwave-alone.

19 The longest-running title is the Australian edition of *Rolling Stone*. Other monthly magazines being published today include *triple j magazine* (formerly *jmag*) and *Blunt*.

20 Marc Brennan, 'This Place Rocks! The Brisbane Street Press, Local Culture, Identity and Economy' (2007) 21(3) *Continuum: Journal of Media & Cultural Studies* 433; Sean Sennett

and Simon Groth, *Off the Record: 25 Years of Music Street Press*, St Lucia: University of Queensland Press, 2010.

21 The US tradition of the 'resident' music critic for a respected publication is not as widespread in Australia, though notable exceptions exist. Robert Forster, lead singer of the much-loved 1970s/1980s pop band The Go-Betweens, writes long-form reviews for *The Monthly*; and the *Sydney Morning Herald* employs full-time music journalist Bernard Zuel.

22 *FasterLouder* is particularly interesting for its explicit prosumer model in which a large number of readers submit all editorial for free: it is seen as the most basic entry-point into music writing in Australia.

23 This is indicative of the small scale of many niche genres: most promoters are deeply embedded in the scene and are avid readers of its key publications, while more than a few readers are involved in the industry themselves, through dabbling with music production, promotions, touring, et cetera. It also reflects the 'symbiotic' as well as osmotic tendencies of many contemporary music scenes. See Keith Negus, *Producing Pop: Culture and Conflict in the Popular Music Industry*, London: Arnold, 1992.

24 Angela McRobbie, 'Clubs to Companies: Notes on the Decline of Political Culture in Speeded up Creative Worlds' (2002) 16(4) *Cultural Studies* 520.

25 Andrew Ross, *Nice Work If You Can Get It: Life and Labor in Precarious Times*, New York: NYU Press, 2009.

26 The exception to this rule is the daily newspaper publishers and their online arms which still pay respectable rates for music-related content (though their treatment of freelancers is frequently criticised).

27 Hesmondhalgh's example is the system of unpaid internships. See David Hesmondhalgh, 'User-Generated Content, Free Labour and the Cultural Industries' (2010) 10(3–4) *Ephemera* 278.

11 Swedish subtitling strike called off!

Fan-to-fan piracy, translation and the primacy of authorisation

Eva Hemmungs Wirtén

On February 27, 2010, 'Filippa', the administrator of the Swedish fansubbing site divXsweden ('dXs'), posted the following announcement:

> The strike is called off!
>
> As you are all aware of, some of our translators have been on strike for a while. This action has been carried out to protest against the changes that are made in the text files when they are posted on other subtitling sites. The translators on strike have now decided to call off the strike in the hope that their message has been received. We, who only want to watch movies with quality texts from dxs, are of course very grateful for this. DivXsweden is a small subtitling site. Because of this we should not really pose a threat to other subtitling sites. What makes us unique is that we only post texts produced by ourselves and of the very best quality. We therefore have a hard time understanding why we cannot be proud of our work by keeping our texts untouched. Now, however, the strike has been called off and we look forward to many new quality texts from DivXsweden. Welcome back all translators on strike. I have missed you, but understand and support you!!![1]

Striking fansubbers? There's something you don't see every day. In this chapter, I consider the events leading up to the strike and its aftermath, events described in the dXs forum as the result of a 'text war',[2] in which the three competing sites dXs, Undertexter ('UT') and SweSub, all were embroiled.[3] The purpose of such a micro-historical approach is to query some of the implied norms produced in the fansubbing community in respect to the activity of translation, and particularly to consider the repercussions of having these norms challenged from within the community itself. Beyond providing an insight into the rationales of fansubbing, the web-walkout also illustrates the often convoluted and conflicting importance of creativity, ethics and norms involved in fandom more generally.

Two main aspects of the hostilities that ultimately ended in the web-walkout are highlighted. First, I take into account the rationales of what I call 'fan-to-fan' piracy, the conduct unbecoming that provoked the 2009 strike and a similar action three years earlier. 'Piracy' is an exceedingly familiar term in a context such as this. Yet, our familiarisation rests on tacit assumptions about the relationship between right holders and copyright pirates that are, regardless of the complexities of the ongoing copyright wars, depressingly recognisable and cookie-cutter. Considering piracy that takes place *fan-to-fan* strikes me as a less explored and potentially rewarding terrain that perhaps could tell us something new about the practices of online fan communities. But such lessons are not the only – or perhaps the most important – ones we can draw from this idiosyncratic subbing-strike.

Furthermore, I want to address how the fansubbers implicated in the 'text war' related to the one issue that above all others brought about the strike: authorisation (including its genealogy to *un-authorised* and *authorship*), a cornerstone in the edifice of early international copyright. Largely associated with the world's first multilateral copyright treaty, the Berne Convention for the Protection of Literary and Artistic Works from 1886,[4] at the end of the nineteenth century the boundaries of authorial authority were inextricably bound up with translation, fansubbers' primary practice and a constant 'stumbling block',[5] in the evolutionary history of Berne.

My overarching ambition is not only to situate the Swedish fansubbing strike within a general discussion on fandom, but also within a much longer history of translation and copyright which, I believe, offers a complementary, productive and still largely unexplored approach into the persistent authorship/ ownership dilemma that is of such interest to copyright scholars.

Fansubbing and the logic of fan-to-fan piracy

Fansubbing has been defined as 'the practice whereby groups of overseas fans of Japanese animated films and TV shows ("anime"), digitise, translate, add subtitles to and make available online unauthorised copies of TV series and films'.[6] Simply put, the Swedish fansubbers that prefigure in the following write subtitles to popular movies and TV series, text files subsequently posted on fansubber sites such as dXs, 'by fans for fans'. Situated in relation to the two other contributions in this section, the work of the fansubbers can be read and interpreted against the many complex relationships described by David Hesmondhalgh in his overview of the notion of 'creative labour'. Narrowed down from the larger contextual framework of the cultural industries, the amateur practices of fansubbing illustrate well the committment that goes into cultural practices that straddle the professional and the amateur, and that take place on the border between the legal, illegal and semi-legal. Ramon Lobato and Lawson Fletcher's contribution on popular music writing in Australia is an important reminder that the larger tendencies and structural power-relations embedded in digitisation and globalisation also must be studied empirically, mapped out in the shared norms and codes of conduct of specific communities, be they those of Swedish fansubbers or Australian music writers.

On the topic of the pros and cons of subtitling versus dubbing, Tessa Dwyer and Ioana Uricaru bring up the interesting question if the former is not somehow associated with linguistic and cultural cosmopolitanism, whereas the latter comes laden with connotations of cultural chauvinism and even xenophobia.[7] Being a subtitling nation, Sweden frowns upon dubbing. Without having anything more than anecdotal evidence in support of the claim I am about to make, I would still argue that Swedes who travel to 'dubbing countries' such as France or Germany tend to find the voice-overs on familiar US/UK TV series a source of mild ridicule, evidence of an outdated tradition. By the same token, the simultaneous entertainment value that stems from watching the unsynchronised lip movements of a 'right' character speaking in the 'wrong' language, should not be underestimated. The simultaneous comparison between original soundtrack and subtitles has been referred to as a 'double spectatorship',[8] which, in the case of dubbing, might carry over into another 'double', where sight combines with sound.

However, in order to understand something of the turf upon which the 'text war' was fought, the Swedish fansubbing sites must initially be located on a 'fandom scale' of disinterestedness and commitment. Founded in 2002, dXs is the oldest, most quality-oriented and hardcore 'translation' site. Translations are vetted and controlled carefully, all in line with how administrator Filippa describes the dXs founders as 'happy amateurs', driven by an incentive to 'provide the people with high-quality subtitles'.[9] This commitment to exclusivity also makes dXs the smallest of the three sites. SweSub is similar to dXs in terms of outlook on translations and ideology and started in 2006 as a breakout operation from UT. Financed by advertising revenue and the largest of the three sites, UT claims to be 'visited daily by 35,000 unique visitors who for the past 6 years have downloaded 56,000,000 subtitles'.[10]

A quick glance at the websites reveals designs befitting their respective self-image as non-commercial/high quality/slow versus commercial/low quality/fast. Visually speaking, dXs is pure internet Stone Age. Text centred rather than image focused, old school rather than flashy, it displays all the hallmarks of dedication and seriousness in a sea that overflows with digital dilettantes. With banners, pop-up windows, advertising and a contemporary look-and-feel, SweSub and especially UT, are more immediately accessible. In a response to a posting on the dXs forum that the dXs website design, 'quite frankly, is boring', 'Mephisto' answers that it would of course be possible to develop the site and make it more attractive, but, as he says, 'we work with texts.'[11] Period.

Signed by then dXs translator administrator 'Earl of Oxford', the strike was first announced in a long and emotional posting from 12 November 2009, entitled 'Enough is enough NOW!' As a parenthesis, in early 2010 Earl of Oxford announced that he would cease all his subbing activities, ending his slightly downcast sign-off with a call to 'boycott UT'.[12] As I write this, Earl of Oxford's 'membership title' on the dXs forum is 'Translatoradmin Emeritus', an interesting choice of words that speaks volumes on the dXs discursive environment. In this environment, the rhetorical arsenal draws on a sense of professionalism and ethical credo which seeks (and finds) legitimation in the old-school textual universe of literary history and in an equally old-school visuality. The less high-tech, the better.

In 2009, Earl of Oxford was still on the barricades, however, and in his call to arms he targeted the infamous 'Eu65', founder of UT and archenemy to dXs and SweSub both:

> UT has today only a very marginal production of own subtitles. Net-texts published on the website are to an overwhelming degree taken from SweSub and divxsweden.net (dXs). Despite that UT's survival depends on texts from dXs and SweSub have Eu65 never given an inch of his arrogance towards translators and representatives of these websites. Eu65 and his lackeys make changes in the texts, take out original references and replace these so that it will look like UT produced them. [...] A couple of years ago the translators at dXs and SweSub tired of this bullying and initiated a common strike. The lack of new texts, combined with fears that advertising revenue would go down, made Eu65 back down. In the agreement that followed it was noted that UT would be entitled to publish the texts, only if texts and references would stay untouched.

Earl of Oxford remarked that this agreement has been breached regularly and that UT for a long time 'honoured' it by consistently changing references in texts originating from SweSub. Noting that many qualified translators now began to feel despondent, he concluded:

> Having no other means at our disposal a number of translators from SweSub and dXs will limit the public's access to newly produced texts. By doing so, we hope to stop these from reaching UT. This will continue until UT promises to respect the agreement that has been made. [...] We make no complicated demands. All we ask is the right to our own texts, that is, to have our texts unchanged. [...] We understand that this action will hit third party. Direct your anger accordingly. We're not the ones that started the fuss. We're not the ones who slowly suffocate the creative spark of the Swedish net-movement of amateur translators.[13]

Twenty-two minutes later, the SweSub site began a thread entitled 'Action against UT and Eu65', leading off with Earl of Oxford's posting. The thread eventually consisted of 642 postings, many of which were shouts of support in the vein of 'Keep it up folks!' dotted with the familiar iconography of hearts and smileys.[14]

Earl of Oxford focused renewed attention on a situation that the dXs and SweSub translators had struggled with for many years. Eugen Archy, the person behind the Eu65 nickname, was seen as the source of the trouble brewing in the fansubbing community since 2003. At that time, Archy launched www. magic-planet.net, a gaming website constituting the embryonic beginnings of what the dXs and SweSub communities in 2009 felt had escalated into rampant fan-to-fan piracy by UT. Archy was the mastermind behind UT ripping subtitles done by the dXs or SweSub subbers, then removing the translators' names and posting them as if they were actually authored by UT.

In 2006, Archy landed the number 3 spot on the tabloid *Expressen*'s list of '15 hottest names in Media-Sweden',[15] but he was also the target for the first strike called by the dXs translators, this time announced in a collective posting entitled 'Translatorstrike' signed on 23 March 2006.[16] The arguments given by the dXs translators for their drastic action was the tsarist behavior of Eu65, whose blatant stealing of dXs translators' work, they argued, made them less and less motivated to produce the high-quality subs for which they were known. Three days later, the UT site administrator 'homaNN' posted 'Decision regarding Strike!' on the UT forum, where he stated that '[myself] & Eu65 have decided that from now on the site will work according to the earlier agreement with dXs. Translated by: 'translator' and source: address (divxsweden) will remain in all forthcoming subtitles originating from dXs.' Just to be on the safe side, he ended with: 'There is no use discusssing [sic] this further in the forum, as it is a final decision.'[17] That the March 2006 truce between UT and dXs/SweSub never really materialised is perhaps obvious from the fact that a strike was called again three years later. Speaking about the situation in 2009, SweSub's 'Incubator', was less than impressed with Eu65's track-record so far: 'We hate him. We really do. He's destroyed so much for so many people.'[18] The strike therefore worked as something of a 'shaming' action, once again attempting to disclose just how disloyal Eu65 had been to the informal norms established by the community. 'Incubator', who dedicates three–four working days in order to text a normal feature film, or SweSub devotee 'Sigge McKvack', who spends 15 hours a week on his subtitling,[19] are typical examples of the devoted fansubber. Although there are a few women that take active part in the discussions, most of the fansubbers are male, and it is their submersion into fandom that produces the finely calibrated skills that in turn produces a superior translation. In his contribution to this volume, David Hesmondhalgh raises the issue of how to understand the notion of 'good and bad work', within the cultural industries today. Fansubbers develop the skill to distinguish between 'good and bad work' within their community as a way to determine the quality of good or bad translation. The Australian music writers that prefigure in Ramon Lobato and Lawson Fletcher's contribution, publish in different fora, including those we traditionally associate with a larger public sphere. The Swedish fansubbers, however, remain within a highly specialised community that cannot expand too much, because if it did, it would no longer be a domain of fandom. While the rationales differ between these two groups, both develop tacit expertise that allow them to articulate and develop their views on what constitutes quality (or not) in their respective communities.

The self-image of dXs and SweSub fansubbers rests on an identity where they constantly repeat that they are motivated, not by money, but by passion

for what they do and peer recognition. It is one of the main points of contention for the striking subbers that the motivations of Eu65 are less 'pure'
and that he is a money-grabbing pirate whose setup only exploits translation
in order to profit. 'An amateur-translator', on the other hand, 'doesn't get
paid, choose[s] their jobs, and seldom works with a deadline, and that is the
reason why it becomes better', all in the words of Sigge McKvack.[20] However,
the question of the economy of fansubbing seems slightly more complex than
the simple dichotomy between 'amateur' and 'businessman' that the dXs/Eu65
controversy hints at. Yes, as subber 'Overdrive' says about the dXs amateur-
credo, 'we couldn't care less about money'. But at the same time as Overdrive
negates money as an incentive, he/she insists that money is the gold standard
of comparison: '[M]oney should be compared to downloads instead. We don't
lose money but we lose downloads.'[21]

Downloads are the currency with which fansubbers barter. Downloads work
like money in the sense that they buy you a more high-ranking position on
the fansubbing credometer. But money and downloads are not the same.
Because fansubbers invest so much in time – in their own brand (or authorship, if you will), and in what they see as the general well-being of the
community – Eu65's behaviour has negative implications for their sense of
authorship, their sense of community, but also for their sense of reward and
value. The dXs and SweSub translators are incensed when they see their subs
ending up on the UT site under another name, where they will generate
10,000 downloads as opposed to the expected 500 on dXs. Cred can thus
be calculated and measured in very real numbers as the subbers experience the
underbelly of digital excess and speed; the fact that, as one subber put it,
'80% of all who download a text from UT or DXS don't give a damn where
the text comes from.'[22]

In a scenario where fast and so-so always trumps slow and good, it might
not help that dXs translators would never let slip the kind of UT translation
in which the line 'nobody will see the fucking dailies' from an episode of
Entourage becomes 'nobody sees more daisies'. This is symptomatic, perhaps,
of Eu65's own spelling problems, which are so prolific as to make you slightly
suspicious, and which remain a constant source of amusement on the dXs and
SweSub forums.[23] For some in the UT-camp, it is the QC (quality control)
that dXs have instituted that causes new users to abandon dXs and instead
turn to UT.[24] It is part of the granularity of fandom that in response to UT's
practices, dXs and SweSub both develop their more exclusive, hardcore side.
Membership in SweSub's new, blue-colored 'SweSub Group' ('SSG') is by
invitation only. Once you are allowed to enter SSG, however, you are part of
an exclusive elite of the 'very best of the SweSub translators'.[25]

The work and its many authors

SSG member Sigge McKvack uses the term 'amateur' in a positive sense, but
others definitely feel more comfortable using 'pirate' in conjunction with

fansubbers. Sara Lindbäck at *Svenska Antipiratbyrån*[26] has given her take on translation, explaining that '[w]hen you are translating someone's work you need the permission of the rights holder. If not, you are infringing on the copyright.'[27] It might seem clear-cut to the Anti-Pirate Bureau today, but to those invested in the making of modern international copyright it was not; translation was a kind of work that seemed to be two things at once, an independent creation and a derivative work. Translation is one of the first instances of transformative uses of cultural works and their treatment in international copyright. Translation made new works out of old. A prerequisite for the continued circulation of texts, at the end of the nineteenth century it was the primary vehicle by which authors multiplied their works; more importantly, it produced new readers. Yet, translation was a double-edged sword, a problem in search of a legal solution. On the one hand, there was the promise of new markets and readers, but, on the other, there was the possibility that unless somehow regulated, the transformation into a new language could result in substandard or even corrupt texts that by extension alienated the author from his or her work.

How to come to terms with this paradox proved a major challenge for the small group of Old World diplomats, lawyers, and professors who met in Berne during three diplomatic conferences (1884, 1885 and 1886) with the aim of returning home signatories of the first ever multilateral copyright treaty.[28] Few problems caused them as much headache as translation. Two nations in particular, France and Sweden, would disagree on whose interests translation served – authors' or readers'? Based on a strong author-centred tradition and as the leading nation in early international copyright, France wanted to subsume translation rights under reproduction. Sweden, by way of contrast, did not. Seeing itself as a developing nation in need of a steady influx of culture and knowledge, Sweden advocated freedom of translation.

Fansubbers argue that one of the main motivating factors behind their unauthorised amateur translations is that they are better than the official, authorised versions. In French as well as in English, 'authorisation' connotes not only a more general authority but also direct legal sanction.[29] At the end of the nineteenth century the French argued that it was absolutely necessary to subsume translation rights under the right to reproduction, and that the author was the only trustworthy guardian of the work. A sanction of this kind was perhaps on the French diplomat René Lavollée's mind when he, in 1884, called attention to what he considered the undeniable right of authors to protect their works to avoid the travesty of translation. 'On this last point', he noted, 'the interests of the author are the same as those of the public, which needs to be assured of the fidelity of interpretation given to the original work.'[30]

Alfred Lagerheim, the Swedish delegate at the same conference, pointed out that any direct analogy between authorisation and quality was tangential at best and 'one has to entertain the possibility that even an authorised translation can be bad'. In such a case, 'the public has a right not to be deprived of all possibility to get to know the original work in a form that corresponds better to the thoughts of the author, where the author's honour cannot but benefit from the freedom of translation given after a certain period of time.'[31] Advocating freedom of translation was the kind of stance that made Sweden a pariah in the nascent international copyright regime a century before the Pirate Bay. It might seem like a mere parenthesis in international copyright history, and yet up to the present time, freedom of translation would make regular and turbulent appearances in the global governance of copyright.[32]

Why? Partly because translation was such an obvious element of international relations, partly because it called into question the nature and stability of the work. Of course, the question of how to define the boundaries of a work has long occupied scholars in literary studies, art history and other branches of the humanities, and it is also an ongoing problematic within copyright law and scholarship. Even the Swedish fansubbers, who regularly consider the legality or illegality of their activity, devote considerable time and energy to questions of this kind. One of the key issues debated by the dXs community during the 2006 strike was the nature of the work they produced. 'Fjodor' even cuts and pastes ten paragraphs from the Swedish copyright law (from 1960 at this juncture) into his post, after which he 'translates' legalese into fansubbing talk, arguing that:

> As soon as a work (sub) is published (here on dXs) it is owned by the author (the person who translated the text). To publish in other places (undertexter.se) without the consent of the author (the translator) is a crime according to Swedish law. Making changes in the work (sub) and then publishing it is also forbidden according to Swedish law. [...] So ... to end this posting, translators who have had their texts published on a site other than the one they have authorized can subsequently report that site for copyright infringement and have it closed down ...
> Isn't Sweden a wonderful place to live, huh.[33]

Fourty-five minutes later, 'Fjodor' receives a reply from 'halm', a subber who understands things very differently:

> You cannot copyright something you do not have the right to copyright. This is called legal error. A translator here does not have the right to translate another's work without their permission. Read the law again and you'll see that it is illegal to translate somebody else's work. Yes, to my mind what what's done on this site is illegal. That's why a translator cannot have the copyright on the subtitle.[34]

According to Fjodor, subbing is legal, an argument he will repeat a few days later when he continues: 'A sub is a work in itself, [...], a sub does not alter the original work because it is a work in itself.' And he continues, 'Hosting a sub approved by its author is not illegal, but hosting a sub somewhere the author has not approved of is an illegal action.'[35] Before the thread is closed down on 22 June, there is no record of halm returning to the discussion, but others step in where he/she left off. 'Pechblände', for instance, raises the issue of translating a book from English and asks Fjodor sceptically, 'are you saying that this would be an independent work?'

As we know, this question was 'solved' at the Berne Revision Conference in Berlin in 1908. 'Solved', because while translation was completely assimilated under reproduction rights at that time, translators were also given the rights to their translation, 'without prejudice to the original'. This begs Salah Basalamah's question: 'How can the original remain present within the translation, when the change in language constitutes a major change in form, and it is the form alone – the expression – which is protected under copyright?'[36] In light of the various takes on the process of translation vis-à-vis the original/new work relationship, the most interesting of 'Pechblände's' suggestions is when he/she counters that a translation does not have to be made from a print-based original, but can actually be made directly from an audio book. This possibility will leave 'Fjodor' puzzled as well as speechless, and the whole thing is just left hanging. It is important to remember that what we tend to think about as 'old' media – for instance the physical book – was never the kind of stable entity it is sometimes made out to be today, just as little as the digital work is completely unstable. As David Hesmondhalgh also notes, we must take great care to remember just how complex the relations between producers and consumers were *before* we found ourselves in the informational/digital present. Translation is one of the first instances of transformative use of cultural works and their treatment in international copyright, but it is not the last. To consider the discussions on the legal and cultural ramifications of translated work in an analogue space could shed light on how we view the instability of digital works and their relationship to authors and readers, or, to use a more updated terminology, 'users'.

Conclusion

In this chapter, I have tried to establish that fansubbing is a new branch on an old tree. So is Google Translate or any other machine translation that allows us to ask old questions in new settings. Many of the issues with which today's fansubbers engage echo a much older discussion in the international copyright community. As 'authors' of a new work that has a value by itself but that simultaneously somehow relates to an underlying work, fansubbers are – for good reason – confused about the way works collide or overlap in translation. Most of us are. Even, as it were, those involved in the global governance of copyright since the end of the nineteenth century.

One of the problems caused by translation in early international copyright had to do with authorship, or rather, the power of the author to authorise, to exercise control of his/her work. Anxieties over the perceived instability of the text in print culture are now exponentially increased thanks to digitisation, and the importance of being identified as the 'author' remains central to fansubbing. What the striking fansubbers were concerned with vis-à-vis Eu65's behaviour was not that their texts were posted on the UT website, but that this was done under a false pretence, where dXs translators no longer could be identified as authors. There is something fascinating going on when the dXs and SweSub subbers, superficially associated with file-sharing and piracy, express their identity as authors by articulating an almost text-book defence of moral rights and the importance of attribution. Conversely, another group of subbers find authorship irrelevant and argue that real cred attaches not to individuals, but to the UT or dXs site. It is the site or the brand that acts as author, not 'Incubator' or 'Sigge McKvack'. As anyone venturing into the maze of forum postings will know, most of what is out there is actually not that interesting. Yet, in the jungle of snippets announcing the latest subbed episode of *Lost* or that makes fun of Eu65 and his little 'popes', there is also a fascinating debate about translation, authorship, control, piracy and the work.

Finally, the context within which all three contributions in this section find themselves is in the global discourse of the English language, a language which is simultaneously the language of the cultural industries and the language of the critique and interpretation of the cultural industries. It remains an important scholarly challenge to query the consequences of this hegemony on the terrain where object and subject intersect. Although such hegemony is neither all-encompassing nor uncontested within the larger Anglo-Canadian– Colonial–Australian–American family tree – Ramon Lobato and Lawson Fletcher for instance problematise the Australian experience in their contribution – the power relations of language should make us more, not less, willing to engage with comparative approaches. The most worrying effect of a monolingual tendency where all primary sources must be in English, or suffer the con- sequences of oblivion, is that it produces a mono-epistemological outlook, a skewed history where alternative experiences, told in other languages and offering other interpretative frameworks, remain un-accounted for. Given the historical and theoretical links mobilised by translation in the juncture of language and law, paired with the fact that the story of the Swedish fansubbers must be translated into English in order to be 'seen' at all, tells us something about the rich and untold copyright history that is out there as well as something of the problems we face in telling it.

Notes

* All URLs were last visited on 15 April 2011.

1 'Filippa', *The Strike is Called Off!* [Strejken avblåst!] (27 February 2010) http://forum. divxsweden.net/index.php?s=599135c6ac48af571f117ae9af9c3d43&showtopic=23911.
I have decided against including the original Swedish quotes in my notes partly because of space, partly because readers whose language skills include Swedish can consult the original posting via the links and there also check the veracity of my translation.

2 'Text war' [Textkrig] is the title of a discussion-thread created on the dXs forum by 'Sati-fullah', on 22 March 2007: http://forum.divxsweden.net/index.php?showtopic=21670&hl= strejk,and,eu65& st=0.

3 See *divXsweden*: http://forum.divxsweden.net/ipdl.php; *Undertexter*: www.undertexter.se; *SweSub*: www.swesub.nu. For a comprehensive introduction (in Swedish), to the fansubbing war, see Magnus Västerbro, 'Översättarkriget', *Magasinet Filter* (online), 18 March 2009: www.magasinetfilter.se/magasin/filter-7-09/film7–09.aspx.

4 *Berne Convention for the Protection of Literary and Artistic Works*, opened for signature 9 September 1886, as last revised at Paris on 24 July 1971, 1161 UNTS 3 (entered into force 10 October 1974).

5 '[P]ierre d'achoppement': Daniel Vignes, 'Aide au développement et Droit D'auteur: Le Protocole de L'acte de Stockholm pour la protection des œuvres littéraires et artistiques' (1967) 13(1) *Annuaire Français de droit international* 722.

6 Ian Condry, 'Dark Energy: What Fansubs Reveal about the Copyright Wars' (2010) 5 *Mechademia* 194.

7 Tessa Dwyer, 'Slashings and Subtitles: Romanian Media Piracy, Censorship, and Translation' (2009) 63 *The Velvet Light Trap* 46.

8 Ibid.

9 'Filippa', *Divxsweden – why should we come here?* [Divxsweden – Varför ska vi komma hit?] (1 July 2010): http://forum.divxsweden.net/index.php?showtopic=23981.

10 See www.undertexter.se.

11 'Mephisto', *The Strike is Called Off {2006}* [Strejken avblåst] (30 March 2006): http://forum.divxsweden.net/index.php?showtopic=20040&hl=strejken%20avbl%E5st&st=0.

12 'Earl of Oxford', *Thx & goodbye* (16 January 2010): http://forum.divxsweden.net/index.php?showtopic=23876.

13 'Earl of Oxford', *Enough is Enough NOW!* [Det är nog NU!] (12 November 2009) http://forum.divxsweden.net/index.php?showtopic=23775&hl=det+%E4r+nog+nu!.

14 'Incubator', *Action against UT and Eu65* [Aktion mot UT och Eu65] (12 November 2009): http://forum.swesub.nu/viewtopic.php?f=3&t=8984&st=0&sk=t&sd=a&hilit=strejk.

15 '15 hetaste namnen i Media-Sverige', *Expressen* (online), 26 September 2006: www.expressen.se/nyheter/1.426587/15-hetaste-namnen-i-media-sverige.

16 'Translatorgroup' [Översättargruppen], *Translatorstrike* [Översättarstrejk] (23 March 2006): http://forum.divxsweden.net/index.php?showtopic=20002&hl=%F6vers%E4ttarstrejk.

17 'homaNN', 'Decision regarding Strike' [Beslut ang Strejk!] (23 March 2006): http://forum.undertexter.se/viewtopic.php?f=1&t=17356&p=113340&hilit=beslut+ang.+strejk#p113340.

18 Quoted in Västerbro, 'Översättarkriget'.

19 Helene Nordgren, 'Passion för att översätta till nätet', *Lokaltidningen* (online), 9 September 2010: http://lokaltidningen.se/passion-for-att-oversatta-till-natet/20100909/artikler/100909731/1028.

20 Quoted in Nordgren, 'Passion'.

21 'Overdrive', *The Strike is Called Off {2006}* [Strejken avblåst] (30 March 2006): http://forum.divxsweden.net/index.php?showtopic=20040&hl=strejken%20avbl%E5st&st=0.

22 'Suzack', *The Strike is Called Off {2006}* [Strejken avblåst] (29 March 2006): http://forum.divxsweden.net/index.php?showtopic=20040&hl=strejken%20avbl%E5st&st=0.

23 Despite his prominent role in the strike, Eugen Archy is not that visible in the discussions. In mid-April 2007, however, he enters into a long discussion with 'Leffe', the translator admin at dXs at the time. Perhaps intended as a defense of his position, many of his postings are nonetheless strikingly filled with spelling errors. See 'Funny email' [Lustigt email] (18 April 2007): http://forum.divxsweden.net/index.php?showtopic=21785&st=0.

24 'halm', *The Strike is Called Off {2006}* [Strejken avblåst] (30 March 2006): http://forum.divxsweden.net/index.php?showtopic=20040&hl=strejken%20avbl%E5st&st=0.

25 'Sigge McKvack' quoted in Nordgren, 'Passion'.

26 The 'Swedish Anti-Pirate Bureau' is the most well-known pro-copyright organisation in Sweden.

27 Quoted in Nordgren, 'Passion'.

28 8–19 September 1884, 7–18 September 1885 and 6–9 September 1886.

29 See the second definition of 'authorise' in *The Oxford English Dictionary*, Oxford: Oxford University Press, 2nd edn, 1989: 'to give legal force to; to make legally valid'; and consider

the meaning of 'authoriser' in *Le Grand Robert de la langue Française*, Paris: Dictionnaries Le Robert, 2nd edn, 1992, vol. 1, sid 732: 'autoriser qqch' as 'rendre licite, permettre' as in 'Autoriser l'exécution d'un act'.

30 *Actes de la conférence internationale pour la protection des droits d'auteur réunie a Berne du 8 au 19 Septembre 1884*, Berne: Imprimerie K.-J Wyss, 1884, p. 48.

31 Ibid.

32 For an overview, see Eva Hemmungs Wirtén, *Cosmopolitan Copyright: Law and Language in the Translation Zone* (Meddelanden från Institutionen för ABM, 4. Uppsala University, 2011).

33 'Fjodor', *The Strike is Called Off {2006}* [Strejken avblåst] (30 March 2006): http://forum. divxsweden.net/index.php?showtopic=20040&hl=strejken%20avbl%E5st&st=0.

34 'halm', *The Strike is Called Off {2006}* [Strejken avblåst] (30 March 2006): http://forum. divxsweden.net/index.php?showtopic=20040&hl=strejken%20avbl%E5st&st=0.

35 Ibid.

36 Salah Basalamah, 'Translation Rights and the Philosophy of Translation: Remembering the Debts of the Original', in Paul St-Pierre and Prafulla C. Kar (eds), *In Translation: Reflections, Refractions, Transformations*, Amsterdam/Philadelphia: John Benjamins Publishing Company, 2007, p. 122.

12 Have amateur media enhanced the possibilities for good media work?

David Hesmondhalgh

Discussions of amateur media need to pay attention to the meaning of work, and the quality of working life. I begin by arguing that celebrations of the creative possibilities of digital media have unwittingly repeated the sidelining of questions of work in studies of cultural production. I then introduce two strands of analysis that have helped to improve this situation by addressing work in digital and cultural industries. The first is particularly germane to discussions of amateur media: critiques of 'free labour' (unpaid work) in IT and cultural industries. The second has generally been concerned more with paid work and employment in these industries. It points to the fact that, alongside autonomy and relatively good working conditions, these sectors are often characterised by casualisation, precariousness and overwork. In this second strand can be found a welcome emphasis, missing from the first, on quality of working life in media production. But these studies have paid little sustained attention to other, more rigorous conceptualisations of quality of working life in sociology and philosophy. To correct this, the next section then presents a normative framework for what constitutes 'good work' and 'bad work' in modern societies. I then draw on this framework to consider the other case studies in this section of the book. These case studies affirm that amateur media can enhance media production and consumption. But they also, in my view, show how tentative and limited such enhancements may be. Maintaining amateur careers alongside professional ones can lead to people making excessive demands on themselves. In commercial systems, amateur work oriented towards high quality can be exploited by the less scrupulous.

Marginalisation of employment and occupation by digital optimists – and critiques of 'free labour' as a response

Media production has been the subject of thousands of studies. But until recently, only a very small proportion of these studies focused on the creative labour upon which media production depends. The forgetting or devaluation of work in analysis of media production has taken a number of different forms. One, apparent in some arts and humanities studies, is a focus on individual producers rather than on the complex division of labour which, as the sociology of culture has shown,[1] is the basis of most cultural production. Another is an emphasis within certain schools or traditions, notably some types of cultural and media study, on consumption, at the expense of production.

More recently, though, the devaluation of work in communication and cultural research has taken a new shape. Digitalisation has led to a proliferation of new forms of amateur and semi-professional production; blogs, Wikipedia, citizen journalism and various forms of interactive games were the most cited examples during the 2000s. Many commentators have heralded this supposed explosion of non-professional cultural production as evidence of a new era of cultural production, and as a democratisation. Axel Bruns, for example, claims that production and consumption are old-fashioned 'industrial age' concepts, and that in the internet age, where access to the means of producing and distributing information is 'widely available', consumers can become cultural producers and distributors, bypassing 'traditional' organisations via peer-to-peer and 'many to many' (rather than 'one to many') communication systems, leading to a new form or model known as 'produsage', a mixture of production and use.[2]

Phenomena such as Wikipedia and open source software are, without doubt, fascinating examples of cultural activity that attempt to base themselves on the pleasures and rewards of co-operation rather than competition. It is certainly the case that the cultural industries in the digital era, like many other kinds of firm, increasingly seek to draw upon the participation of their users and consumers.[3] But too many of these discussions of transformations associated with new digital media rely on caricatured portrayals of supposedly bypassed eras. The 'industrial age', for example, involved much more complex relations between production and consumption than is implied by Bruns's account. What's more, many of these discussions are discomfortingly reliant on business and journalistic commentary regarding the impact of digital technologies on economies and societies in the twenty-first century. The list of neologisms and buzz phrases goes on and on: 'the new economy', 'the digital economy', 'wikinomics', 'crowdsourcing', 'collective intelligence', 'the long tail', 'the wisdom of crowds', 'smart mobs', et cetera.

Yet some critics have drawn attention to problems associated with work in these accounts of digital media. An important strand of critique points to problems associated with unpaid work in IT and cultural industries. In a seminal essay, Tiziana Terranova wrote about the phenomenon of 'free labour', which she described as 'an important, yet unacknowledged, source of value in advanced capitalist societies'.[4] Free labour was, wrote Terranova 'simultaneously voluntarily given and unwanted, enjoyed and exploited' and on the internet included 'building web sites, modifying software packages, reading and participating in mailing lists and building virtual spaces'.[5] Others have applied similar perspectives to other forms such as television and games. Mark Andrejevic, reacting against celebratory accounts of 'active audiences' in media studies, has written powerfully about 'the ways in which creative activity and exploitation coexist and interpenetrate one another within the context of the emerging online economy'.[6] In earlier work, Andrejevic had discussed how 'reality TV anticipates the exploitation of ... the work of being watched, a form of production wherein consumers are invited to sell access to their personal lives in a way not dissimilar to that in which they sell their labor power.'[7] Andrejevic went on to explore how online viewer activity serves television producers in two ways, by providing feedback, which saves the producers from having to undertake expensive market research, and by, in effect, publicising television programmes, which saves marketing costs.[8] Andrejevic critiques the equation of participation and activity with real democratisation and shared control, and claims that regimes of surveillance and imperatives of profit-making hugely compromise the pleasures and progressive elements of online participation. In the world of games, Greig De Peuter and Nick Dyer-Witheford have explained how, from the 1990s onwards, 'authoring tools' have been increasingly packaged with computer games, helping to foster a vibrant participatory culture of game 'modding', or modification.[9] They argue that the work of such modders is a kind of free labour, a 'space-defying' process of exploitation of 'collective intelligence' which also serves as a kind of informal training for the future game development workforce.[10]

A further way in which analysts have pointed to the contribution of free labour to the cultural industries is the way in which the latter draw on pools of talent outside their boundaries, and employ professionals to manage crossings of those boundaries, and to negotiate the creativity–commerce dialectics that are at the heart of modern cultural production. All this is familiar from political economy and sociological analysis of cultural industries[11] but recent critics have linked this to the free-labour debates by emphasising the way that creative professionals draw on the unpaid 'mass intellectuality' (see later) of alternative and underground scenes. Adam Arvidsson, in an effort to counter the celebratory discourses associated with modern creative industries policy, even uses the rather dubious phrase 'creative proletariat' to refer to the underground cultural producers that some creative professionals draw upon as part of their work.[12] Elsewhere, Arvidsson has extended discussion of free labour into debates about consumption, claiming that brand management exploits the 'immaterial labour' of consumers by drawing on resources of ideas and styles generated in contemporary urban environments.[13] Clearly, this is a more critical account of 'user-generated content' than is to be found in academic management studies and journalistic hype.[14]

Critical accounts of creative employment

The critique of free labour is not the only way in which critical analysis has sought to pay attention to creative labour in recent years. Alongside these developments, there have also been discussions of professional and semi-professional workers in the cultural industries and in related industries such as web design. Various recent critical accounts have suggested that professional workers in the (digitalising) cultural industries and in related industries are involved in forms of labour that are characterised by high degrees of autonomy, creativity and 'play', but also by overwork, casualisation and precariousness. Andrew Ross observed how, in the eyes of a new generation of business analysts in the 1980s, Silicon Valley 'appeared to promote a humane workplace not as a grudging concession to demoralised employees but as a valued asset to production'.[15] 'New economy' firms, he argued, aimed to provide work cultures that 'embraced openness, cooperation and self-management'.[16] Ross showed that such features were in fact closely linked to long working hours and a serious blurring of the line between work and leisure. Whilst the dot.com working environments of the 1990s offered 'oodles of autonomy along with warm collegiality' they also enlisted 'employees' free-est thoughts and impulses in the service of salaried time'.[17] This process of involvement has been described as 'self-exploitation'. Similarly, also writing about new media work, Andreas Wittel saw there a paradigmatic case of an emergent form of community that he calls 'network sociality', one which appears to be individualistic and instrumental, involving an assimilation of work and play.[18] Ros Gill, in a study of European freelance new media workers, found evidence that features of the work that seemed superficially attractive, such as its informality and high levels of autonomy, were, in fact, particularly problematic for women because of the lack of clear criteria for evaluating work and especially because of the difficulties such informality caused when seeking new contracts.[19]

Such insights, often developed in relation to the IT sector, have been increasingly applied to the cultural and creative industries. Gillian Ursell's early contribution noted 'an intensification of the self-commodification processes by which each individual seeks to improve his/her chances of attracting gainful employment'[20] and analysed how television workers had, in the era of casualisation and increasing freelance work, come to take on the work of organising their own labour markets. This element of 'apparent voluntarism' needed to be acknowledged, Ursell claimed, and she turned to Foucauldian theory not to dispense with labour-process theory concerns but 'to approach them more substantially'.[21] In particular, she drew on Nikolas Rose's idea that, in advanced liberalism, freedom is redefined as 'a capacity for self-realisation which can be obtained only through individual activity'.[22]

Discussing how notions of creativity, talent and work are being redefined in those burgeoning micro-businesses of the cultural sector associated with young people – including fashion and design, but also entertainment industries such as clubbing, recording and magazine journalism – Angela McRobbie echoed Ursell in pointing to the 'utopian thread' involved in the 'attempt to make-over the world of work into something closer to a life of enthusiasm and enjoyment', and in focusing on how this leads to a situation where, when things go wrong, young people entering these creative worlds of work can feel they only have themselves to blame.[23] In this respect, McRobbie usefully broadened the study of creative work to include a wider set of conditions and experiences, including the way in which aspirations to and expectations of autonomy could lead to disappointment, disillusion and 'self-blaming'. She also pointed to the gendered aspects of these conditions, with women now expected to find full-time work, uninterrupted by family commitments, satisfying and enriching.[24] The context for McRobbie's critique was the then UK Labour government's creative industries policy, and their general valorisation of labour, where 'work comes to mean much more than just earning a living; it incorporates and takes over everyday life'.[25] McRobbie was usefully questioning the 'ideal of self-expressive work' and its place in Labour's advocacy of 'a new youth-driven meritocracy', involving a labour of love and self-exploitation.[26]

Later writers have built on these contributions. A helpful and important synthesis is provided by Mark Banks in his book *The Politics of Cultural Work*.[27] In the article discussed earlier, De Peuter and Dyer-Witheford showed how the creativity and playfulness highly valued by the games workers that they interviewed served to offset extremely long and demanding working hours.[28] In a series of articles and chapters Matt Stahl has brought legal, political and cultural theory together to suggest that the incorporation of subjectivity into capitalism acts as a kind of pacifying device in the era of neo-liberalism and that popular music's democratic promise that 'you can do this too' is a particularly salient way in which 'liberal society' promises an end to alienation and appropriation by promising independence and autonomy.[29]

Quality of working life

Some of the key concepts raised in these recent debates about paid employment in the IT and cultural industries (such as self-exploitation and the hidden costs of autonomy) are germane to discussions of free labour in the digitalising media industries. Yet the free labour debates have paid only rather passing attention to questions concerning employment, occupations and careers in media production, other than to make brief reference to moments of resistance to oppressive working conditions.

Discussions of amateur media and unpaid labour need to pay careful attention to questions regarding the quality of working life. This needs to be linked to questions of social justice and the distribution of possibilities for living a good life. In a fuller version of this chapter, published elsewhere,[30] I apply these two assumptions somewhat critically to key contributions about free labour. Are we really meant to see people who sit at their computers modifying code or typing out responses to TV shows as 'exploited' in the same way as those who endure appalling conditions and pay in Indonesian sweatshops? Surely not – and this raises the question of how to integrate such analysis into more satisfactory understandings of capitalism, exploitation, power and freedom. To what kinds of political demand might objections to free labour give rise? In that earlier article, I address those issues by examining the political origins of the debates about free labour in autonomist Marxism. Here, though, in the remainder of this much briefer chapter, I simply want to address the question of how we might best consider work in the cultural industries, in terms of its quality, and ask what this might mean for discussing the rise of amateur media production. Doing so allows us to take seriously the lives of workers, in a way that the focus on 'prosumers', 'produsers' and even free labour sometimes seem to discourage. This is not just a question of politics, it is also one of theoretical breadth and depth. We need to connect the analysis of cultural and creative labour much more explicitly to the sociology of work in general, and to a richer and diverse body of social theory than has been used in critical work.

In the book that Sarah Baker and I recently published on work in the cultural industries we argue that an important issue for those concerned with creative labour in the present conjuncture is to think about good and bad work in general, and what differentiates jobs, occupations and careers from each other in terms of their quality.[31] To pursue this issue, we asked the following question: what kinds of experiences do jobs and occupations in the cultural industries offer their workers? We drew on sociology of work and political theory in an attempt to conceptualise more fully what might constitute good and bad jobs, occupations and careers. Table 12.1 brutally summarises the framework Sarah and I developed in Chapter 2 of our book. It simply lists the factors that, in our view, drawing on philosophy and sociology of work, should be considered in discussing quality of work. Note that there is a deliberate ambiguity in the terms 'good work' and 'bad work': they refer to products as well as process, to the quality of outcomes, and their potential contribution to the flourishing of others, as well as to the quality of life for the worker(s). Our primary concern though is with the experience of work for workers. Underlying this approach is a desire to put questions of well-being and flourishing – concepts central to Aristotelian and other traditions of thought[32] – at the centre of debates about social justice, equality and democracy.

Table 12.1 Criteria for thinking about what constitutes good and bad work

	Good work	Bad work
Process:	Good wages, working hours, high levels of safety	Poor wages, working hours and levels of safety
	Autonomy	Powerlessness
	Interest, involvement	Boredom, detachment
	Sociality, friendship, collegiality	Isolation, conflict, animosity
	Esteem of others and self-esteem	Self-doubt, shame
	Self-realisation	Frustrated development
	Work–life balance	Overwork
	Security	Inappropriate levels of risk
Product:	Excellent products	Low-quality products
	Products that contribute to the common good	Products that fail to contribute to the well-being of others

First of all, let me briefly report on the findings from our study of workers in three media industries – music, television and magazine journalism – using the criteria indicated in the table. This will help to fill out the bare abstractions in the table. I'll then discuss how these criteria, and our research, might relate to unpaid work and amateur media.

It was clear from our research that many cultural-industry jobs and occupations are riddled with problems and inequities. Many are offered on a short-term basis, making it difficult to plan ahead with any certainty, and constraining workers' abilities to make their work the basis of meaningful self-realisation. Although many people respect art, learning and knowledge, some see them as mere ornamentation, and creative labour as a kind of social luxury. This limits the degree to which workers in these industries can feel sure of social respect and recognition. Autonomy is always limited, but many creative workers have little control over the products they are involved in, especially in terms of how they are distributed, marketed and publicised. The 'autonomy' involved in freelance work can provide freedom to combine work with childcare and family life, but it can also involve isolation and a lack of solidarity with other creative workers. The returns for creative work are highly uneven, and many struggle even to get a foothold in the cultural industries. By contrast, a successful few enjoy considerable benefits in terms of financial reward and recognition, in ways that distort the minor differences in talent that might lead some to succeed more than others. Many workers tolerate poor pay, long hours and difficult conditions in order merely to gain jobs with very poor levels of security and protection. In other words, to achieve the possibility of self-realisation through creative work seems to require what some recent critics have called self-exploitation. In the light of these dynamics, many workers leave the cultural industries at a relatively early age, burnt out by the need to keep up to date with changing ideas of what is fashionable, relevant and innovative, a process that requires not only hard work at work, but also a blurring of work and leisure. Many cultural industries now seem to their workers to be more competitive than ever, and staying ahead requires long hours and an intense relationship to the work. Autonomy is a desirable feature of creative work, but it comes hand in glove with self-reliance and an uncertainty about career paths. All in all, there are good reasons, it seems, to think of creative work as – to quote the title of a track by British rap musician Mike Skinner, who performs under the name The Streets – 'The hardest way to make an easy living'.

As we saw earlier, these negative factors have led some critical commentators to interpret positive aspects of creative work in the cultural industries as, ultimately, control mechanisms that serve to discipline or seduce workers into putting a great deal of themselves into what they do, and tolerating precariousness and insecurity. Such critical accounts have been an important counter to the complacent portrayal of creative work in creative industries policy. Yet in the form that they have often been presented, such criticisms may leave something of a normative vacuum. For to treat these positive components of creative work as mere sugar coatings for the bitter pill of precariousness is surely too dismissive of the genuinely positive experiences that some creative workers have in their jobs and careers. It is worth recalling that jobs, occupations and careers in the cultural industries rarely involve gruelling physical demands or tasks that endanger the person undertaking them. They hardly ever involve work of a kind that many others will find disgusting or disdainful (such as a toilet attendant, or nurse who has to care for incontinent patients). In fact, cultural-industry jobs are often thought of as desirable and intriguing, even glamorous. They involve expressive and communicative forms of endeavour which are highly valued by many people in modern societies. Although this of course depends very much on industry and genre, in principle at least this suggests that they are capable of providing a basis for respect and recognition from others, which in turn can help nourish the worker's sense of self-esteem, and over time, contribute to projects of self-realisation. Cultural-industry organisations also tend to be structured in such a way that some workers are able to gain high levels of autonomy, in two different senses: workplace autonomy and creative autonomy deriving from ambivalent Enlightenment and romantic conceptions of the value of art and culture. This means that they have the possibility of shaping outcomes, and producing good work in the sense of work that contributes to the common good. There are also significant spaces where excellence is valued and encouraged. We shouldn't forget, then, that as well as the negative dynamics I've already outlined, the cultural industries provide significant opportunities for good work.

This can only be a very brief summary, and readers are referred to the detailed discussion of these questions in *Creative Labour*.[33] The point here is to think about how to apply some of these notions of 'good' and 'bad' work to amateur media and unpaid labour. To what extent might the massive growth of amateur media production allow people who wish to centre at least some of their lives around symbol making to live thriving, flourishing lives? How might they undertake activities – whether rewarded financially or not – which allow them to have positive experiences of the kind listed under 'good work' in Table 12.1, and to produce work that might enhance the lives of others? The two other chapters in this section provide valuable case studies that can help us to consider these questions – questions which Sarah Baker and I did not have the opportunity to address in our analysis of paid work and occupations in our book.

Ramon Lobato and Lawson Fletcher seek to move discussions of amateur and semi-professional creative labour away from narratives of decline associated with the critiques of authors such as Andrew Keen in their insightful and illuminating discussion of Australian music writing. I want to extemporise on their fine piece here, relating their concerns to the model of good and bad work presented here, as a way of exploring some of the difficult normative questions raised by amateur media. They note the diffusion of rock/pop music writing beyond the Anglo-American specialist music magazines where such journalism formed as a field in the 1960s to 1990s and into the vast, somewhat internationalised spaces of the internet, but with nationally based magazines continuing to provide important long-form journalism, alongside a new breed of local, city-specific publications. How, they ask, do Australian music writers understand their work in this new configuration of the field: as a stepping stone to a future paid career, or as final destination? This is closely connected to a second question: to what extent do writers feel contented to conduct music writing as an unpaid hobby? They also explore questions of product, arguing that this form of amateur media production is marked by surprisingly high standards of quality, inherited from professional journalism.

Lurking beneath those questions of career trajectory (stepping stone or final destination?) and satisfaction (are they content with music writing as an unpaid hobby?) are deeper questions about the place of work in people's lives. To what extent are music writers able to find in present labour market conditions a means by which they might feel themselves to be successfully developing as a person over time? (This is a question concerning self-realisation in terms of the model presented.) This in turn is closely linked to questions of self-esteem and recognition by others. To what extent does our work allow us to feel that we are fulfilling and developing our potential in ways that might be appreciated by others, and by ourselves, so that we might gain a sense that we are living our lives well?

Music writing is a highly desirable job, but it is simply not available to that many people in Australia. The potential consequences of this should not be understated. It is true that conducting music writing as an unpaid hobby will allow writers greater freedom than their professional counterparts. But in terms of the lived experience of individuals, there is no getting away from the fact that they will almost certainly have to, or will want to, gain income from other sources of employment. And if they have a strong commitment to their music writing, that might end up creating problems in terms of reconciling a strong commitment to amateur writing with commitment to other forms of paid work – the work–life balance criterion comes into play here. Success in activities associated with media production commonly requires quite high levels of dedication, so this will not be easy. In the case of music writing, for example, it will be necessary to keep on top of an enormous amount of music and discourse, to keep ahead of the game. So here we encounter problems of work–life balance and overwork. Is amateur media production sustainable for individuals over a long term in the way that, at least at their best, professional careers might be? Professional careers, ideally, will involve the learning and gaining of skills over time – potentially contributing to a sense of healthy self-realisation. This is certainly possible for amateurs too, as Stebbins shows in his brilliant sociology of serious amateurs.[34] And many professional jobs don't involve that sense of an accumulation of knowledge. But, as Richard Sennett's recent work has suggested, the fact that flexible capitalism has eroded possibilities for enriching work that is sustained over time does not mean that this is not a desirable goal, for large numbers of people (not everyone).[35] There are other reasons too why professional, paid work might be desirable and valuable, even if it means handing over some of our freedom in return for pay. For example, work can provide us with important experiences of sociality and collectivity, which might be difficult to obtain elsewhere: jokes, laughs, and shared experiences with people who we might not otherwise have the chance to know. Of course, amateur writing via the internet might foster a sense of community. Many introverted people will enjoy the privacy and control that such communication will bring. But most people need a considerable amount of interaction with other people, in the same space, and at the same time. A smiley icon in a blog posting is not the same thing as sharing a laugh with people in the same room.

Lobato and Fletcher's portrayal of a relatively successful set of amateur media practices is convincing. But by focusing on participants' own accounts at a particular time, rather than looking at people's working lives over time, and in the context of broader structural conditions, we may sometimes fail to see ways in which people's efforts to live good lives, including good working lives, might be constrained. In this case, isolation, unsustainability and overwork might be the downsides of the positive picture of autonomy and recognition afforded by amateur music writing.

The chapter by Eva Hemmungs Wirtén raises a somewhat different set of issues regarding the relationship of amateur work to human flourishing. Wirtén provides a fascinating account of disputes and rivalries among 'fansubbers', who add subtitles to (often Japanese) film and TV shows, making available the copies online. Fansubbers associated with sites such as dXs and SweSub see the fact that they carry out their work for free as meaning that they are motivated by quality, rather than money. They despise the translations made available on a rival site, UT, for their poor quality, and attribute this poor quality to its profit-seeking ethos. What's more, dXs subbers accuse UT of stealing their freely given work, and making money out of it (through sales of advertising on the UT website).

These disputes and rivalries concern questions of ethics and law, but just as significant are battles over quality and recognition. It might be possible to see the dXs subbers as motivated by a desire for mastery, a will to power, but what seems impressive to me is their commitment to a gift economy, where Japanese films and television programmes are made available to non-Japanese speaking audiences, and with high-quality subtitles attached. The aim is not only recognition for the high-quality work they do, a battle for credibility; it is surely also about a desire to contribute to the common good by making these translations of interesting anime freely available.

It seems to me that, although she does not make this argument herself (she is understandably and interestingly focusing on questions of authority and authorisation), Wirtén's account demonstrates the constraints imposed on amateur production by the fact that such amateur production nearly always exists in fields where commercial imperatives can prevail. I may be misreading the situation, but the UT site seems parasitical on the freely given labour of subbers, and careless about the issues of translation quality that the fansubbers admirably prioritise. Admittedly, a commercial site such as UT seemingly makes it easier for consumers to access anime through its better designed website. However, the cost of this access for consumers is lower quality, and on the part of other producers (that is, the fansubbers) the price of such access is a justifiable sense that they are not being adequately respected or recognised. This commercial parasitism[36] makes good unpaid work harder to achieve, in two senses. It makes it harder for amateurs to gain a sense of reward and satisfaction from their labour. And it makes good work in the sense of high-quality outputs produced for the common good harder to achieve as well.

Conclusions: how might we live good working lives in a digital age?

I have been reading these excellent essays slightly against the grain, not to criticise them, but to suggest further possibilities for assessing amateur media, in terms of their relationship to people's ability to live good lives. But discussions of amateur media production that take questions of labour, employment and occupation seriously would, I am arguing, benefit from assessing how possible it is for people (including the quantitative issue of how many people, and which ones) to achieve generally good combinations of paid and unpaid work, of self-realisation, autonomy, work–life balance, esteem and recognition, and so on. People's conceptions of good lives and good work will obviously vary. Some will value autonomy over security and high wages, some will value self-realisation over work–life balance, and so on. And most of us will be confused about what we want! Crucially, our choices are constrained by structural conditions, including labour markets, education, and the class, gender, ethnic and other relations that cut across them. This is surely at the heart of politics: how we might make good lives – and good work as a crucial component of good lives – as available as possible for as many people as possible, balancing collective and individual needs and desires.

If all this is right, then it becomes important to ask: to what extent has the rise of amateur media production made good lives – and good cultural work – more available for people (and which people)? That is a very tough question to answer, like most important questions. But what strikes me about the debates on prosumers, crowdsourcing, networked media production, et cetera is how rarely anything resembling that question has been posed. What some recent critiques rightly point to is how contemporary acceptance of 'sacrificial labour'[37] paves the way for de-unionisation, and contributes to the depression of wages and the erosion of working conditions. Yet we still need to value unpaid labour, in spite of the way it is bound up with power.[38] So we are left with quite challenging political dilemmas regarding media work. But these can best be identified and addressed by at least being clearer about what our objectives are.

Notes

1 In valuable accounts such as Howard Becker, *Art Worlds*, Chicago: University of Chicago Press, 1982; and Janet Wolff, *The Social Production of Art*, Basingstoke: Macmillan, 2nd edn, 1993.

2 Alex Bruns, *Blogs, Wikipedia, Second Life and Beyond*, New York: Peter Lang, 2008, pp. 13–14. A similar but older phrase, 'prosumer', coined by Alvin Toffler in 1980, involved the claim that production and consumption had been separated in the era of mass production, and that increasingly, in order for firms to achieve customisation, a post-Fordist economy would require the increasing integration of consumers into the process of production. Ritzer and Jurgenson argue that Web 2.0 facilitates a much more intensified version of 'prosumption', one which generally empowers consumers and which is characterised by the end of scarcity and an economy of abundance: George Ritzer and Nathan Jurgenson, 'Production, Consumption, Prosumption: The Nature of Capitalism in the Age of the Digital "Prosumer"' (2010) 10 *Journal of Consumer Culture* 13. The millions of workers who are currently losing their jobs in the wake of recession might question what is meant here by 'abundance'.

3 Of course some firms and industries have opted for prohibition of certain kinds of participation, rather than engagement, notably the early efforts of the music industries to address digitalisation: see David Hesmondhalgh 'Music, Digitalisation and Copyright' in Peter Golding and Graham Murdock (eds), *Unpacking Digital Dynamics*, New York: Hampton Press, 2009, p. 63. Some have tried a mixture of the two strategies – see Joshua Green and Henry Jenkins, 'The Moral Economy of Web 2.0: Audience Research and Convergence Culture' in Jennifer Holt and Alisa Perren (eds), *Media Industries: History, Theory and Method*, New York: Wiley-Blackwell, 2009, p. 213.

4 Tiziana Terranova, *Network Cultures*, London: Pluto Press, 2004, Ch. 4 'Free Labour', p. 73. Note that this essay was originally published in 2000, but was reprinted in only a slightly revised form as part of Terranova's book in 2004.

5 Ibid., p. 74.

6 Mark Andrejevic, 'Watching Television Without Pity' (2008) 9 *Television & New Media* 24, 25.

7 Mark Andrejevic, *Reality TV: The Work of Being Watched*, Lanham, MD: Rowman & Littlefield, 2004.

8 Mark Andrejevic, 'Watching Television Without Pity'.

9 Greig De Peuter and Nick Dyer-Witheford, 'A Playful Multitude? Mobilising and Counter-Mobilising Immaterial Game Labour' (2005) 5 *Fibreculture* http://five.fibreculturejournal.org/fcj-024-a-playful-multitude-mobilising-and-counter-mobilising-immaterial-game-labour/.

10 Ibid.

11 See, e.g., Bernard Miège, *The Capitalization of Cultural Production*, New York: International General, 1989.

12 See Adam Arvidsson, 'The Ethical Economy of Customer Coproduction' (2008) 28 *Journal of Micromarketing* 326.

13 Adam Arvidsson, 'Brands' (2005) 5 *Journal of Consumer Culture* 235.

14 Facebook has recently come to be seen as the archetype of a business that relies on the activity of its users as the basis of profit, and it has become increasingly common to hear remarks made on this among critical scholars. For a thoughtful analysis of Facebook in relation to debates about free labour, see Nicole Cohen, 'The Valorization of Surveillance: Towards a Political Economy of Facebook' (2008) 22 *Democratic Communiqué* 5.

15 Andrew Ross, *No Collar: The Humane Workplace and its Hidden Costs*, Philadelphia, PA: Temple University Press, 2003, p. 9.

16 Ibid.

17 Ibid, pp. 17, 19.

18 Andreas Wittel, 'Toward a Network Sociality' (2001) 18 *Theory, Culture and Society* 51.

19 Ros Gill, 'Cool, Creative and Egalitarian? Exploring Gender in Project-Based New Media Work in Europe' (2002) 5 *Information, Communication and Society* 70.

20 Gillian Ursell, 'Television Production: Issues of Exploitation, Commodification and Subjectivity in UK Television Labour Markets' (2000) 22 *Media, Culture & Society* 805, 807.

21 Ibid, 809.

22 See Nikolas Rose, *Powers of Freedom: Reframing Political Thought*, Cambridge: Cambridge University Press, 1999, p. 145.

23 Angela McRobbie, 'Clubs to Companies: Notes on the Decline of Political Culture in Speeded Up Creative Worlds' (2002) 16 *Cultural Studies* 516, 523.

24 Ibid., 521.

25 Angela McRobbie, 'From Holloway to Hollywood: Happiness at Work in the New Cultural Economy?' in Paul du Gay and Michael Pryke (eds), *Cultural Economy*, London: Sage, 2002, p. 97, p. 99.

26 Ibid, p. 101.

27 Mark Banks, *The Politics of Cultural Work*, Basingstoke: Palgrave, 2007.

28 De Peuter and Dyer-Witheford, 'A Playful Multitude?'.

29 Matt Stahl, *Reinventing Certainties: American Popular Music and Social Reproduction* (PhD thesis, University of California, San Diego, 2006), p. 23.

30 David Hesmondhalgh, 'User-generated Content, Free Labour and the Cultural Industries' (2010) 10 *Ephemera* 267.

31 David Hesmondhalgh and Sarah Baker, *Creative Labour: Media Work in Three Cultural Industries*, Abingdon and New York: Routledge, 2010.

32 See Martha Nussbaum and Amartya Sen (eds), *Equality of Life*, Oxford: Clarendon Press, 1993.

33 David Hesmondhalgh and Sarah Baker, *Creative Labour*, Ch. 2.

34 Robert A. Stebbins, Amateurs, Professionals, and Serious Leisure, Montreal: McGill-Queen's University Press, 1992.

35 Richard Sennett, *The Corrosion of Character*, New York: Norton, 1998; Richard Sennett, *The Craftsman*, London: Allen Lane, 2008.

36 I am not saying that all commerce is parasitical on unpaid labour – just that this is an example of such parasitism.

37 Ross, *No Collar*.

38 See Hesmondhalgh, 'User-generated Content'.

Part V

Property and play

13 *Minecraft* as Web 2.0

Amateur creativity and digital games

Greg Lastowka

This chapter considers how the digital game *Minecraft* has both enabled and benefited from various Web 2.0 practices. I begin with an explanation of the concept of Web 2.0 and then consider how that concept applies to the space of digital games. I then look at *Minecraft* specifically. As I explain, *Minecraft's* surprise success as an 'indie' game is largely attributable to the ways in which it tapped into the dynamics of amateur creativity. I conclude by suggesting that more games like *Minecraft* may be socially desirable, but noting how current laws discourage the creation of these sorts of games.

Web 2.0

The media landscape of the twentieth century featured a range of media formats: television shows, movies, books, newspapers, periodicals, music and digital games. The media trajectory during that time was largely dominated by the growth of past industries and the new creation of others. Specialised firms introduced a variety of new technologies (for example, radios, televisions, cassette tapes) to consumers that provided new capabilities for one-to-many media. Both old and new forms of media showcased, primarily, the works of professional writers, actors, artists and musicians who were employed by the media production industries.

'Professional' creators played a central role in this media environment in part because the various technologies of media creation (for example, movie cameras, sound mixers and lithographic presses) were expensive and therefore purchased primarily by commercially motivated firms. The technologies of media distribution (for example, broadcast stations, printing presses, delivery trucks) were also expensive. Firms who created media recouped their expenses by licensing their content to distribution companies, who recouped their expenses by either selling content directly (the model for books), supporting distribution with advertising (the model for radio), or pursuing a combination of these strategies (the model for newspapers). Notably, many forms of new media were dependent on the profusion of receptive consumer technologies (for example, televisions, radios and turntables). These technologies were one-way receivers of media – they built audiences.[1] Technology thus drew a stark line between artist and audience, creator and consumer, author and reader.

In this world, few 'amateurs' were significant. Amateurs are creators who produce primarily (or exclusively) because they enjoy the act of production.[2] Professionals may enjoy their work, but they labour in expectation of a significant financial return. Amateurs do not. The professional/amateur distinction, like the work/play distinction, has a blurry boundary, but the ability of a professional to produce a work of commercial value seems to be the key delineating factor.

The labour of a creative 'professional' is commercially valuable within a market. Professional works are packaged and sold within the media industry. Those who are not successful at gaining entry into the commercial marketplace (the gallery, the book store, the television network) must be described as amateurs. Amateurs have traditionally had more limited means for making their creativity available to the public.

'Web 2.0' is the term used to describe the recent shift in this landscape. *Internet* technology, and the World Wide Web in particular, have supplemented the one-to-many media model with a many-to-many model. Web 2.0 describes online forms of 'participatory media' in which former audiences assume significant agency in content creation and distribution.[3]

Web 2.0 is commonly associated with specific technologies and platforms that enable amateur content creation and distribution. They include blogs, wikis (Wikipedia especially), photo-sharing forums, video-sharing forums and other sites where individuals upload media in ways that permit mass distribution. A term often associated with Web 2.0 is 'user-generated content' or 'user-created content', which highlights the value of 'user' (audience) contributions to Web 2.0 platforms.[4]

The terms 'Web 2.0' and 'user-generated content' are hardly the only neologisms used to describe this shift. Every commentator seems to have a different way to describe some aspect of Web 2.0. For instance, even before the term Web 2.0 was coined, law professor James Boyle was describing the 'commons' of culture and creativity.[5] Lawrence Lessig, in many popular books, described concepts like 'remix culture', where cultural products are (digitally) adapted and transformed by the public.[6] Clay Shirky has celebrated 'crowdsourcing', where communities use their 'cognitive surplus' to create new content and share it with each other.[7] Henry Jenkins heralds the dawn of a 'convergence culture' where 'fans, bloggers, gamers' help to shape the media.[8] Jonathan Zittrain praises the 'generativity' of the internet.[9] Eric von Hippel celebrates the role of user communities in 'democratizing innovation' by adding new ideas and value to many products.[10] Don Tapscott and Anthony Williams have promoted the term 'prosumer' as a way of describing productive consumers who add value to commercial platforms.[11] Yochai Benkler argues that prosumers are participants in a new economy of 'peer production' that draws on the 'wealth of networks'.[12] This is hardly a complete catalogue of the Web 2.0 terminological buffet,[13] but it certainly suggests that many commentators believe that something new is afoot in online media.

Of course, the new is usually an evolution of the old, and veteran digerati might view Web 2.0's emphasis on user agency, innovation, community and creativity as embodying the 'hacker ethic' and the 'open source' philosophy that has been part of computing culture since the 1960s.[14] And, as some commentators have noted, the contemporary movement towards participatory media might be seen as a revival of the folk culture displaced by the mass media. Web 2.0 is certainly modelled, in many ways, on pre-digital amateur practices (for example, letters to the editor, art enthusiast clubs and garage bands).[15]

Like the earlier shift to a mass media model, the shift to Web 2.0 has technological underpinnings. Cheap digital machines combined with the internet's decentralised architecture have led past motivations and practices to take on a new power.[16] As Ithiel de Sola Pool observed over 25 years ago, certain technologies, once in place, exert a sort of 'soft technological determinism' on the shape of the culture that uses those tools.[17]

As the next section explains, the emergence of Web 2.0 amateur creativity has gone hand in hand with the emergence of the most popular forum of participatory media, the digital game.

Digital games as Web 2.0

Oddly, digital games are often excluded from discussions of Web 2.0. To some extent, this may be attributable to the lower cultural status of digital games. Despite broad consumption demographics, there is still a cultural bias against digital games. Erroneously, digital games are often seen as the exclusive domain of young boys.[18] The academic treatment of digital games sometimes reflects this stereotype or does nothing to challenge it. Digital games are rarely studied today in most humanities programmes and are often excluded from the universe of legitimate art forms by critics. Ironically, the prejudice against digital games may be attributable to their amateur roots.

Video games as a form of media were birthed with the technology of Web 2.0, the computer. In the 1960s and early 1970s, due to the high cost of computing equipment, there was little chance of marketing digital games to consumers, so most game creators had no prospect of securing a financial return for their creative labour.[19] *Space War*, for instance, was one of the first multi-player shooter games and is a lineal ancestor of contemporary shooting games, such as *Starcraft II*. *Space War* was written collaboratively by graduate students at MIT.[20] Its creators saw very little in the way of an economic return for their efforts – but they did enjoy making and playing their game. One of the most popular early text-based computer games, *Adventure*, was also not written for sale, but for the author's children. *MUD*, one of the first multi-player online games, was written as a graduate student project at the University of Essex.

The first computer games were not only written by 'amateurs', they also incorporated amateurism into their structure. Digital games depend on constant interactions between the game player and the program that produce the game's 'text'.[21] A film is a crafted work to be enjoyed and deciphered, with every detail attributed to the genius of the author or the production crew. A game, by comparison, turns the 'reader' into a 'player' and offers her a chance to influence the direction of the text.[22] Digital game designers must build in room to accommodate diverging paths of play. This may explain, in part, why the digital game genre is not a favourite of traditional critics – the text of a game varies based on the capabilities of the player. This makes criticism a much more difficult (and time-consuming) task.[23]

Despite the amateur roots of digital games and the amateur agency they entail, digital-game production today is certainly a professional activity. As the computer and digital-game industry matured and consumer-technology costs were reduced, amateur inventions were made profitable by professional firms. *Space War*, *Adventure* and *MUD* all gave birth to commercialised versions of these same games with these same names.[24] Companies like Atari and Infocom effectively profited from making cheaper versions of amateur games and introducing them to consumers.[25] Today, sizeable corporations like Sony, Nintendo, Microsoft and Electronic Arts dominate the landscape of digital gaming and the cost of producing digital games has expanded tremendously.[26] Many companies spend millions or even tens of millions of dollars to develop new titles.

Game design is clearly 'professional' today, which may be why we think of game players not as amateurs, but as consumers. We have learned that forms of professional media entail the existence of an audience, so players fill that role for games. Additionally, our failure to recognise the creative nature of gameplay may be the converse of the suspicion of the aesthetic merit of the digital-game genre. If digital games are less culturally worthy due to their inclusion of amateur participation, then it follows that game players, to the extent they are creative, are less authorial due to their engagement with the work of the game's creator. We may also assume that playing a digital game produces no commercially valuable content and therefore is not a form of amateur creativity.

To the extent that game play is not recorded, this may be true. However, digital games have often been associated with substantial amateur creativity in fixed forms. Since their earliest origins, users of digital games have found ways to creatively 'remix' the games they enjoy by rewriting portions of their code. In some cases, tools for this sort of user creativity have been built into the games. Since the 1980s many computer games have allowed players the ability to design customised 'levels' or 'maps' and share these with other players. Many of the earliest digital games were fully 'remixed' by later creators, starting from the very early programs of the 1960s and 1970s. For instance, Don Woods essentially revised and edited the amateur game of *Adventure* as it was developed by Will Crowther, making the game's canonical version an early act of amateur remixing.[27] An early Atari 2600 version of the same game was another 'remix' of that title. Starting in the 1980s, many computer-based games gave rise to communities of 'modders' who augmented and developed the software to introduce new content and functions.[28] In some cases, these later modifications became as popular as the original games.

Given the interactive nature of gaming, it is natural that many producers of digital games have also experimented with ways of facilitating amateur creativity by building design tools into their software. As Aphra Kerr has noted, '[d]igital games also encourage their users to become "authors" and to produce game content which can be circulated and played by other users.'[29] In the 'sandbox' genre of games, for instance, the game is often primarily about the pleasure of exercising creative power over a complex simulation. *SimCity*, for instance, is a game about building and maintaining a simulated city. The developer of *SimCity*, Will Wright, is perhaps the best-known creator of sandbox games. His most recent game is *Spore* (distributed by Electronic Arts).

In standard *Spore* gameplay, players must customise the appearance of their creatures and environments. This creativity is shared with other players, who can encounter copies of user-generated content in their own games. If players wish to search for new objects and creatures, *Spore* provides a built-in platform for doing so. In one *Spore* expansion pack (*Galactic Adventures*), users can design adventure challenges for other users. Players can that rate those challenges and leave notes for the amateur authors who created them.

In addition to sandbox games, massively multiplayer online role-playing games (MMORPGs) are another genre of games often associated with a high level of user-generated content and amateur creativity.[30] As Sal Humphreys, T. L. Taylor,[31] Thomas Malaby[32] Mira Burri-Nenova and others have noted, this is often true, although the exact sort of user-generated content created varies considerably between gaming platforms. In the game *City of Heroes*, for instance, players are given extensive tools to develop the appearances of their avatars, which can lead to considerable creativity.[33] In *The Lord of the Rings Online*, players can write their own musical notation to be played on virtual instruments. And even in an MMORPG like *World of Warcraft*, which offers very few in-game creative tools to the player, 'user-generated content' of a certain stripe plays a role. In *World of Warcraft*, players often enjoy playing in groups or in social proximity and use the game's platform as a tool for conversation and community.

The game of *Second Life* (which is arguably not a game at all) is often described as a leading example of a platform for user creativity. *Second Life's* marketing materials often describe it as a virtual world built by its users and this is largely a true statement.[34] *Second Life* combines the features of a sandbox game with the social nature of an MMORPG. It has also thrown in the additional element of an authorised virtual economy, which has allowed many of the 'amateur' authors in *Second Life* to obtain 'professional' status by selling their content to other *Second Life* users. In a few cases, this marriage of creativity and a virtual economy has led to user-initiated lawsuits complaining of the infringement of intellectual property rights within *Second Life*.[35]

Of course, not every game is like *Second Life*. Many popular digital games today, such as *Angry Birds* or *Portal II*, offer few built-in tools for user creativity.[36]

However, even in the absence of creative tools, digital games often spur user creativity outside the game. Since the 1980s (at least), players of all manner of digital games have shared information and commentary about their favourite games. In the 1980s game discussion was often found on electronic bulletin boards, which exemplified Web 2.0 practices well before the creation of Web 1.0.[37] Today, a simple online search for any game title reveals a wealth of content, much created by amateurs, relevant to almost every digital game on the market. These sorts of works include gameplay videos, tutorials and wikis, artwork, forums – there is even a YouTube video that captures a playable *Angry Birds* birthday cake.[38]

While not all digital games prioritise amateur creativity in their design, many do, and even those that don't are often swept up into the emerging culture of Web 2.0. Arguably, the most popular and vibrant marriage of amateur creativity and the digital-gaming genre has been achieved by a recent 'indie' game: *Minecraft*.

Minecraft

Minecraft is a computer-based game written in the Java programming language.[39] The first ('Alpha') version of *Minecraft* was created in Sweden in 2009 by Markus 'Notch' Persson. Since that first release, Persson has regularly updated the software (often several times per month) and expanded it to include new features. *Minecraft* can currently be played for free, although the 'Beta' version costs €14.95. *Minecraft* was only 'officially' released in November 2011.

Minecraft's level of sophistication reflects its inexpensive development. The graphics are emphatically retro. Avatars have very crude block-shaped heads and rigid bodies. The world they explore is made up of huge cubic blocks of various materials: for example, trees, grass, stones and water. The website of the game features rather clunky text and graphics and looks like a throwback to the web of the 1990s. Its most prominent feature is an embedded YouTube video clip entitled 'This Is *Minecraft*'.

Though Persson created the game alone, he was soon able to form a small company, 'Mojang', based on the proceeds of *Minecraft*'s early sales. With no advertising, by the summer of 2011, Mojang had sold over three million copies of *Minecraft* and registered over ten million player accounts, translating into well over 60 million dollars in revenue.[40] This level of success is rare in the professional games industry and almost unprecedented in the 'indie' game sector, the umbrella term used to describe games made by solo creators or small studios.

Minecraft's indie roots lend the game a Web 2.0 flavour. Indie games often tend to be more aligned with amateur sensibilities. Since they are created by solo authors or small teams, they are often more authentic expressions of the ideas of their creators. Persson is certainly more intimate with *Minecraft* players than most game developers are with their audiences. Like all indie developers, his public statements are not mediated by corporate marketers or supervising producers. Yet Persson is not a Web 2.0 amateur, by any means. He is certainly profiting from *Minecraft*. The amateurs of *Minecraft* are its players.

To play *Minecraft* is to use the game as a creative tool. One can't really 'win' at *Minecraft*, since there are no required goals and no dramatic plot that must be followed. Players spend most of their time simply 'mining' and 'crafting' blocks of virtual materials, hence the game's name. Once players have gathered and crafted a sufficient inventory of resources, they use these virtual acquisitions to design customised homes and landscapes, often building all manner of blockish structures. *Minecraft* has been called a 'building block game'. It is analogous to a digital box of Lego – one with a healthy dash of *The Lord of the Rings* thrown in.

Minecraft requires players to be creative, even if that creativity is limited to designing a crude shelter or tunnelling the layout of a mine. But most players don't stop there. Digging a mineshaft leads almost inevitably to the creation of large underground caverns and mountainside fortresses. Building a simple house leads to the construction of another story for that house, and then a tower, then villages, then monumental sculptures, and finally feats of complex engineering, such as dams, bridges and roller-coasters.

Many *Minecraft* players want to share their creativity, but unlike players of *Spore*, they have no built-in content-sharing technologies to rely upon. To remedy this, they have turned to video-capture software and YouTube. A search for '*Minecraft*' on YouTube in the summer of 2011 returned almost two million responses. The most popular of those videos were viewed over a million times. Many of the *Minecraft* offerings on YouTube are tours of user-built structures. These range from a full-scale model of the Starship *Enterprise* to a functioning giant-sized whack-a-mole arcade game built out of *Minecraft* blocks and circuitry. Certain video commentators, such as 'Yogcast' and 'Captain Sparklez', are well-known for their mastery of *Minecraft* 'machinima': that is, using *Minecraft* as an animation platform to create audiovisual stories.[41]

In addition to YouTube videos, *Minecraft* players have filled the web with a wealth of wikis, forum posts and other sites that offer specialist advice and commentary about *Minecraft*. Some sites offer tutorials for *Minecraft* building or mining while others explain how to rig basic electrical circuits in the game. There are also a variety of third-party software modifications. These include multi-player servers, 'skins' for adding custom textures to the game and mod packages that add additional features (for example, animals, guns, planes) to the game. There are sites that feature pictures, comic strips and costumes based on *Minecraft*. There is even one website that serves as a forum for elementary school instructors who are seeking ways to use *Minecraft* as a teaching tool.[42] One can also find college course weblogs about game aesthetics that offer student reflections on the experience of playing *Minecraft*.[43]

Players use *Minecraft*'s software as a locus for generating their own creative content both in the game and outside of it. They use cheap digital content creation tools (digital video, wikis, blogs) for the sharing and promotion of their creations. They host their creative content on webpages and cloud-based content-sharing sites (for example, YouTube, Facebook, Twitter). Their creations work in lieu of traditional advertising by popularising the game with new users and adding to the game's value. This viral dynamic makes *Minecraft* a subject of fascination in the more traditional gaming industry, which leads to stories about the game in mass media, further contributing to the growth of *Minecraft*'s user base.

This sort of creativity can certainly be folded into the standard story of Web 2.0. The millions of *Minecraft* YouTube videos, for instance, are one small piece of the (presumably) billions of amateur videos hosted by YouTube. The written text of a *Minecraft* tutorial or wiki might be seen as analogous to the many online amateur 'fan fiction' works inspired by *Star Wars*, *Harry Potter*, *Twilight*, and countless other films and books. Reading a blog posting about *Minecraft* may certainly substitute for reading a 'professional' paperback or magazine. Yet to conflate *Minecraft* creativity with other forms of amateur content is to lose sight of how the game itself draws the player in and initiates the creative process. The way in which a game like *Minecraft* generates amateur creativity is unique.

Minecraft is not just media content that became the focus of fan attention. The game is a creative tool. But it is not the same sort of tool as a word-processing program or a digital painting program. *Minecraft* does not present new users with a blank page or space. Instead, it presents a simulated landscape and a set of tools to manipulate a fictional space. All creativity in *Minecraft* derives from and furthers the fiction presented by the game. To build something from wood blocks, once must first cut down trees. To build from stone, one must mine the blocks from the ground. *Minecraft*'s creative tools are enmeshed with its simulated world.[44]

Minecraft additionally demands creativity outside the game. In its first two years of development, *Minecraft* offered barely any instructions to the novice player. As a game-design decision, this was arguably an unforgivable error – standard game-design doctrine is that the player should be taught, by the game, how to play and be successful. However, even the most rudimentary gameplay in *Minecraft* (for example, chopping down a tree, making a mining pick) is a nearly impossible task if one simply plays the game as written. The new player must look outside *Minecraft* for answers.

Initially, *Minecraft*'s lack of an instruction manual may have been a consequence of Persson's lack of interest in writing one. However, in retrospect, this 'mistake' was an ingenious design decision. When *Minecraft* players look for help online, this introduces them to the wikis, videos, blogs and other forums that are devoted to the game. This introduces players, at the outset, to the importance of the independent online community.

By turning to the web, new players find (perhaps inadvertently) examples of what *Minecraft* is about. A web page featuring basic instructions for crafting a *Minecraft* bed, for instance, might also feature a link to a formula for crafting a diamond breastplate, which may send the novice in search of information about where diamonds are hidden in the virtual landscape. A search on

Google for that answer may include, in its results, a video showing a player-built roller-coaster, inspiring the novice to learn how to build a basic roller-coaster. YouTube, web forums, and other sites thus emulate an artist's colony – new players can appreciate what has been done in *Minecraft*, comment on what others have done, imitate the techniques of others and ultimately share their own work with *Minecraft* players.

Minecraft does very little to aid or direct players in this process. Often, new players see things in the community that appeal to them, yet seem outside their capabilities. In some cases, this is because they have not modified the game's software. Adding customised content is not easy and requires additional forays into web-based instruction and downloading files and programs from third-party websites.

Minecraft's mode of amateur content sharing is much less packaged than what can be found in *Spore* and much further from the control of Mojang. *Minecraft* is therefore much more open to user-created innovations. The lack of sophistication and slickness in the tools used for content sharing signals the greater authenticity of the user community, which also leads users to feel empowered to seek and create new ways to share content. The community's existence and enthusiasm are viewed as independent of Mojang's corporate efforts to promote the game.

By making *Minecraft* players rely on each other, Mojang effectively introduces new players to other amateur creators and enthusiasts. By regularly updating and revising *Minecraft* – and giving fairly laconic details about the content of these updates – Mojang ensures that players return to their online communities to share information. By making community participation intrinsic to the game, Mojang builds social networks around the game. All this, plus its indie origins and its nature as a 'sandbox' game, would seem to make *Minecraft* a paradigm for the marriage of amateur creativity and digital games.

Minecraft clearly exemplifies Web 2.0. The question we might ask is the same one that has been asked about Web 2.0: is this a good thing? And, if so, what is the future of *Minecraft* and games like it?

Valuing amateur creativity

Not everyone thinks that Web 2.0 and the amateur creativity it entails is a good thing. Some popular critics have assailed Web 2.0 as detrimental to the profits and viability of 'professional' content creation. In his book *The Cult of the Amateur*,[45] former Silicon Valley entrepreneur Andrew Keen argues that an amateur-centric culture threatens both the important role of expert gatekeepers and the quality of information produced. Like many critics of amateur creativity, Keen also accuses amateur creators of groupthink and egoism, states that amateur creativity is derivative (if not piratical) of professional content, and laments the coarseness and vulgarity of amateur tastes. Keen is probably the best-known detractor of Web 2.0, but many other critics (for example, Nicholas Carr,[46] Jason Lanier[47] and Mark Helprin[48]) share some of his views and have published book-length attacks on Web 2.0 enthusiasm along similar lines.

Much more ubiquitous, however, are the popular commentators mentioned earlier who celebrate the various upsides of mass amateurisation of the media. The list of benefits depends on the observer, but they seem to break down into roughly three categories: promoting democracy, promoting diversity and promoting autonomy.[49]

Web 2.0's promotion of democracy is certainly seen as a key value by many commentators. As Ithiel de Sola Pool noted years ago, the profusion of technologies enabling popular communication allows the public to 'speak back' to mass media.[50] From the standpoint of engaged democracy, a public sphere injected with a healthy dose of popular expression should be superior to a public sphere dominated exclusively by the passive receipt of 'elite' and 'professional' content. Indeed, as Aphra Kerr has noted, digital games should be particularly appealing to us, politically, because '[a]s a cultural practice they embody the liberal ideals of individual choice and agency'.[51]

Cultural diversity is also claimed to result from Web 2.0 practices. A broad set of amateur creators, by the sheer magic of numbers, is more likely to offer the public forms of media content that speak to unique perspectives, both in terms of locality and in terms of cultural diversity.[52] Web 2.0 is seen as a remedy to the homogenisation and exclusion of culture which is found in globalised professional media.

Even putting aside these two civic values associated with amateur creativity, many commentators argue that there is an intrinsic and non-instrumental value to amateur creativity. Amateur creators are not passive audiences, but active participants in their own micro-groups. The experience of crafting and delivering public expression through online media builds communication skills, allows creators to experience freedom and autonomy and lends creators a new perspective on the nature of professionally produced content.

Finally, it is worth noting that amateur culture, due to its lack of profitability, has greater authenticity – it is more expressive of the creator's ideas. Whereas professional content is often allied with the goals of advertising and persuasion, amateur content is more likely to be non-manipulative in its objectives. This actually goes hand in hand with popular criticisms of amateur expression as unmarketable and unappealing. This is true: many amateur works may not be of interest to any particular audience, given that amateur producers are not restricted to creating commercially viable commodities. And, arguably, this is a good thing. Amateur projects can be experimental, personally expressive, and politically controversial.

Although there are certainly critics of Web 2.0, the consensus of commentary seems to be that the inclusion of amateur creativity in popular media is a beneficial development. Ideally, therefore, those who promote the public interest through policy and law would work to craft laws that value amateur creativity. At the very least, they would do nothing to hinder the current flourishing of amateur media.

Many of today's laws, however, are firmly rooted in a pre-Web 2.0 world. Despite several years of academic and popular enthusiasm over Web 2.0, amateurs have little political traction in the world's legislatures. 'Professional' media are still the media that make money and therefore the media that count. Companies that create and distribute books, music, software and movies have grabbed the attention of lawmakers and law-enforcement agencies. The reaction of executives in the entertainment industry to amateur media is, at best, indifference.

Although the United States is arguably the birthplace of Web 2.0, it is also the birthplace of Hollywood. Legislators have focused largely on the latter fact and devoted themselves to protecting the profits of the entertainment industries against commercial piracy. In the international arena, the same trade-based concerns seem to dominate. The revenues derived from entertainment media play an important part in trade negotiations and treaties, probably because US films and music are a key American export.

The legislative take on Web 2.0 in the United States is not too surprising: few elected representatives are early adopters of new technologies, many are dependent on the contributions of private firms to run their campaigns and many are keen (especially in the current economic climate) to prioritise job creation. It follows that lawmakers would be more inclined to favour the stability of traditional content 'industries' rather than embrace this shift toward Web 2.0 amateurs who threaten to destabilise the commercial landscape. While Web 2.0 companies, such as Google and Facebook, might be seen as worthy civic actors (creating potential tax revenues and jobs), the creative fuel that feeds the balance sheets of both companies – amateur creativity – is generally ignored.

Yet it might be noted that Web 2.0 did not rely on the market or the government for its birth. Web 2.0 itself was an accident just as *Minecraft's* success was an accident. The infrastructure of the internet may have been built through state and private investments, but very few of those who built that infrastructure understood that they were laying the groundwork for Web 2.0. If that were the case, the business models of Web 2.0 would have been quickly adopted by the publishing, recording and motion-picture industries. Instead, Web 2.0 was not even anticipated by the first wave of dot-com titans; America Online and Yahoo! were both taken by surprise. Even the most recently minted technology companies have often had a blind spot with respect to amateur creativity. Much like *Minecraft*, each new business built on the energy of amateurs seems to come as a surprise.

There are good reasons for this blind spot. Traditional media companies view media as commodities they offer to consumers, not something consumers produce for themselves. And when amateur creators produce, they rarely produce work that is entirely original (who does?). As a result, when companies give substantial creative leeway and creative tools to fans, it is inevitable that fans will use those tools to create derivative forms of content. This can create legal problems for those who provide the tools, since the laws of copyright and trade mark treat the work of online amateurs in the same way that they treat the work of professionals.

Copyright law deems new works that are substantially similar to protected works as infringing unless authorised by the owner of the copyright. J. K. Rowling, for instance, owns a copyright in her books and therefore has the exclusive right to make stories and films set in the *Harry Potter* universe.[53] Copyright law gives Rowling the right to sue and recover damages from authors who make and sell new works of fiction set in her world. A cursory search of Web 2.0 sites, however, reveals a surfeit of amateur stories, artworks and videos that are all based on Rowling's books. Many of these would appear to infringe her copyright.

As a matter of public relations, it would be unwise for Rowling to sue everyone who dresses up like Harry Potter in a YouTube video or posts a short story about Harry on the internet. As a practical matter, Rowling (and the owner of any popular fiction) would find it incredibly time consuming and all but impossible to entirely prevent the circulation of amateur works based upon her creativity. However, existing law also makes it problematic for her to permit amateur creativity based on her stories.

The chief problem is that fans who create authorised new works should, by default, own exclusive rights to whatever creative labour they have added. Fan rights in new works based on *Harry Potter* may ultimately work against the financial and creative interests of Rowling. For instance, some fans of *Harry Potter* have written unauthorised stories where characters from Rowling's books travel to New York City. If Rowling were, at this point, to give a blanket licence to all derivative works by her fans, she might ultimately find herself subject to a fan's copyright claim if she were to write or authorise a new *Harry Potter* work set in New York. Copyright law therefore operates in a way that makes it problematic for the content industries to work with amateur creators without some sort of clear guidelines about the ultimate ownership of intellectual property rights.

The space of video games has encountered these same problems. Fans of *World of Warcraft*, for instance, are currently permitted to submit fan art and machinima to the company's website pursuant to written policies that specify the terms and conditions of the licence and generally provide the game company with the right to commercially exploit user creations. Many sandbox games, like *Spore*, have similar extensive licensing provision for the use of the tools that they provide. In some cases, like other Web 2.0 companies, game companies have responded to complaints of copyright infringement by users. For instance, certain creatures in *Spore* have been removed by Electronic Arts when they presented concerns about copyright infringement. And the makers of the MMORPG *City of Heroes* complied with demands by Marvel Comics to delete certain avatar costumes created by users that were claimed to infringe Marval's copyrights.[54]

Navigating the interplay of copyright law and user-generated content in games is therefore a rather messy proposition. The difficulties may explain the reluctance of many established players in the games industry to full embrace tools for amateur creativity.

Once again, though, *Minecraft* provides an interesting case study due to its nature as an independent game. At present, *Minecraft* is eschewing legalese and approaching intellectual property issues in its characteristic (primitive and authentic) manner. On Minecraft.net, there is a page labelled 'terms of use' and signed by 'Markus Persson and friends'. The terms page is no more than 500 words long, incredibly short compared to almost any similar set of terms on a similar game. Under the heading 'The One Major Rule' it states:

> Do not distribute anything we've made. This includes, but not limited to, the client or the server software for the game. This also includes modified versions of anything we've made. In order to ensure integrity of the game, we need all game downloads to come from a single central source: us. We hope you understand. It's also important for us that 3rd party tools/services don't seem 'too official' as we can't guarantee their quality. If you wish to make something pertaining to anything we've made we're humbled, but please make sure that it can't be interpreted as being official.[55]

Immediately after that, under the heading 'What You Can Do', Persson goes on to say that:

> [i]f you've bought the game, you may play around with it and modify it. We'd appreciate it if you didn't use this for griefing, though, and remember not to distribute the changes. Any tools you write for the game from scratch belongs to you. You're free to do whatever you want with screenshots and videos of the game, but don't just rip art resources and pass them around, that's no fun.[56]

Finally, in the third section of the short document, entitled 'Other,' Persson states:

> We reserve the right to change this agreement at any time with or without notice, with immediate and/or retroactive effect. Any suggestions made are assumed to be offered for free unless otherwise agreed before the suggestion was made. We're not going to put up a huge EULA. We're trying to be open and honest, and we hope people treat us the same way back. If there's anything legal you're wondering about that isn't answered from this page, don't do it and ask us about it. Basically, don't be ridiculous and we won't.[57]

While the first sentence in the above quote reveals that Persson is not completely cavalier about what he is doing with the document, his later refusal to 'put up a huge EULA' is well in keeping with the indie ethos of *Minecraft*. The permissions statement – [y]ou're free to do whatever you want with screenshots and videos' – is decidedly not the language of copyright law, but is incredibly succinct compared to the multi-part agreement that *World of Warcraft* uses to permit its players to submit fan art or post machinima.

On the whole, the 500-word document also seems to reflect Persson's political views about intellectual property: he is a member of the Swedish branch of the 'Pirate Party'. During the closing session of the Indie Games Summit in 2011, he captured some media attention in the game industry by stating 'piracy is not theft' and advising games creators to view those who copy their games without authorisation as potential customers. As one critical reporter/blogger (writing for Forbes.com) explained, this tolerance for unauthorised copying is hardly a common perspective in the games industry.[58] To critics of Web 2.0 who associate the trend with piracy, it may be positive evidence of the connection. But Persson is part of the digital-games industry and *Minecraft* is his own creative work. Despite his refusal to condemn piracy, he has been incredibly successful at monetising his game while retaining a rather sceptical view of intellectual property protections.

Persson's minimalist approach to controlling his game may also help him avoid potential run-ins with other intellectual property owners. As stated before, *Minecraft's* lack of content-sharing tools pushes much of the community's creative activity to the open web. The player-created 'infringing avatars' in *City of Heroes* became a copyright problem for the game's creators because they hosted and claimed intellectual property rights in the amateur content created within the game. However, a *Minecraft* rendition of the Starship *Enterprise* posted on YouTube would not be a problem for Mojang, since the company claims no rights in user creations and does not host the (potentially infringing) content. By sending players to third-party sites (such as YouTube) to share their creativity, Mojang effectively removes itself from the tricky questions of digital copyright, foisting those concerns off on third parties, such as the Google-owned YouTube.

It is ironic that, if *Minecraft* is an example of the benefits of Web 2.0 for culture and popular media, its success has been accompanied by a rather dismissive and sometimes antagonistic stance toward the intellectual property laws that, in theory, should be Mojang's best friend. From the vantage point of Web 2.0, copyright law seems to be a hurdle laid down in the path of amateur creativity. Governments probably won't remove the hurdle any time soon, but *Minecraft* has shown that, at least in one case, it has been surmountable.

Conclusion

Given the contemporary politics of intellectual property, it is highly doubtful that many governments will make much of an effort to support the growth of amateur creativity, much less the niche realm of amateur creativity in games. Although the growth of Web 2.0 seems to be socially desirable, the threat that is poses to the business models of the traditional entertainment industry is significant. The support of amateur practices, when amateurs engage in remixing, reference, parody and other derivative practices, is also threatening to the coherence and consistent enforcement of intellectual property laws.

While some game companies will make efforts to embrace Web 2.0 in their games and platforms, according users creative leeway may lead to more problems than benefits. A large part of the problem is copyright law, but it is doubtful that companies that depend on intellectual property rights for profits (other than Mojang) will lobby governments or design user tools that operate to weaken the strength of those rights.

Minecraft has succeeded by mining the rich gap in our media between games and tools. It offers players not only something considerably more than a conventional 3-D sketching program, but also something considerably more creative than what most games offer. Persson, inadvertently or not, struck gold by calling on *Minecraft*'s players to collaborate, deeply, in the process of creation (including the creation of the game itself). Millions of amateur creators responded eagerly to this challenge by embracing a game that let them be more than an audience and a little more than players too.

Mojang's dependence on an amateur community makes it a highly unusual success. The game industry is surely studying it carefully now. It seems very likely that other companies will offer new games that tap the creative energies of amateur communities. So while *Minecraft* is a breakthrough at the intersection of amateur creativity and digital games, it remains to be seen how this interesting combination of the marketplace, the agora and the magic circle will evolve.

Acknowledgement

My thanks to Danielle Lapidoth-Berger for helpful comments on an earlier draft.

Notes

1 Henry Jenkins, *Convergence Culture: Where Old and New Media Collide*, New York: New York University Press, 2006, p. 13 (discussing 'delivery technologies').

2 The word 'amateur' originates from the Latin *amator*, or 'lover'.

3 See, e.g., Sal Humphreys, 'The Concepts and Conditions of Governance in Massively Multiplayer Online Games' in Christoph Beat Graber and Mira Burri-Nenova (eds), *Governance of Digital Game Environments and Cultural Diversity: Transdisciplinary Perspectives*, Cheltenham: Edward Elgar, 2010, p. 113; Clay Shirky, *Cognitive Surplus: How Technology Makes Consumers Into Collaborators*, New York: Penguin Press, 2010, p. 19.

4 Mira Burri-Nenova, 'User Created Content in Virtual Worlds and Cultural Diversity' in Graber and Burri-Nenova (eds), *Governance of Digital Game Environments and Cultural Diversity*, p. 74.

5 James Boyle, 'A Politics of Intellectual Property: Environmentalism for the Net' (1997) 47 *Duke Law Journal* 87.

6 Lawrence Lessig, *Remix: Making Art and Commerce Thrive in the Hybrid Economy*, New York: Penguin Press, 2008.

7 Shirky, *Cognitive Surplus*.

8 Jenkins, *Convergence Culture*.

9 Jonathan Zittrain, *The Future of the Internet and How to Stop It*, New Haven, CT, and London: Yale University Press, 2008.

10 Eric von Hippel, *Democratizing Innovation*, Cambridge, MA: MIT Press, 2006.

11 Don Tapscott and Anthony D. Williams, *Wikinomics: How Mass Collaboration Changes Everything*, New York: Penguin Group, 2010 expanded edition.

12 Yochai Benkler, *The Wealth of Networks: How Social Production Transforms Markets and Freedom*, New Haven, CT, and London: Yale University Press, 2007.

13 See, e.g., Dan Hunter and Greg Lastowka, 'Amateur-to-Amateur' (2004) 46 *William and Mary Law Review* 951.

14 Steven Levy, *Hackers: Heroes of the Computer Revolution*, Garden City, NY: Anchor Press/ Doubleday, 1994.

15 Ramon Lobato, Julian Thomas and Dan Hunter, 'Histories of User-Generated Content: Between Formal and Informal Media Economies' (2011) 5 *International Journal of Communication* 899.

16 See Shirky, Cognitive Surplus, 19.

17 Ithiel de Sola Pool, *Technologies of Freedom*, Cambridge, MA: Harvard University Press, 1983, p. 5.

18 Aphra Kerr, '(Girls) Women Just Want to Have Fun: A Study of Adult Female Players of Digital Games' (paper presented at Level Up: Digital Games Research Conference, Utrecht University, 4–6 November 2003).

19 Steven L. Kent, *The Ultimate History of Video Games*, New York: Three Rivers Press, 2001; Aphra Kerr, *The Business and Culture of Digital Games: Gamework and Gameplay*, Sage, 2006, pp. 13–15.

20 Stewart Brand, 'SPACEWAR: Fanatic Life and Symbolic Death among the Computer Bums', *Rolling Stone*, 7 December 1972, p. 50.

21 David Myers, *The Nature of Computer Games: Play as Semiosis*, New York: P. Lang, 2003; Kerr, *The Business and Culture of Digital Games*, pp. 21–41.

22 Espen Aarseth, *Cybertext: Perspectives on Ergodic Literature*, Baltimore, MD: Johns Hopkins University Press, 1997.

23 Espen Aarseth, 'Playing Research: Methodological Approaches to Game Analysis' (2003) 17 *Fine Art Forum* (available at http://hypertext.rmit.edu.au/dac/papers/Aarseth.pdf).

24 Greg Lastowka, *Virtual Justice: The New Laws of Online Worlds*, New Haven, CT, and London: Yale University Press, 2010, pp. 37–43.

25 Nick Montfort and Ian Bogost, *Racing the Beam: The Atari Video Computer System*, Cambridge, MA: MIT Press, 2009, pp. 8–12.

26 Christian Reimsbach-Kounatze and Sacha Wunsch-Vincent, 'Online Games and Virtual Worlds: Business and Policy Developments' in Beat and Burri-Nenova (eds), *Governance of Digital Game Environments and Cultural Diversity*, p.3.

27 Nick Montfort, *Twisty Little Passages: An Approach to Interactive Fiction*, Cambridge, MA: MIT Press, 2003.

28 Hector Postigo, 'Video Game Appropriation Through Modifications' (2008) 14 *Convergence: The International Journal of Research Into New Media Technologies* 59.

29 Kerr, *The Business and Culture of Digital Games*, p. 2.

30 T. L. Taylor, 'Whose Game Is This Anyway? Negotiating Corporate Ownership in a Virtual World' (paper presented at Computer Games and Digital Cultures, Tampere, Finland, 6–8 June 2002) 227; Sal Humphreys, 'Productive Players: Online Computer Games' Challenge to Conventional Media Forms (2005) 2 *Communication and Critical/Cultural Studies* 1; Erez Reuveni, 'Authorship in the Age of the Conducer' (2007) 54 *Journal of the Copyright Society of the USA* 285.

31 T.L. Taylor, *Play Between Worlds: Exploring Online Game Culture*, Cambridge, MA: MIT Press, 2006.

32 Thomas M. Malaby, *Making Virtual Worlds: Linden Lab and Second Life*, Ithica, NY: Cornell University Press, 2009.

33 Lastowka, *Virtual Justice*.

34 Ibid. As Malaby's book *Making Virtual Worlds* explains, however, certain *Second Life* users are more creative than others.

35 See Lastowka, *Virtual Justice*, pp. 192–93.

36 *Portal II* actually does offer users tools for creating new levels, but these tool must be downloaded separately.

37 Mia Consalvo, *Cheating: Gaining Advantage in Videogames*, Cambridge, MA: MIT Press, 2007.

38 Electricpigtv, *Playable Angry Birds Birthday Cake* (20 February 2011) YouTube: www.youtube.com/watch?v=-hwVRzaQNkA.

39 See http://www.minecraft.net/&.

40 See Tim Edwards, 'The Game's Industry's Massive Fail: Where Are All the Minecraft Clones?', *pcgamer.com* (online) 20 September 2011: www.pcgamer.com/2011/09/20/the-game's-industry's-massive-fail-where-are-all-the-minecraft-clones/.

41 See *BlueXephos's Channel*, YouTube: www.youtube.com/user/BlueXephos; *Captain Sparklez's Channel*, YouTube: www.youtube.com/user/CaptainSparklez.

42 See *Massively Minecraft: A Community for Educators*: http://socialmediaclassroom.com/host/MassivelyMinecraft/See Sidsel, *I Feel Free* (2 March 2011) Digital Game Theory: http://digitalgametheory2011.tumblr.com/post/3617136120/i-feel-free.

44 The current game does feature a 'creative mode' where players can build freely without gathering resources, but the original 'canvas' for this mode is still a simulated natural landscape.

45 Andrew Keen, *The Cult of the Amateur: How the Internet is Killing Our Culture*, New York: Doubleday, 2007.

46 Nicholas Carr, *The Shallows: What the Internet Is Doing to Our Brains*, New York: W.W. Norton & Company, 2010.

47 Jaron Lanier, *You Are Not a Gadget: A Manifesto*, New York: Alfred A. Knopf, 2010.

48 Mark Helprin, *Digital Barbarism: A Writer's Manifesto*, New York: HarperCollins, 2009.

49 Cf. Burri-Nenova, 'User Created Content', p. 98 (pointing to the value of 'increased user autonomy, increased participation, and increased diversity').

50 de Sola Pool, *Technologies of Freedom*, 5.

51 Kerr, *The Business and Culture of Digital Games*, p. 1.

52 Aphra Kerr, 'Beyond Billiard Balls: Transnational Flows, Cultural Diversity, and Digital Games' in Graber and Burri-Nenova (eds) *Governance of Digital Game Environments and Cultural Diversity*, p. 47.

53 With some exceptions – parodies, for instance, might be allowed in the United States if they fall within the scope of 'fair use' doctrine.

54 See *Marvel Enterprises v NCSoft*, 74 USPQ 2d 1303 (CD Cal, 2005).

55 *Terms of Use*, Minecraft: www.minecraft.net/terms.

56 Ibid.

57 Ibid.

58 Paul Tassi, 'Minecraft's Notch: "Piracy is Not Theft"', *Forbes* (online) 4 March 2011: www.forbes.com/sites/insertcoin/2011/03/04/minecrafts-notch-piracy-is-not-theft/.

14 Cosplay, creativity and immaterial labours of love

Melissa de Zwart

In June 2011, 7690 people attended the AVCON event in Adelaide, Australia AVCON is a popular culture convention which celebrates all things related to the anime and digital-game genres. A key focus of the two-day event is cosplay, both for competition and merely for the 'lolz' of dressing up and having your photo taken with a range of other people in costume. Although it is impossible to measure, it appears to the casual observer that the majority of people attending AVCON attend in costume, and although no official rules apply (excepting those relating to nudity and the safety of weaponry), not just any costume will do. Costumes must relate to Japanese culture, anime, manga or computer games, with some concessions to the sci-fi genre at large.

The Adelaide experience is not unique. Cosplay competitions are a growing phenomenon across Australia, the US, Europe and of course Asia. Cosplay originated in Japan and still focuses predominantly on Japanese culture. Thus it reflects and generates some of the issues related to Japanese culture generally, such as portrayal of women, sexual and violent content.[1] Interestingly there is significant inter-city rivalry between the various conventions hosted in each Australian capital city, and also a significant number of people who attend one or more conventions outside their home state. Participation in cosplay, like many other manifestations of amateur creativity, can be both time consuming and expensive.

This comment will consider the importance of cosplay as an exemplar of user-generated content emanating from digital games. In particular, it will address similar themes to those raised by Greg Lastowka in his chapter, namely the consideration of the importance of user interactivity and the level of immersion of users in game culture.

Cosplay is a perfect manifestation of amateur creativity, as despite the proliferation of online commercial cosplay producers, only those who have made their costume themselves may enter the competitions. It involves key elements of user-generated content (being the costume and the accompanying skit or dance), the ambivalent legal relationship to the intellectual property owner, the willingness and desire to share the content with other creators and the social element. Whilst cosplay is not a manifestation of Web 2.0

creativity, the ability to share, discuss and network using Web 2.0 platforms has been essential to the flourishing of cosplay in Australia. Although, as Norris and Bainbridge highlight, mainstream and niche retailers have been essential in providing consumers with local access to content and fuelling their desire for more.[2]

What is cosplay?

Cosplay is a portmanteau word from 'costume' and 'play'. Actually coined in Japan, despite the use of these two English words, the term refers to dressing up and acting as a character from manga, anime or a digital game. As Norris and Bainbridge note, the word 'play' is crucial to the definition, as cosplay goes beyond merely dressing up in an often very elaborate costume, and involves play with race, age and gender.[3] Cosplayers are expected to act in character at all times when dressed in their costume. As Duchesne notes: 'the audience expects effort and passion from the performers and rewards them for creativity and commitment.'[4]

Cosplay is important as a 'portal' into the digital-game environment, reflecting both the importance to fans of engaging deeper with their game platform of choice. However, it also serves as an alternative arena for players to express their mastery and skill. This accessibility explains the popularity of cosplay both in Japan and in the countries to which this essentially Japanese pastime has migrated. As Hjorth notes: 'In order to understand why cosplaying has become a vehicle for young females to enter the male-dominated games industry we need to comprehend how gender within Japanese technocultures provides alternative spaces for perform-ativity, creativity and expression.'[5] In particular, cosplay enables players to transcend the more commonly known 'otaku' stereotype of the geek, loner male.[6]

Cosplay then enables players, new and old, proficient, excellent or merely fans, to engage with the text of the game, transforming the passive player to the participatory prosumer.[7] First-time cosplayers are always identified and applauded at AVCON and there is a strict 'no heckling' rule during all cosplay parades. It is an excellent example of Henry Jenkins's 'active' and participatory fan.[8] It is also an active demonstration by the cosplayer that they have achieved some mastery or control over the game. It involves both consumption and performance.[9]

Beyond this, cosplay also allows socialisation in a game-related context outside of the game. In fact, socialisation is a key function of cosplay. Socia-lisation occurs between cosplayers, but any competition of course also requires an appreciative audience.[10] Players or users dress up as the avatar and, in this character, interact with others at the convention. Thus cosplay, like the play-ers' response to Minecraft discussed by Lastowka, reflects another way in which digital content may be actively and socially used in order to be actively consumed, rather than passively absorbed.[11]

Amateur creativity

Two key questions arise at this point:

- Do cosplayers challenge or reinforce the dominant narrative of the game?
- How do we characterise cosplay as part of the commercialisation of the game?

Responses to these issues will be discussed in the next two sections of this comment.

Cosplay is, like many aspects of amateur creativity, a merger of commercial and personal interests.[12] It is essential, in order for the cosplay to work, that the costume appears as authentic and recognisable as possible. Therefore, it could be said that the message conveyed by the cosplayer is pure homage. However, this would be to misunderstand the subversive element of cosplay. Several authors stress that the 'play' element of cosplay facilitates cross-dressing, subversion of the dominant narrative and experimentation with gender stereotypes.[13]

Norris and Bainbridge argue that cosplay can be more disruptive than other forms of 'dressing up'.[14] One aspect of this disruption is the avenue it provides for exploration of gender. Cosplay provides a reason for teenage boys to dress up in highly stylised costumes. Outside of this context it is difficult to imagine any other environments where so many teenage boys would be prepared to parade around in costumes. The link to gaming prowess and the warrior-like nature of the costumes may certainly help.[15] However, gender performance is freely accepted in the cosplay world.[16] For example, bishōnen, highly feminised male characters, are popular in Japanese manga. Ouran High School Host Club, a very popular manga and now anime series, specifically plays upon gender ambiguity, by having a girl as its main protagonist, who is initiated as one of the 'hosts' due to her boyish appearance. Each of the other (male) hosts reflects a specific 'shōjo' style to appeal to a broad range of readers.[17] For this reason, the Ouran High School Host Club is a popular focus for groups of male and female cosplayers. A very popular manga which has also been picked up as a favourite of cosplayers is Ikeda Riyoko's the Rose of Versailles, which focuses on the adventures (romantic and otherwise) of Lady Oscar, who was raised as a man. Oscar attracts the romantic interest of males and females alike and provides the cosplayer with the capacity to explore gender differences through one character, but multiple costumes.

Sara Gwenllian Jones observes that 'fandom needs to be understood as a liminal, fetishistic and highly engaged consumer culture that is both born of and fully implicated in the cultural processes it supposedly "resists"'.[18] By adopting and experimenting with these forms, cosplayers gain ownership of the cultural properties they reflect, embrace and embody.

Free labour

The enthusiastic take up of cosplay in countries outside of Japan reflects the successful export of Japanese media culture. Cosplay events frequently take place in conjunction with celebrations of Japanese food and culture. Hjorth's study of Melbourne female cosplayers highlights the interest of cosplayers in broadening their understanding of the Japanese language and culture. However, the unlicensed reproduction of costumes, images and music from the games and anime of choice of course represents a challenge to the intellectual property owner.[19] By the same token, as a popular and pre-digested version of these cultural products, cosplay may also be said to serve as a marketing device for the items they present. Many fans will be encouraged to expand their consumption of certain manga, anime or game on the basis of seeing it portrayed in a cool cosplay.

The creation of a costume is likely to reflect a significant investment of love and labour. The costume thus embodies – like most pieces of fan art such as fan fiction, machinima and even computer-game mods – an investment of time, energy and emotion. Cosplayers will be flattered by requests to take their photo and to pose for group shots that might combine groups of players from the same or very different games, manga or anime. It is possible that many of these cultural items would not have been promoted to western audiences outside the cosplay context.

Duchesne explores the interesting phenomenon of cosplayers actually serving as promotional devices for the corporate owners of the cultural property. In the absence of the real stars of a film (or game, etc.) people will seek to have their photo taken with the most 'authentic' looking cosplayer.[20] This becomes even more relevant in the context of characters from games, where the human, in a strange reversal of fate, becomes the embodiment of the avatar.

Ownership and control

So what is the interest of the intellectual property owner in regulating or controlling cosplay? Whilst at one end of the spectrum the intellectual property owner may appear to at least have an interest in the costume market, true cosplayers make their own costumes, so this would appear at best to be a small ancillary market. Any attempt to restrict players' abilities to make their own costumes through the control of intellectual property rights would be counter to encouraging the further uptake of the character, restricting the free advertising generated by cosplay events.

Certainly in a genre that is seeking to develop its market share, it appears that intellectual property owners are prepared to support cosplay competitions. Madman Entertainment, a major Australian niche provider of Japanese content, including manga and anime, sponsors several cosplay competitions, including sending the winner from an Australia-wide competition to compete in Japan.[21]

There has been little litigation with respect to copyright in characters, and more importantly in this context, the physical appearance of characters, divorced from their context or storyline.[22]

The recent case brought by *Star Wars* creator George Lucas in the UK Supreme Court against designer Andrew Ainsworth with respect to his manufacture and distribution of Stormtrooper helmets provides an interesting case study. Whilst successful in a copyright infringement in the US, Lucas had pursued Ainsworth through the UK courts, in order to enforce the US judgment and to establish Ainsworth's liability under UK law. Lucas had been unsuccessful in the copyright claim under UK law at first instance and on appeal to Court of Appeal.[23] The Court held that the helmet was not a sculpture but rather a utilitarian object.[24] The Court confirmed the opinions expressed in the lower courts regarding the nature and function of the helmets, concluding that 'the helmets are there as (in the judge's words) "a mixture of costume and prop" in order to contribute to the artistic effect of the film as a film'.[25] Lord Walker and Lord Collins concluded: 'it was the *Star Wars* film that was the work of art that Mr Lucas and his companies created. The helmet was utilitarian in the sense that it was an element in the process of the production of the film.'[26]

Another example is the litigation threatened, but ultimately settled, between Marvel Enterprises, the owners of intellectual property rights in a range of well-known superheroes including Captain America, Spiderman, the Incredible Hulk, Iron Man and Wolverine, and NCSoft, the creators of the superhero/supervillain MMOG City of Heroes. Marvel claimed, that through the provision of customisable characters, NCSoft was authorising players to infringe copyright in Marvel's characters.[27] Essentially Marvel claimed that NCSoft was facilitating the creation of infringing avatar costumes and that it was deriving a financial benefit from those infringements. The District Court refused to grant NCSoft a motion to dismiss the infringement claim, and appeared to accept that it was possible that the avatar costumes may infringe Marvel's intellectual property rights.[28] However the matter was settled on undisclosed terms, possibly in part due to allegations that Marvel employees had created the allegedly infringing avatars.[29]

An alternative mechanism for looking at cosplay in the copyright context is of course as parody. Under Australian copyright law, users are permitted to make a fair dealing with a literary, dramatic, musical or artistic work, 'if it is for the purpose of parody or satire.'[30] It is uncertain though, that the majority of uses would constitute parody or satire in a strict sense. Rauch and Bolton note that '[l]ike fan fiction and dōjinshi parodies, cosplay is part of the feedback loop that allows fans to enter into a text and transform it, turning readers into authors and blurring the distinction between fan and critic, as well as reader and text.'[31] Such interaction is unlikely to be recognised as a parody of the target work.

Conclusions

So, ultimately, what is the value of cosplay as amateur creativity? Does it add to our understanding of user interaction with digital games?

As noted by Lastowka, Henry Jenkins and others have argued that user-generated content allows the audience to engage with, critique and become involved in the subject matter of popular culture. This participation, it is argued, facilitates engagement that goes beyond mere passive reception, and thus allows the UGC creator to feed back into the creative process. Cosplay reflects another way in which digital worlds may be actively and socially used in order to be consumed.[32]

The extension of participatory media characterised by Web 2.0, which as Lastowka indicates is one where 'former audiences assume significant agency in content creation and distribution', is embraced by cosplayers. Drawing their inspiration from print-based, video- and digital-game platforms, cosplayers rework and perform their chosen characters in the convention domain and then feed back those performances into Web 2.0 platforms by posting photographs and video to Facebook, Twitter, fan forums, YouTube, deviantART and Flickr.[33] These contributions can then be further distributed, remixed, commented upon and used as inspiration for new cosplayers.

Further, the organisation and promotion of cosplay events relies significantly on Web 2.0 platforms. Drawing largely on volunteer labour, events are planned and advertised online. Pre- and post-event discussion on dedicated lists hosted on services such as Facebook encourage the sense of community. Like much immaterial labour, it is dependent upon distributed networks and significant amounts of unpaid labour. The practice of cosplay thus exemplifies the importance of the relationship between the development and maintenance of social networks and amateur creativity.[34]

Therefore the creative labour of cosplayers reflects a deep connection with the text or the game and also the contribution of a significant amount of intellectual capital which benefits the cosplayer, through a sense of achievement and engagement, and the intellectual property owner through the exposure (and implicit endorsement) of the text to the market. It also engenders customer loyalty by embedding that text in the minds of the audience. As Lastowka concludes with respect to games, it is unlikely that copyright laws will be rewritten to clearly accommodate such creativity, but it is important that such uses be respected as non-commercial, creative embodiments of the immaterial labour facilitated by Web 2.0.

Notes

1 For a further discussion of these issues, see Melissa de Zwart, 'Japanese Lessons: What Can Otaku Teach Us About Copyright and Gothic Girls?' (2010) 35(1) *Alternative Law Journal* 27; Mark McLelland, 'No Climax, No Point, No Meaning? Japanese Women's Boy-Love Sites on the Internet' (2000) 24(3) *Journal of Communication Inquiry* 274; Mark McLelland, 'The World of Yaoi: The Internet, Censorship and the Global "Boy's Love" Fandom' (2005) 23 *Australian Feminist Law Journal* 61.

2 Craig Norris and Jason Bainbridge, 'Selling Otaku? Mapping the Relationship between Industry and Fandom in the Australian Cosplay Scene' (2009) 20 *Intersections: Gender and Sexuality in Asia and the Pacific* 1.

3 Ibid.

4 Scott Duchesne, 'Stardom/Fandom: Celebrity and Fan Tribute Performance' (2010) 141 *Canadian Theatre Review* 21, 24.

5 Larissa Hjorth, 'Game Girl: Re-imagining Japanese Gender and Gaming via Melbourne Female Cosplayers' (2009) 20 *Intersections: Gender and Sexuality in Asia and the Pacific*: intersections.anu.edu.au/issue20/hjorth.htm [4].

6 For a discussion of the evolution of the otaku stereotype, see, de Zwart, 'Japanese Lessons'; Sharon Kinsella, 'Japanese Subculture in the 1990s: Otaku and the Amateur Manga Movement' (1998) 24 *Journal of Japanese Studies* 289; and Alisa Freedman, 'Train Man and the Gender Politics of Japanese "Otaku" Culture: The Rise of New Media, Nerd Heroes and Consumer Communities' (2009) 20 *Intersections: Gender and Sexuality in Asia and the Pacific*: http://intersections.anu.edu.au/issue20/freedman.htm.

7 See Greg Lastowka, '*Minecraft* as Web 2.0: Amateur creativity and digital games', in this volume. See also Greg Lastowka, 'User Generated Content & Virtual Worlds' (2008) 10 *Vanderbilt Journal of Entertainment and Technology Law* 893; and Dan Hunter and Greg Lastowka, 'Amateur-to-Amateur' (2004) 46 *William & Mary Law Review* 951.

8 Henry Jenkins, *Textual Poachers, Television Fans and Participatory Culture*, New York: Routledge, 1992; Henry Jenkins, *Convergence Culture: Where Old and New Media Collide*, New York: New York University Press, 2006.

9 Mizuko Ito, 'Mobilizing the Imagination in Everyday Play: The Case of Japanese Media Mixes' in Stefan Sonvilla-Weiss (ed.), *Mashup Cultures*, Vienna and New York: Springer, 2010, p. 79.

10 Theresa Winge, 'Costuming the Imagination: Origins of Anime and Manga Cosplay' (2006) 1 *Mechademia* 65, 68–69.

11 See Lastowka, 'User Generated Content'.

12 Scott Duchesne, 'Stardom/Fandom'.

13 See, for example, Hjorth, 'Game Girl'; and Winge, 'Costuming the Imagination'.

14 Norris and Bainbridge, 'Selling Otaku?'.

15 Popular cosplays include, for example, characters from the *Final Fantasy* range of games, *Naruto, Deus Ex, Neon Genesis Evangalion*, and *Bioshock*, as well as a host of other games, manga and anime.

16 For a discussion as gender as a performance, see Judith Butler, *Gender Trouble: Feminism and the Subversion of Identity*, New York and London: Routledge, 1990, p. 177.

17 'Shōjo' means manga marketed directly at girls between the ages of ten and eighteen, but the term is frequently used to refer to all female-oriented manga. See further Matt Thorn, 'Shôjo Manga—Something for the Girls' (2001) 48 *The Japan Quarterly* 43.

18 Sara Gwenllian Jones, 'Web Wars: Resistance, Online Fandom and Studio Censorship' in Mark Jancovich and James Lyons (ed.), *Quality Popular Television, Cult TV, The Industry and Fans*, London: British Film Institute, 2003, p. 165. See also Mark Deuze, 'Convergence Culture in the Creative Industries' (2007) 10 *International Journal of Cultural Studies* 243.

19 Koichi Iwabuchi, 'Undoing Inter-national Fandom in the Age of Brand Nationalism' (2010) 5 *Mechademia* 87.

20 Duchesne describes the Fan Expo Canada Masquerade (a space for costumed fan performance with prizes awarded in various categories) at which a fan dressed and acting as Heath Ledger's Joker (from *The Dark Knight*) took the place of the recently deceased Ledger: 'With the absence of the star, Entry #56's FTP [Fan Tribute Performance] functioned as a symbolic "form of capital" that created social and economic profit at the convention': Duchesne, 'Stardom/Fandom', 24.

21 Norris and Bainbridge, 'Selling Otaku?'

22 For an extended analysis of copyright in characters in the game context, see Melissa de Zwart, 'Angel(us) is my Avatar! An Exploration of Avatar Identity in the Guise of the Vampire' (2010) 15 *Media & Arts Law Review* 318.

23 *Lucasfilm Ltd v Ainsworth* [2008] EWHC 1878 (Ch); [2009] FSR 103; and [2009] EWCA Civ 1328; [2010] Ch 503.

24 *Lucasfilm Limited and others v Ainsworth and another* [2011] UKSC 39 (27 July 2011).

25 Ibid., at [43].

26 Ibid., at [44]. The Court did however allow the appeal on the question of justiciability of the US copyright claims in the UK.

27 *Marvel Enterprises v NCSoft*, 74 USPQ 2d 1303 (CD Cal, 2005).

28 Greg Lastowka, *Virtual Justice: The New Laws of Online Worlds,* New Haven, CT, and London: Yale University Press, 2010, pp. 166–68.

29 See further, de Zwart, 'Angel(us) is my Avatar!', 338–39.

30 See *Copyright Act 1968* (Cth) s 41A, and s 103AA which deals with audiovisual material.

31 Eron Rauch and Christopher Bolton, 'A Cosplay Photography Sampler' (2010) 5 *Mechademia* 176, 177.

32 See Lastowka, 'User Generated Content'.

33 See, e.g., *Manifest*, Facebook: www.facebook.com/MelbourneAnimeFestival; *AVCon: Adelaide's Anime and Video Games Convention*, Facebook: www.facebook.com/TeamAVCon>; *AVCon 2011 – Official Cosplay Pic Thread*: https://avcon.org.au/forum/showthread.php?550-Avcon-2011-Official-Cosplay-Pic-Thread (all accessed 17 October 2011).

34 Mark Coté and Jennifer Pybus, 'Learning to Immaterial Labour 2.0: MySpace and Social Networks' (2007) 7(1) *Ephemera* 88, 89. For a further analysis of affective and immaterial labour, see Michael Hardt and Antonio Negri, *Multitude: War and Democracy in the Age of Empire*, London: Penguin, 2005. Hardt and Negri define affective labour as 'labour that produces or manipulates affects such as a feeling of ease, well-being, satisfaction, excitement or passion' (at p. 108). Discussion of immaterial labour in the digital game context can be found in Greig de Peuter and Nick Dyer-Witheford 'A Playful Multitude? Mobilising and Counter-Mobilising Immaterial Game Labour' (2005) 5 *Fibreculture*: www.fibreculture. org/journal/issue5/depeuter_dyerwitheford.html.

15 Web Zero

The amateur and the indie-game developer

Christian McCrea

Amateur economies loom large in video-game production; in fact, the category of the 'indie' or independent developer/company more accurately reflects the economic and creative structures of the games industry as a whole. Success is hard to measure even in base economic terms, as games production is built around highly idiosyncratic funding structures and extremely volatile labour markets. In his contribution to this book, Greg Lastowka examines the success of *Minecraft*, a game funded largely by its development team, and which had sold four million copies (at €10–15 each) before it had even officially been released. *Minecraft* is a crucial moment in the independent games sector because its outsized success coincides with vast changes at the peak of commercial production. The pressures that are dismantling the models of games funding and production – such as the changes brought about by the Apple App Store and Web 2.0 phenomena – can be assumed to be the source of great opportunities for 'indies'. However, in game development the distinctions between amateurs and professionals, and between independents and professional developers, are highly idiosyncratic. While the independent and the professional developer are blurring roles in some senses, the amateur-game developer and the independent-game developer are increasingly distinct, a division which might be instructive in looking at other media sectors. In this chapter, I take a closer look at these co-dependent relations in game development, with specific reference to two earlier games that played a pivotal role in the *Minecraft* success story: *Infiniminer* and *Dwarf Fortress*.

What makes games so crucial in understanding contemporary amateur cultural production is that wholesale resistance to some of these changes can also provide opportunities. Commercial and independent games have flourished in the new gated publishing environment of the App Store. However, the social media games sector is dominated by Facebook games such as *Farmville* and *Cityville*, run by companies which are new to the games sector and employing addiction techniques which are considered, at best, gauche. It is fashionable, and highly profitable, to resist the shift to social games and represent a hardcore, intensive game-design philosophy. Players, too, benefit from a culture of taste and distinction in which innovation of different kinds flourishes as a response to the commercialised (and ironically often financially precarious) mainstream industry. At the centre of Lastowka's engagement is the blurry middle ground between *Minecraft* players and producers. The game is emblematic of the changes across the sector, but also of its rich history and legacy in focusing on audience creativity.

Kenji Ito's 2007 essay 'Possibility of Non-Commercial Games: The Case of Amateur Games Designers in Japan' describes the role a particular program – RPG Tkool 2000 by Enterbrain, Inc – in the continuance of the amateur-game-design space in Japan. An intricate lineage of magazines, subcultures, discussion forums, early web bulletin boards and software development is outlined in which game players exist on a spectrum of creativity and technical skill.[1] Dabbling in the production of games is natural in these contexts, where playing with games means playing with software. In turn, this means that expert players often become fans who have special knowledge of the production process, and then eventually grow interested in taking their play-ing habits into a new hobby of game design and development. Ito notes that in the Japanese context, 'while motivations vary, but as long as creating a game is not technically too challenging, gamers report ample reasons to devote their time and enjoy doing it without seeking material compensation.'[2]

The software Tkool 2000 (and its precedents and antecedents) allowed a particular set of subcultures to emerge around particular sets of amateur-game design. But crucially, Ito highlights that amateur-game design is by and large the norm by which game development occurs, and out of which commercial-game production continually emerges, reacts and shifts. Market economics of course dictate that the large production capacity of major game publishers will dominate, but throughout the history of computer games, amateur designers and developers have existed alongside that industry. It is important to note that in the case of particular game genres, the amateur is not replicated by commercial entities. For example, the 'bullet hell' or 'bullet curtain' shooter genre – the top-down two-dimensional shooters that usually feature flying planes, bullets and enemies – have become a completely closed and fervent niche. With no viable commercial market, they are pursued only by small teams or individual developers. This point is echoed by Olli Sotamaa, who notes that it becomes difficult to make meaningful distinctions between player and producer, even within the same software environment or gamer subculture.[3]

Amateur-game production is often seen as a historical quirk; an acknowledge-ment that early game development culture was chaotic and diverse and has slowly been commercialised, alongside which a trace of the original amateur production ethos exists. However, many of the market structures that under-pin this distinction are being radically inverted by recent changes to digital culture. Surprisingly, it is not merely the broad phenomena of Web 2.0 that is driving the changes. If games are not often part of the discussion of Web 2.0 phenomena, it is because the games industry and culture are undergoing vast shifts of their own which tempt us to make connections to the broader chan-ges online and throughout technology culture. These changes are distinct and, importantly, at least partially antithetical to the common understanding of the social media paradigm. Games have an amateur dimension spanning the spectrum from player to developer; but this dimension has several and distinct intersections.

First, the traditional games market is splintering underneath enormous pressures both internal and external. Spiralling development costs and poorly managed speculative game-publishing practices have built a boom–bust cycle that turns over companies, which in turn is constantly disrupting or ending the careers of developers. Parts of the game-publishing business are dysfunctional by any measure; publishers fund expensive development in a hostile and volatile consumer landscape, reliant on hardware changes that need to be expertly managed on a global scale. In response, top-tier games are routinely released with post-release paid content in mind, known as DLC (downloadable content). Depending on the game, this can be episodic single-player segments, paid multiplayer systems, online passes meant to extract a little more from those who bought the game second hand, game variants such as options or items, or purely cosmetic changes such as character costumes.

Second, the Apple App Store for iPhone and iPad, while only lightly cannibalising previously measured consumer spending in games, figures heavily in the planning of contemporary game development. While *Angry Birds* by Rovio sells for as little as a chocolate bar, much of the rest of the industry is entirely reliant on expensive packaged goods and marquee digital downloads. Mobile-game development (or more accurately, App Store and Android game development) intersects with the epiphenomena of 'social games'. This describes first and foremost a specific type of game played through or in concert with social networks. The most famous examples would be *FarmVille* and *CityVille* by Zynga Games and *The Sims Social* by EA/Playfish. The most important attribute of these games is their utterly addictive and abusive payment systems, where game progress is continually impeded until further payment is made. Social games can also refer to a wide range of digital and non-digital games, but in practice, it is this abusive/addictive game design which is the foremost feature of social games.

If Web 2.0 has impacted games, it is along these pressure lines. However, it is crucial to understand that these changes are fragments of a vast and complexly changing picture that includes a precarious global industry and volatile commercial forces. For traditional game developers and players, Web 2.0 is most accurately described as an existential threat, not an emerging trend along which one is willingly swept. It represents, through games like *CityVille*, a virulently destructive force that diverts player time, money and corporate position from traditional games developers and creators.

Greg Lastowka's chapter connects the phenomena of indie games and the broader circles of cultural and community formation around games. *Minecraft* is situated as a pivotal example of the broader changes in web and digital culture, amateur engagements and game production. For Lastowka, the way in which *Minecraft* players build community relationships, and the fact that the game is wildly successful, naturally feeds into an inquiry about how it might interrelate with Web 2.0 phenomena. The success of the game can illuminate a great deal about amateur and indie creativity within games production.

However, that illumination is only partial without a consideration of the game's peculiar history and place in recent indie-game development, since *Minecraft* exists in relationship to two games that are utterly niche, but without which the game's development would have been absolutely impossible. First, *Infiniminer*, a very similar-looking mining and creating game. Second, *Dwarf Fortress*, an incredibly rich text interface (where regular text characters are used to represent environments and objects, or what is sometimes called 'ASCII style', after the text encoding system of the same name). *Infiniminer* is the product of a single developer, Zachary Barth, who has since become known for a series of highly complex puzzle games which use Rube Goldberg-esque physics and complex visual modelling. *Infiniminer* uses randomly generated environments made of cubes on a grid, and puts rare blocks below ground. The game was never completed, but allowed players to find and 'mine' the rare blocks to build structures. *Dwarf Fortress* – played within this highly unusual text character interface – uses randomly generated environments and gameplay, allowing players to send several characters to perform simple tasks and set up contraptions, defences and living quarters. The minor success of these games not only inspired the design of *Minecraft*, but the latter game was also able to use its passionate fan bases as a launching point for the long and public development process. However, it is *Infiniminer* and *Dwarf Fortress* – not *Minecraft* – that represent the amateur component in this history. *Minecraft*, in fact, is the commercialisation of their amateur innovation.

In the 2009 article 'The Independent Production of Culture: A Digital Games Case Study', Chase Bowen Martin and Mark Deuze describe the peculiar history of independence in games as 'something quite different from what the literature on independent, alternative, oppositional, radical, or otherwise nonmainstream media tends to suggest or advocate'.[4] Using a sociological outline, Martin and Deuze propose that independence in games was concerned with the production of culture and the inhabiting of social position much more than it was about economic relationships. Their model sought to examine how indie-game development and identity emerges out of, not despite, the structuring elements of the industry. These elements, which they identify as 'technology', 'laws and regulation', 'industry structure', 'organizational structure', 'occupational careers' and 'the market', all proposed a complex set of opportunities from a spectrum of corporate, out-sourced, minor contract and truly independent work.[5] The unique organisational structures of game-publishing companies, who seek games to finance across cost and platform types, allows companies to describe themselves as independent even as they produce highly successful corporate products set out in contracts. The differentiators between commercial and independent are more often about stylistic choice, the romance of precarious unfinanced production and claims to authenticity.

Crucially, Martin and Deuze argue the following:

> With an increasing prevalence of digital distribution of free SDKs [software development kits], the design of games with built-in level editors and other customization tools, and social networks becoming incorporated into games and game production itself, it is difficult to draw effective lines between what is production or consumption in gamework. What is specifically interesting here is the way that indie games serve their audience, not just as providers of entertainment experiences but also as call to engagement with (and a professed loyalty to) a specific cultural identity.[6]

Andreas Jahn-Sudmann remarked in 'Innovation NOT Opposition: The Logic of Distinction of Independent Games' (2008) on the crucial fact that independent games are the source of gameplay innovation, sound innovation and visual innovation that the commercial industry cannot produce.[7] Jahn-Sudmann then adds that many independent-category games constitute a kind of ongoing critique of the mainstream commercial industry, reacting to the pursuit of visual spectacle and the closing off of interactivity in favour of cinematic excess with another culture entirely – difficult, intricate games requiring pre-existing knowledge and building/referencing lineages far outside the commercial paradigm. The 'specific cultural identity' in question here is highly negotiated, but certainly one marked by an embodied discomfort with commercial-game structures, and a celebration of older complex game types. This identity is a taste category inhabited by a spectrum of positions.

'Amateur-game developers' is a useful category once released from the need to describe amateur games in turn. The amateur-game producer may be best understood as the producer of game content regardless of the taste categories at stake, and produced without over-determined market position. *Infiniminer* is by all means an amateur game; a prototype released, explored and then discontinued. It embodies the prototype model of software development that is so crucial to game-development culture. It may also be considered an 'indie' game in retrospect because of its antecedent relationship to *Minecraft*. *Dwarf Fortress* is made by people who exist outside the commercial structures of industry, but again it is less useful to describe its production as 'amateur'. In fact, it is more complex and allows for rich articulated gameplay that, while lacking the visual flair of commercial titles, constitutes a product that outclasses the bulk of commercial games in interactive quality terms. Though there are certainly hundreds of thousands of amateur games released every year, the lines of production can be so blurred as to make the distinction meaningless. Rather, it is more accurate to speak of an independent economy (of which amateur-game developers are a part).

Beyond games-specific discourse, however, it becomes entirely possible to discuss a game such as *Minecraft* in terms of amateur economies. Players, not producers, embody the amateur position. Mastery of the *Minecraft* toolset, which may take a dozen hours or so, quickly gives way to a more freeform style of play in which construction of buildings, terraforming and exploration of cave systems become the norm of play. One of the key factors in the sudden growth of the game is the use of the same random world generation principles as *Infiniminer* and *Dwarf Fortress*. Players can enter text or numbers into a 'World Seed' entry field before starting the game – for example, the text 'Gekko Farm' – and *Minecraft* will generate the same world for two players, even as their play is offline. This allows a player to find interesting landscapes and share the World Seed with friends who can then explore the same landscape, even as the two games are perfectly separate. This has led to huge numbers of World Seed sites, video collections and trading communities. Lastowka analyses these opportunities for players to communicate with each other as exemplifying Web 2.0 phenomena; social relations built upon aggregate networks.

Given the idiosyncrasies of the 'indie'-game environment, we might also consider that many of these relationships are occurring in response to, rather than as a result of, Web 2.0 phenomena. For example, *Minecraft* has zero identity-specific social features, and its multiplayer function is organised by a simple IP address entry field. That is, players have to go outside of the games, find the address of a *Minecraft* server hosted somewhere, and type in the numbers themselves. More modern and conventional ways of allowing players to play online would be possible, so this archaic model is clearly by design. This IP address system, however, is reminiscent of early internet-enabled games that would require no small degree of technical knowledge to connect and play properly. Lastowka importantly remarks that 'the website of the game features rather clunky text and graphics and looks like a throwback to Web of the 1990s'. It is, of course, intended as such – as *Minecraft* embodies the indie category of reply, resistance and rejection of contemporary games culture.

If that contemporary games culture is heavily suffused with the contemporary culture of the web, diffuse social networks and identity practices, then *Minecraft* is notable for what it doesn't include, for the ways in which it defies contemporary purpose-driven software culture. It is possible to describe software that rejects or confronts the contemporary social media paradigm as a kind of 'Web Zero', rather than a throwback to the 1990s. *Minecraft* and games like it distinguish themselves by remaining resolutely modern, while drawing on their rich game-specific history. *Minecraft* is a success because it speaks to nostalgia about what has been lost in contemporary-game design, and wraps its experience in the tropes of older games. Yet at its core, it is an innovation built on the technical and stylistic ground of earlier games in a very recent and creative niche.

The category of the amateur is incredibly important in games development. Amateur-game developers and hobbyists form a huge international college of peers for those looking to transition into independent production. From the outside, this distinction may seem slight, but it defines contemporary games production.

In turn, independent games are a category of taste more than they are a category of economics. With commercial-game production so volatile and hit-driven, independent games are a more convincing and holistic long-term view of the production model of video games. This inversion has now become culturally self-aware; people who self-identify as 'gamers' will support independent games as a response to their own history with commercial products. This is perhaps a very traditional view of taste and distinction, but it is having a very unique impact in games culture. Just as the App Store, Facebook and other Web 2.0 phenomena overturn the opportunities and economics of game development, independent-game development continues to deploy and develop on its own trajectories. Independence may now mean selling directly to consumers, but in practice the authority of the independent game is in its culture – often, an elegant nostalgia while expressing current technology.

Notes

1 Kenji Ito, 'Possibilities of Non-Commercial Games: The Case of Amateur Role-Playing Game Designers in Japan' in Suzanne de Castell and Jennifer Jenson (eds), *Worlds in Play: International Perspectives on Digital Games Research*, New York: Peter Lang Publishing, 2007, p. 129.
2 Ibid., p. 135.
3 Olli Sotamaa, 'Who's Game Is This Anyway? Creative User-centred Design Practices among Gaming Cultures' (paper presented at The Good, the Bad and the Irrelevant: The User and the Future of Information and Communication Technologies', Uiah, Helsinki, 1–3 September 2003) pp. 257–59. See also Leslie Haddon's chapter in this edited collection ('What is Innovatory Use? A Thinkpiece', ibid., pp. 99–102), which addresses the role of innovation in the home and as a leisure practice.
4 Chase Bowen Martin and Mark Deuze, 'The Independent Production of Culture: A Digital Games Case Study' (2009) 4 *Games and Culture* 276.
5 Ibid., 279.
6 Ibid., 291.
7 Andreas Jahn-Sudmann, 'Innovation Not Opposition: The Logic of Distinction of Independent Games' (2008) 2 *Eludamos: Journal for Computer Game Culture* 5.

Part VI

Anonymity, identity and publicity

16 Anonymous speech on the internet

Brian Murchison

Introduction

The US legal community is engaged in a serious but inconclusive dialogue on issues relating to anonymous speech on the internet. To be sure, several basic questions relevant to internet speech have been settled: in a 1997 case, the Supreme Court determined that strict scrutiny applies to internet content regulation,[1] and in a 1995 case, the Court recognised a First Amendment right of anonymous speech.[2] Yet the 1995 case did not arise in an internet setting, and the scope of expressive freedom in certain internet scenarios remains disputed. Over the past ten years, courts and commentators have grappled with anonymous blogging cases, proposing a spectrum of legal standards for pretrial discovery of bloggers' identities.[3] As experience accumulates, this legal doctrine should stabilise, and doctrine affecting related issues should emerge as well. This chapter argues that the stabilising process will depend on clear analysis of the relevant First Amendment value. The truth-seeking value should guide the formulation of rules for anonymous internet speech.

Such rules are increasingly necessary as the internet becomes society's central pathway of communication and harms arising from that pathway become common. Part of the challenge for courts may be the dazzling variety of creators, receivers and subjects of anonymous speech. Can a jurisprudence develop that fairly accommodates this diversity? The anonymous speakers in recent high-profile US cases include a voter accusing an elected official of paranoia; a fashion student impugning the sexual morals of a *Vogue* model; jurors blogging about an ongoing trial or revealing later how jurors deliberated; a college student berating her home town for its conventionality and prejudice; a public employee blogging about the failings and stresses of government. These speakers hardly fit the negative stereotype of the pyjama-clad blogger/podcaster vapidly flooding the web with talk, neither do they precisely conform to the positive image of the citizen journalist dutifully relaying facts that mainstream media have ignored. Perhaps the only generalisation that can apply to such speakers is that they are amateurs – in the sense of being new to public or semi-public participation, perhaps not anticipating the potential audience and impact of a posted comment or observation, and certainly lacking the experience necessary to avoid litigation.[4] Like budding tennis players over-hitting the ball, at least some anonymous web participants enter the vibrant new market of ideas with rackets swinging and slicing at full strength, only to find themselves accused of defamation, invasion of privacy, breach of confidence, infliction of emotional distress, or other wrongs.

In the US, the thrust of discussion has been that legal rules for this developing area must protect the participatory impulse yet allow for at least a measure of accountability. In reflecting on what that measure should be, this chapter examines three scenarios. The first is the most familiar: a party believes that an anonymous blogger has defamed or otherwise injured him, but the party cannot pursue a tort claim because he does not know the blogger's identity. The legal task is to formulate a test for obtaining a judicial order that would force a website or internet service provider to disclose the blogger's identity and thus enable the plaintiff to bring his claim.

The second scenario is less familiar but flows from the test applicable to the first. Since that test is likely to be highly speech protective, the second scenario involves a party who has been defamed or otherwise injured but cannot meet the test for obtaining the blogger's identity. The party therefore resorts to self-defensive counter-speech, even language that infringes a common-law interest of the blogger or of a third party. How far can this party go without risking liability?

The third scenario relates to the first two and is based on a recent English decision, *Author of a Blog v Times Newspapers Ltd*.[5] If a party discovers an anonymous blogger's identity and plans to make it public – either self-defensively while rebutting the blogger's content, or simply to provide information thought to be newsworthy – the blogger who learns that he is about to be unmasked may petition a court to enjoin the disclosure. How should the court rule? Presumably the blogger insists that his future dispatches will cease or at least be adversely affected by the disclosure, yet even the chance of a shut-down would not likely rebut the strong presumption against prior restraint in US law.

This chapter urges courts to reflect on the relevant First Amendment value in fashioning frameworks for each scenario. Of the four values, or valued functions, generally associated with expressive freedoms of speech and press, the one most identified with the informational potential of the internet is the search for truth.[6] That value generates doctrine protecting opinion as well as true and false speech, depending on context and competing interests. The chapter posits that consideration of the truth-seeking value is the element missing from much of the commentary and judicial decision-making thus far. Creating satisfactory frameworks for each of the three scenarios may well depend on getting this consideration right.

Scenario 1: forcing disclosure of a blogger's identity

Chroniclers link the rise of the web to perceived limitations of traditional media. In the days following the events of 11 September 2001, 'many [in the

US] looked to the Web for a sense of connection and a dose of truth' that seemed unavailable elsewhere.[7] The sense of connection was important to both internet commentators and their readers, making possible a surprising new experience of 'tell[ing] the story together'.[8] And the 'dose of truth' was provided by copious 'eyewitness accounts and personal diaries of the aftermath' of the attacks, providing a 'rude honesty that [had not often made] its way through the mainstream media's good-taste filter'.[9] Connectedness and joint truth-seeking would become hallmarks of web use, even if the continuous cascade of speech on all possible topics ultimately has produced as much 'pettiness and discord' as harmony and enlightenment.[10]

Eric Boehlert's lively book *Bloggers on the Bus*[11] details the impact of blogs on the 2006 and 2008 US national elections. It recounts how 'liberal bloggers', marginalised by what many regarded as the conservative dominance of talk radio, and eager to 'drive Fox News out of the mainstream of American media', found their niche on a new medium – the web – and collectively 'expanded well beyond the traditional role of journalist or commentator'.[12] Many sought 'to stitch together a kind of coherent narrative from the liberal perspective, which wasn't there before'.[13] Boehlert reports that in the 2008 campaign, bloggers (whether anonymous or not) not only expressed viewpoints but also uncovered and disseminated facts that captured national attention. For example, one blogger exposed a McCain-endorsing pastor's bizarre interpretation of the Holocaust,[14] while another published candidate Barack Obama's comments, made in a supposedly off-the-record meeting with campaign donors, that unemployment had made many 'small-town' Americans 'bitter', causing them to 'cling to guns or religion'.[15] In these and other instances, internet writers engaged in basic fact-finding and reporting of news. Others focused on commentary, exercising 'the power of explanation'. As one put it, '[e]xplaining is defining, and if you do it effectively, it can be very powerful. And with the blogs, we've got a place to do it now'.[16]

With power and prominence comes potential for liability. Although both plaintiffs and defendants have sought to unmask anonymous speakers, most of the cases involve efforts by plaintiffs in civil actions. These include public officials suing detractors for online defamation, usually comments about an official's job performance or fitness for office;[17] private plaintiffs suing anonymous commentators for offensive factual assertions, often sexual in nature, posted on a bulletin board or blog;[18] corporations or their officers suing bulletin-board speakers for defamatory statements about business performance or officers' actions;[19] ex-employees suing employers for unlawful discharge or other acts, and seeking evidence from anonymous third parties who have posted online comments concerning the litigation.[20] In other cases, civil defendants seek an anonymous speaker's identity, maintaining that the information would provide, or lead to, important evidence for the defence.[21]

The cases in which plaintiffs seek a blogger's identity have at least three aspects in common: fierce rhetoric from both sides about what a case is 'really' about; arguments about whether anonymous speakers are adequately protected by existing rules of civil procedure; and, if the answer to the latter question is negative, arguments about the appropriate scope of First Amendment protection.

The first clash in most of the cases is rhetorical, with defendants insisting that the case concerns a censorious plaintiff's effort to 'silence' a legitimate speaker, and plaintiffs countering that the case actually concerns a malicious speaker's attempt to defame and then 'hide behind' constitutional privilege. Each narrative ends with a legal demand. The anonymous defendant's reference to being 'silenced' asks the court not to order identification automatically but to consider the plaintiff's actual need for the information and the consequences of exposure for the defendant. The plaintiff's reference to 'hiding behind privilege' urges the court to respect the plaintiff's right of access to the courts by permitting the plaintiff to discover the defendant's identity and to proceed with a lawsuit whose elements are already shaped by the First Amendment. The parties in effect accuse each other of abusing power: the defendant accuses the plaintiff of setting in motion a frightening legal spectacle of identity exposure and potential financial loss, and the plaintiff accuses the cloaked defendant of sending hurtful speech to unlimited receivers by the mere press of a button. Though dramatically effective, each narrative undercuts itself by omitting a sense of the public's interest in how the question of anonymity should be resolved, perhaps because of the difficulty in calculating, much less in articulating, the public's interest in anonymous speech.

The anonymous blogger cases also have involved a second clash: whether the question presented by an application for discovery of a blogger's identity is fundamentally procedural, requiring application of ordinary rules, or substantive, requiring 'heightened', First Amendment-based analysis. The debate plays out between lawyers invoking craft and prudence,[22] and academics offering theory and doctrine.[23] Judges caught in the crossfire sometimes borrow from both perspectives, recognising that procedural rules incorporate substantive First Amendment standards. In *Cohen v Google*,[24] where a professional model sought an order forcing Google to identify a blogger who had accused the model of lewd practices and dishonesty, a New York judge ordering disclosure noted that state law:

> generally applicable to a[n] application for pre-action disclosure which requires a prima facie showing of a meritorious cause of action, and the legal requirements for establishing a meritorious cause of action for defamation, appear to address the constitutional concerns raised in this context.[25]

Most courts, however, seek a distinct constitutional framework and so confront a third battle, this one concerning the appropriate balance between anonymous speech and common-law interests in reputation, privacy and confidentiality. In *Doe v Cahill*,[26] a city councilman sued four John Doe defendants for postings on a newspaper-sponsored internet blog. The language asserted that the councilman had been 'divisive', that he suffered from 'character flaws, not to mention an obvious mental deterioration', that he was 'a prime example of failed leadership' in need of 'ousting' and that he was 'as paranoid as everyone in the town thinks he is'.[27] To serve process, the councilman petitioned a court for leave to depose the newspaper for the relevant internet protocol address. The councilman then obtained an order requiring Comcast, the owner of the addresses, to disclose the blogger's identity. Notified by Comcast, the blogger moved for a protective order. The case ultimately reached Delaware's High Court, where the justices considered a number of standards for pre-suit discovery of an anonymous speaker's identity.

The court ruled that a plaintiff must meet a summary judgment standard in order to obtain a judicial order forcing disclosure. Two less demanding showings formulated in other jurisdictions – a good faith standard, and a motion to dismiss standard – were rejected as setting the bar 'too low'.[28] On the ground that the First Amendment requires that a libel plaintiff bear a heavier burden in order to protect a defendant speaker's right to speak anonymously, the court adopted a requirement that the plaintiff 'introduce evidence creating a genuine issue of material fact for all elements of a defamation claim within the plaintiff's control'.[29] The court ultimately dismissed the case because the statements at issue constituted non-actionable opinion.

Besides disapproving less rigorous standards, *Cahill* rejected a step that would have added significantly to the plaintiff's burden: 'balanc[ing] the First Amendment right of anonymous speech against the strength of the prima face case presented and the necessity of disclosure'.[30] Maintaining simply that 'the summary judgment test is itself the balance', *Cahill* concluded that no further balancing could be justified.[31] Applying the summary judgment test, the court held that the speaker's First Amendment right to remain anonymous in expressing views about a public official's fitness for office was not overcome by the councilman's interest in vindicating his reputation since an essential element of the plaintiff's prima facie action for libel, one that was 'within the plaintiff's control', was lacking.[32]

Despite assigning a significant showing to plaintiffs in such circumstances, *Cahill* has been criticised for under-protecting anonymous internet speech by failing to add the balancing factor. A student commentator has asserted that without this balancing, known as '*Dendrite* balancing' for a New Jersey decision adopting it, *Cahill*'s framework is 'too easy on plaintiffs who wish to unmask anonymous [speakers]'.[33] At least some academics agree. Despite praising *Cahill* for its 'general' consistency with their preferred approach, Professors Lidsky and Cotter maintain that *Dendrite* balancing is necessary 'as a final piece of insurance that defendant's right to speak anonymously is not too lightly compromised'.[34]

This call for *Dendrite* balancing is unwise for several reasons. First, it jarringly transplants to the internet context a test that several US judges have proposed for use in a quite different setting: a sub-set of reporter's privilege/confidential source cases. In these cases, the government, when investigating a potentially criminal leak of classified information to a journalist, asks the journalist to name her source. When the journalist declines, the government seeks a judicial order. The customary inquiry for judicially ordered disclosure of a confidential source is whether the source's identity is centrally relevant to the investigation and whether the alternative avenues of finding the source have been exhausted. Because this inquiry would almost invariably yield a pre-ordained affirmative answer to both questions, thus necessitating compelled disclosure, two prominent federal judges – Judge Sack of the US Court of Appeals for the Second Circuit and Judge Tatel of the US Court of Appeals for the DC Circuit – have proposed a final balancing test to be conducted by courts to ensure that no First Amendment interest is slighted.[35] Although that test makes sense in criminal leak cases and is included in legislation now before Congress,[36] importing it into a potentially much larger set of cases whose outcomes are *not* pre-ordained is difficult to justify, even as a 'final piece of insurance'. *Cahill's* summary judgment standard itself incorporated First Amendment analysis – that is, the opinion inquiry from the Supreme Court's decision in *Milkovich v Lorain Journal Co*[37] – and the need for anything more is unclear.

Even if additional insurance were considered desirable, the unguided nature of the Sack–Tatel inquiry in the internet/John Doe context poses problems. On what basis would a court calculate the 'news value' of a blogger's speech, and compare that value to the content's harm?[38] In *Cahill*, the harm and value of the posted statements were hardly amenable to clear calculation. It may be that *Dendrite* balancing in *Cahill* would simply amount to a more searching version of *Milkovich* analysis – a question of whether the statements were factual in nature and thus subject to litigation. In any event, it is hard to see how the balancing could be conducted, except very impressionistically, in a defamation action involving anonymous speech. Without addressing this flaw, *Dendrite* asks courts to guess at the news value of specific statements in the process of weighing a speaker's interest against the 'strength' of a plaintiff's case.[39]

Moreover, the *Cahill* framework as it stands is consistent with a core First Amendment value: the truth-seeking value of speech, which broadly protects dissemination of and access to 'information [that] is needed or appropriate to enable the members of society to cope with the exigencies of their period'.[40] Evocations of this value are common in Supreme Court discussions, from Justice Holmes' observation that 'the best test of truth is the power of the thought to get itself accepted in the competition of the market',[41] to Justice White's statement that the First Amendment's 'purpose' is to 'preserve an uninhibited marketplace of ideas', including 'social, political, esthetic, moral, and other ideas and experience'.[42] Like Holmes himself, the truth-seeking value is sceptical, favours experimentation and has no appetite for or illusion about discovering ultimate truth in any philosophical or religious sense. It denotes an incremental and collective search for social fact, perhaps akin to the process described by Justice Frankfurter:

The history of civilization is in considerable measure the displacement of error which once held sway as official truth by beliefs which in turn have yielded to other truths.[43]

The outlook is traceable to John Stuart Mill, for whom truth 'resembles a scientific proposition, which provides a legitimate basis for experimentation until it is successfully challenged and replaced by another proposition that better fits the data'.[44] As a Mill biographer put it, '[d]isproof of any opinion, by way of a new experience, had to be a constant possibility, according to Mill'.[45] Another commentator wrote: 'Mill's concern with self-development and moral progress is a strand in his philosophy to which almost everything else is subordinate.'[46]

The US Congress has considered the internet a medium for such experimentation through speech, noting that it not only provides a forum for 'a true diversity of political discourse' but also creates 'opportunities for cultural development, and myriad avenues for intellectual activity'.[47] Accordingly, the value of internet speech can be seen as its contribution to the 'open-ended pursuit of knowledge' in the Millian sense, and internet speech is part of that pursuit when, true or false, it is subject to evaluation and response by others. As Professor Jane Singer has written, some bloggers – including those dubbed citizen journalists – resemble traditional journalists in that both 'are committed to truth', yet bloggers 'have quite different ideas of how best to attain it and what to do with it'.[48] While old-school journalists see truth 'as the information that has survived the rigorous scrutiny (ideally) of a journalistic process in which verification determines veracity', bloggers 'offer a space for all comers to post what they know or think; to receive a hearing; and to have their ideas publicly debated, modified, and expanded or refuted'. For bloggers, truth 'emerg[es] from shared, collective knowledge – from an electronically enabled marketplace of ideas'.[49]

In adopting the summary judgment standard for anonymous blogger cases, *Cahill* arguably relies on the truth-seeking value and demonstrates the value's range and limits. *Cahill* notes that anonymity serves the search for truth by both the speaker and the public receiving the speech: unsigned expression enters public discourse on its own and therefore avoids the skewing attributable to prejudice or bias based on irrelevant classifications of identity. Like early anonymous pamphleteers, internet speakers fit well into original notions of a marketplace of ideas where content, not the authorship, of facts and opinions is central to the probing, positing and revising of a developing culture. At the same time, the truth-seeking value recognises that at least a measure of accountability is necessary to secure trust in that marketplace – trust sufficient for members of the public to participate in and take seriously the marketplace itself. Arguably, *Cahill* rejected *Dendrite* because the latter's open-ended balancing would work against a predictable, trust-building role for accountability in the scheme of the truth-seeking value. The summary judgment standard, on the other hand, serves accountability not by uncovering a speaker's identity under all circumstances but by doing so when a plaintiff has a credible, supportable claim.

Besides calling for *Dendrite* balancing in defamation cases brought by a public official against anonymous bloggers, commentators have made the even less persuasive argument that *Dendrite* balancing is needed to protect free speech when private plaintiffs sue anonymous bloggers for defamation.[50] In *Does I and II v Individuals*,[51] two female students at Yale Law School sued 28 John Does who had posted statements about them on AutoAdmit, a website frequented by law students and known for its free-wheeling chat about a range of topics. In the Yale Law case, bloggers asserted that one or both women had sexually transmitted diseases and engaged in promiscuous behaviour, among much else. As one observer noted, the anonymous statements were 'sadistic … subjecting the women to what can only be called cyber-stoning, in which participants vied to hurl the biggest rock'.[52] When the women sued and sought their attackers' identities, the district court adopted a multi-pronged framework. The court indicated that *Dendrite* was part of the framework, but any balancing by the court was not apparent. One blogger relied on the argument that succeeded in *Cahill*, that the statements in context were non-actionable opinion: 'AutoAdmit is well known as a place for inane discussion and meaningless derogatory postings, such that one would not take such a statement seriously.'[53] The court rejected the argument, noting that 'not everyone who searched Doe II's name on the internet, or who came across the postings on AutoAdmit, would be aware of the site's alleged reputation'.[54] The court ordered the website to disclose the bloggers' names.

The decision has been criticised as exposing a blogger's identity even where the defamation claim was 'suspect at best',[55] essentially an argument that the challenged statements were protected hyperbole. With explicit *Dendrite* balancing, it is argued, the Yale Law case would have been properly thrown out on the ground that the 'value' of hyperbole, even if offensive, outweighed the 'seriousness' of any claimed harm. The argument seems to ask for a second round of *Milkovich* analysis. Moreover, it fails for advocating an element that, as discussed above, gives courts unguided discretion and is inconsistent with the truth-seeking value. The Yale Law case as decided was correct.

Interestingly, the truth-seeking value works in tandem with the self-governance value. *Cahill* and the Yale Law case recognise this value diversity: that the pre-action issue of identity disclosure concerns the truth-seeking value, whereas the substantive law of defamation stems from the even more protective self-governance value. Accountability – in the sense of identity disclosure and a summons to court – is a function of the truth-seeking value, the value that permits some (but not all) speech to be challenged at law. Once in court, the defendant invokes the freedoms established expansively pursuant to self-governance value in cases such as *New York Times Co v Sullivan* and its progeny, a matrix of rules designed to ensure an all-but-unhindered flow of information.

Scenario 2: talking back to the blogger

Although this chapter maintains that the *Cahill* approach is preferable to *Dendrite*, the latter approach seems ascendant among courts and commentators.[56] In *Dendrite* jurisdictions, a person who has been defamed may shrink from the difficulty and cost of attempting to discover an anonymous blogger's identity. Unable to sue, the defamed person's recourse is 'more speech' – resorting to self-help on the very blog where the original defamation appeared. It is not hard to imagine the defamed person's considerations in deciding what to do: on the one hand, responding would draw attention to the defamation, likely spread it further, and certainly send a signal that the statement has gotten under the skin of the defamed person. On the other hand, a decision not to respond allows the statement to go unchallenged, perhaps signalling that the statement has some truth or that it has done no harm.

In a case like *Cahill*, the utility of a response is questionable. Recall that the blogger had posted a nebulous charge of mental incompetence; it is unlikely that the city councilman would gain much by asserting that he is mentally fine or not 'paranoid'. In the Yale Law case, it is conceivable that the targets would want to post a statement of outrage – but not that they would care to dignify statements about promiscuity and STDs with any kind of 'reply' in the sense of a point-by-point refutation. The decision to 'reply' more likely arises in cases in which a nameless speaker appears to have inside information about a business or other work setting and repeatedly asserts or strongly implies facts that the targeted person feels compelled to answer for purposes of self-defence.[57]

A reply of sorts actually triggered a lawsuit by a partially cloaked speaker in *Moreno v Hanford Sentinel Inc*.[58] The plaintiff, a college student, used her MySpace page to post an 'Ode' criticising the petty provincialism of her home town and high school, telling them, '[e]nvy me [for leaving home], for that's all you can do ... Talk nonsense ... because you are nothing'. The student signed the Ode with simply her first name, but her photo on the website allowed identification. The Ode prompted an unusual response by her former high-school principal: he sent the posting to the local newspaper, which published it as a letter to the editor with her full name as the signature. Appended to the Ode was a reply, seemingly by the newspaper: 'It saddens us to know that a product of this community, a community that takes such pride in its youth, would have such negative thoughts of what was once their home.'[59] Stunned by the fall-out of her outing by the principal and newspaper, the college student sued them for invasion of privacy and intentional infliction of emotional distress. Although the privacy claim was dismissed because the original MySpace posting of the Ode made it 'public', a jury found the principal's conduct outrageous in the second cause of action but awarded no damages.[60] Moreno provides a compelling case study of the inexperience of at least some internet speakers, the hurt feelings and potentially tortious counter-speech that can follow negative postings, the dubious application of old doctrine to new media, and the rough justice of juries.

The risks of replying to anonymous speech can be further illustrated by the following hypothetical. Imagine a place of employment: a trade association for the cable television industry ('Cable Media Association', or 'CMA'). A summer intern, one of ten employed at CMA but the only member of the Mormon faith among them, believes that he is being 'frozen out' by other interns due to his religious affiliation. Late on a Friday afternoon, he complains about his depression and sense of isolation to Mary Thomas, a junior manager at CMA, who among other duties is in charge of the summer internship programme. The intern, Raymond, says he thinks the other interns are pre-judiced against him and his religion. He also confides that part of his unhappiness is the fact that he has just received word from home that his parents are separating. Mary is very sympathetic and offers encouragement and support. She does not contact her supervisor that day but thinks that she will tell her supervisor sometime the following week that there is an issue or at least a question about unfriendly interns. A social event takes place that evening on the premises. Raymond attends and drinks too much, as do other interns, one of whom gets into a noisy disagreement with Raymond about football teams. Raymond looks annoyed by the disagreement, and the other intern apologetically reaches out and grabs Raymond's hand. The other intern's grip is unexpectedly strong, and Raymond recoils and stumbles over a chair, falling down in front of everyone. Raymond accuses the other intern of public humiliation. The following week, Raymond demands that the other intern be fired from the internship. Ultimately the matter is resolved through mediation.

Later an anonymous blogger posts a message on a widely read 'Interns in Business' bulletin board on the internet. The posting says that 'the Cable Media Association is against Mormons, it does not welcome Mormons, and one of its managers, Mary Thomas, showed her bias by doing nothing for a Mormon intern named Raymond when he complained of isolation.' The posting continues that Raymond had been 'publicly shamed' at an office party and that the incident 'showed bias in the company's culture'. The posting concludes, '[t]he manager's inaction made possible this bad public incident, and CMA ought to be ashamed.'

Assume that Mary is devastated by the criticism and horrified that it appeared on an internet bulletin board posting that names her and challenges her professionalism. She worries that the allegations will affect her reputation in the workplace. When she confronts Raymond, he denies authorship of the statement but indicates that he thinks it is essentially true. She then talks to an attorney about bringing legal action. The attorney advises against a law-suit, explaining that the test from *Dendrite* would apply in this case, making it difficult to discover the blogger's identity, and that a court would likely follow the maxim that the First Amendment is all about encouraging 'more speech', that is, responsive speech. Nerve-wracked and against her better judgment, Mary posts the following reply on the same bulletin board where the original message appeared:

> What the blogger says about me and the culture of CMA is a lie. All of us who work here are dedicated to a friendly workplace where somebody's race or religion doesn't matter at all. Has anybody figured out that there are two sides to this story, and that maybe this young intern was hyper-sensitive? And that maybe he fell on his face because he'd had one too many beers? And now is embarrassed and wants this blog to get a little even? The intern came to me not just about other interns at CMA but about his home situation, which is very troubled & has nothing to do with how his summer is going at CMA. I thought his family issues were his main problem, and I counselled him in a caring way. I was happy that he came to me. It's a lie that I wasn't concerned and 'did nothing' for him. We don't have a 'Mormon problem' at CMA.

She signs off, 'Mary Thomas'.

Now assume Raymond sues Mary for her posted reply. First, he alleges libel – that her posted reply defames him by stating that he was hyper-sensitive in thinking there was bias at CMA, that he was intoxicated at the office party, that he was responsible for the anonymous posting and wanted to 'get even'. Second, Raymond alleges invasion of privacy for the statement that he sought counselling from Mary about family issues. Finally, he alleges breach of confidence based on a relationship of counselling that he had with Mary.

Can Mary be held liable for her posted reply? The question is important because it relates to the scope of freedom to reply to an anonymous blogger's speech rather than bring a legal claim. Answering the libel claim, Mary may invoke (among other defences) the common-law privilege of reply, which courts also reference as 'the privilege to speak in self-defence or to defend one's reputation'.[61] The *Restatement (Second) of Torts* recognises this as a conditional privilege that can be invoked 'when the person making the publication reasonably believes that his interest in his own reputation has been unlawfully invaded by another person and that the defamatory matter that he publishes about the other is reasonably necessary to defend himself'.[62] A reply of this kind is protected even if it is 'uninhibited, robust, and wide open',[63] and it can include a 'statement that [the original speaker] is an unmitigated liar'.[64] Moreover, the fact that the person does not know the identity of the blogger or his source is not fatal: case law suggests that 'the privilege is not limited to replies to known attackers'.[65]

In *Foretich v Capital Cities/ABC Inc.*, the United States Court of Appeals for the Fourth Circuit noted that the privilege is lost if abused in any of the following ways: if the reply 'includes substantial defamatory matter that is irrelevant or non-responsive to the initial attack'; if the reply 'includes substantial defamatory matter that is disproportionate to the initial attack'; or if the reply's publication is 'excessive', in the sense that it 'addressed to too broad an audience'.[66] Mary's reply was arguably both responsive to the initial attack and relevant; moreover, impugning motives is fair game.[67] To be disproportionate, a reply must be 'truly outrageous;' honest indignation and strong words do not cross the line.[68] Lacking 'excessive enthusiasm or ceremonial flair',[69] Mary's reply could be defended as proportionate. And because the initial statements were blogged on the internet, her rejoinder could hardly be seen as 'excessive' in terms of audience size. The reply would almost certainly be privileged, and no showing of common-law malice to overcome the privilege likely would be forthcoming.

But a successful defence in the libel action does not mean that Mary can, should, or will avoid all liability. As noted, Raymond's action for public disclosure of private facts focuses on Mary's statement that his parents were separating. Even if this information is known to some who are in Raymond's and his parents' circle of close friends, it is 'private' for purposes of this tort,[70] and its posting on an internet bulletin board surely constitutes providing 'publicity'.[71] If Mary's reply is considered highly offensive to a reasonable person, and not reasonably related to a matter of legitimate public concern, Raymond may complete his prima facie case. Widespread electronic disclosure of information about the marital problems of a couple who are not in the public eye is arguably highly offensive to a reasonable person, and any nexus between that information and the issue of religious bias in the workplace is remote at best. However, the Restatement (Second) of Torts provides that '[t]he rules on conditional privileges to publish defamatory matter [including the reply right] apply to the publication of any matter that is an invasion privacy'.[72] In a 2002 case, the Supreme Court of Nevada rejected a claim for public disclosure of private facts in a workplace setting, citing the defendant's privilege to reply.[73] However, because cases applying the privilege in the privacy context are few, it is hard to predict whether disclosure concerning a couple's plans to separate would be considered 'proportionate' to the blogger's own charge of incompetence and bias. A trial judge might wisely leave application of the elements and privilege to a jury. Even if a jury finds for Mary, a reviewing court considering the fact that Raymond sought counselling from Mary might conclude on policy grounds that she had no privilege to publicize Raymond's private matters, even in self-defence.

A claim for breach of confidence, by way of contrast, appears to be the more appropriate setting for such a policy choice. However, the confidentiality action has had little traction in the United States,[74] and its doctrinal content is undeveloped.[75] Scholars continue to support its wider recognition, and perhaps the action's focus on a violation of trust between parties will resonate in an internet age. In Raymond's case, a key first question would be whether the manager–intern relationship is within the set of relationships giving rise to a duty of confidentiality. If it is, the claim would centre on an alleged violation of trust by Mary in disclosing – on a highly accessible blog – that the intern's family was breaking up.[76] Mary's vague phrasing may limit any compensatory damages, and her motivation may save her from imposition of punitive damages. She may try to argue that Raymond was either the author of the blog or the source and thereby waived any claim of breach of confidence. She may even be able to invoke a privilege comparable to the 'right of reply' discussed earlier. Despite the paucity of cases, one commentator notes: '[a] party may be permitted to breach a confidence to the extent necessary to defend himself against a charge of incompetence, protect himself against fraud, or perhaps collect fees ... '[77] However, policy support for liability would be strong: Mary accepted the role of counsellor, and a court might determine that a minor's reliance on a counselling relationship outweighs other considerations, even waiver and self-defence. If this possibility, along with all the uncertainties of applying the 'emerging' action for breach of confidence, had been conveyed to Mary when she sought a lawyer's advice, she likely would have refrained from mentioning Raymond's family troubles in the first place. At the same time, she would have seen that the truth of Raymond's family troubles was the most compelling fact in her self-defence – that, with no mention of those troubles, any 'reply' would fall flat. Legalities aside, she may also have decided that professionally she should say nothing, concluding that both she and Raymond expected the conversation about his family to be confidential. So it is likely that with further counsel from her attorney and further reflection of her own, she would have remained silent, or at best posted a much shorter, far less revelatory message: 'There are two sides to this story.'

The Raymond–Mary hypothetical is meant to suggest that 'more speech' may not be a practical alternative for one defamed by an anonymous blogger. Where specific facts are at issue, and where a target of anonymous defamation would face legal problems in furnishing a truthful and effective reply, the better part of valour may well be silence. How common such situations are is unknown, but as courts consider *Dendrite*'s onerous showing, they should keep in mind that the option of 'more speech' may not exist in some settings for vulnerable targets of anonymous bloggers.

Scenario 3: moving a court to gag disclosure of the blogger's identity

A third scenario concerns the place of prior restraint in protecting the anonymity of bloggers, specifically whether a blogger can enlist the injunctive power of the courts to protect his identity even when a third party has lawfully and independently discovered his identity and wishes to publish it.

A recent English case provides the factual setting. In *Author of a Blog v Times Newspapers Ltd*,[78] a police officer's anonymous blog, 'Night Jack' (or 'NightJack'), became famous in the United Kingdom. He wrote about his work and related policy issues. He refrained from revealing names or settings, and claimed to write nothing about cases that were pending or subject to reporting restrictions.[79] In May 2009, a *Times* reporter contacted the officer and said that he had discovered that the officer was writing the blog and that *The Times* would publish that information. An agreement was reached that there would be no publication in the next edition, but on receiving word that publication would take place the day following that edition, the officer applied to the court for an interim injunction.

The officer argued that his identity was 'confidential and private'; that his authorship of the blog was 'information about his 'private' writing activities – divorced from the 'public' content of the blog itself'; that anonymity was part of his 'exercise of personal autonomy'; that unmasking him would 'deter him (and other bloggers) from expressing themselves in the future' and thus impede the free flow of information; that exposing his identity would subject him to possible discipline; that any of *The Times*' justifications for publishing based on the public interest were 'flimsy' at best; and that the court must enjoin publication.[80]

The Times argued that the reporter arrived at the blogger's identity by using 'publicly available materials, patience, and simple deduction'; that no breach of confidence or violation of a reasonable expectation of privacy had occurred; that 'there was a public interest in the public['s] knowing the identity of the author of the blog' in order 'to assess the weight to attach' to its content; and that a public interest existed 'in disclosing alleged breaches by the [officer] of Police Regulations by writing the blog'.[81]

Justice Eady employed a two-part inquiry for analysis of claims based on privacy invasions in contravention of Article 8 of the European Convention on Human Rights and Fundamental Freedoms: first, whether the applicant for injunction demonstrates a reasonable expectation of privacy; if so, second, whether 'there is some countervailing public interest such as to justify over-riding that prima facie right'.[82] In the first part, noting 'a significant public element in the information sought to be restricted',[83] Justice Eady concluded that the information lacked the required 'quality of confidence'[84] and that the applicant lacked a reasonable expectation of privacy because 'blogging is essentially a public activity rather than a private activity'.[85] Although this finding was conclusive of the case, Justice Eady addressed the second part, finding a countervailing public interest in the newspaper's disclosure of the information.[86] On the specific matter of whether an injunction should issue, Justice Eady concluded that it was unlikely that the applicant would succeed at trial 'in restraining *The Times* from publishing his identity' on a theory either of confidentiality or privacy.[87]

From a US perspective, these facts implicate several legal strands. The first and most obviously relevant strand is the strong presumption against prior restraint. In case law interpreting and applying the First Amendment, prior restraint carries a heavy burden of justification – perhaps the heaviest burden to be found in the US law of free speech and press. From the historic case of *Near v Minnesota* in 1932,[88] to the *Pentagon Papers* case of 1971,[89] the Court has disfavoured even temporary restraining orders issued to permit parties to present arguments and the court to deliberate. Lower court decisions have followed the Court's lead, finding that countervailing interests lacked sufficient weight to justify prior restraint. In *Matter of Providence Journal*,[90] a federal appellate court found that a trial judge erred in restraining the press from publishing information that first had been unlawfully gathered by the US government and years later disclosed to several media outlets in response to a petition under the Freedom of Information Act 1966. The trial judge restrained publication for two days pending a hearing, justifying the temporary order in part on the ground of privacy. The appellate court found this restraint not only unconstitutional but 'transparently invalid': the privacy interest was patently inadequate as justification.[91]

This tradition may seem to involve case-by-case balancing of interests. Yet its essence is to look at the timing of the restraint – whether previous or subsequent to publication – and if previous, to presume to a virtual certainty that the restraint violates free speech. Questioning this formalism, some scholars have called for revision of the Court's all but unyielding approach, in favour of a subtle practice of balancing. Dean John Jeffries, for example, criticises the Court's dichotomy, arguing that prior restraint and subsequent penalty are functionally indistinct because they have the same impact on speech. Jeffries questions 'the broad and categorical condemnation of injunctions as a form of "prior restraint"'.[92]

Perhaps this moderating perspective lay behind *People v Bryant*,[93] in which the Colorado Supreme Court upheld a prior restraint of an alleged rape victim's in camera testimony in a widely covered criminal case's preliminary hearing. In Bryant, involving criminal allegations against a national sports figure, the victim had given sworn testimony about her sexual history in a closed pre-trial proceeding pursuant to the state's rape shield law. When a court reporter inadvertently emailed transcripts of the sealed testimony to members of the press, the trial judge ordered the recipients not to publish the contents. A newspaper sought relief in the state's high court on the ground of prior restraint – but to no avail. The Colorado Supreme Court acknowledged that the order was a prior restraint but upheld it, maintaining that the victim's sworn testimony about her sexual conduct, some or all of which might not even be admissible in the trial, was intensely private, that her interest in privacy was of the 'highest order', and that the extraordinary remedy of an injunction was warranted on the facts.[94] The US Supreme Court declined review.

Because *Bryant* stands almost alone in upholding an injunction against press publication on the ground of privacy, the decision is not likely a harbinger of things to come. The case explicitly depends on certain facts: (a) the rape shield statute, which for the court magnified the weight of the privacy interest; (b) the worldwide notoriety of the underlying criminal case, ensuring an unlimited audience for any news about the victim; (c) the fact that the private information was sworn testimony from a proceeding held in camera, giving it extra credibility if disseminated; and (d) the likelihood that the prior restraint would be effective, since the testimony had been sent to only a few outlets and had not been further disseminated. But even if *Bryant* on its facts is good law, it is hard to see how it could support a privacy-justified prior restraint in *Night Jack*, where there was no threatened exposure of highly intimate conduct, and no assurance that a non-disclosure order would be effective in keeping the information secret.

On the other hand, perhaps the relevant inquiry in the US would not be the *Bryant* inquiry at all. That case asked whether the victim's interest in privacy of conduct was sufficient to rebut the law's heavy presumption. Perhaps the real question in *Night Jack* is whether the blogger's privacy of speech, or more precisely, the blogger's right to speak anonymously, is a sufficient interest. The right to speak anonymously on matters of public concern is a right to control the content of one's speech – to decide for oneself whether to include one's name or not in communicating with a few others or with the public. Thus, the proper analogy may not be between the *Night Jack* blogger and the victim in *Bryant*, but between the *Night Jack* blogger and a confidential source. Both the blogger and source provide information, often information of public concern, without self-disclosure. On this analysis, the question is whether a prior restraint is constitutional when it protects speech, that is, guards the anonymity of the blogger as a continuing source of information of public concern. A similar question could arise if a news entity planned to identify another news entity's confidential source, and the source sought an injunction from a court in advance of publication. Both sides could voice familiar First Amendment arguments: the news entity seeking to publish could argue that no court can legitimately decide an outlet's content absent a threat of 'direct, immediate, and irreparable harm to the Nation or its people', and the source could argue generally that news sources will dry up and the 'free flow of information' be greatly impeded if 'outing' is permissible. Both arguments would cite the truth-seeking value of free expression.

In resolving the impasse, the Supreme Court would likely emphasise the specific evil – prior restraint of pinpointed information – rather than the general evil that might result from not imposing the prior restraint – the drying up of a source. And the Court's principal reason would centre on the prong that brings a pragmatic consideration into the calculus: effectiveness. Because *The Times* reporter was capable of 'deducing' the blogger's identity from publicly available information, others presumably could make the same deduction. The same information could emerge from another source. A prior restraint against *The Times* therefore would be ineffective in maintaining the secret so as to enable the blog to continue as before. And because the subject matter of the postings was clearly of public concern, it is likely that the court would defer to the newspaper's judgment that publication of the poster's identity, deducible from available information, was beyond the power of the court to block.

Yet the advent of the internet and the remarkable economic decline of the institutional press in the United States may be further complicating factors, as evidenced by a recent federal appellate case featuring a concurrence by Judge J. Harvie Wilkinson, perhaps the First Amendment's most sensitive expositor in the US judiciary. Like the *Night Jack* case, *Andrew v Clark*[95] involved speech about the workings of the police and the relationship of police and citizens from the perspective of an insider. A police officer, Major Andrew, was discharged for taking his concerns to the press after another police officer used deadly force against a suspect and an internal investigation was (in Major Andrew's view) unsatisfactory. Concurring with the panel's decision that the Major's discharge may have violated his First Amendment rights, Judge Wilkinson noted the decline of newsgathering organisations with beat reporters who would specialise in journalism about law enforcement. 'The staffs and bureaus ... of newspapers and television stations alike have been shuttered or shrunk' due to 'the advent of the internet and the economic downturn', causing 'traditional news organisations throughout the country to lose circulation and advertising revenue to an unforeseen extent'.[96] As a result, 'substantial reports on matters of critical public policy are increasingly shortchanged', and 'intense scrutiny of the inner workings of massive public bureaucracies charged with major public responsibilities is in deep trouble'.[97] In this context, scrutiny of public institutions such as the police is 'impossible without inside sources' such as police officers themselves'.[98] Judge Wilkinson concluded, '[i]t is vital to the health of our polity that the functioning of the ever more complex and powerful machinery of government not become democracy's dark lagoon.'[99]

Given the cogency of Judge Wilkinson's concerns, the Supreme Court taking up the *Night Jack* case surely would recognise that the blog consists of 'core' speech and may even acknowledge the changing nature of the news industries. Even so, it is unlikely that the Court would abandon its prior restraint precedents and uphold an order prohibiting *The Times* from publishing facts that are in its possession and that in its news judgment should be published. Behind the Court's intolerance of prior restraint is the truth-seeking value, which follows Mill's belief in the capacity of citizens engaging in the give-and-take of free discourse over time to sort through such speech and identify facts relevant to social progress. The *Night Jack* blogger's own invocation of the truth-seeking value would carry weight, but it is probable that the Court would regard its prior restraint tradition as 'prior' to the blogger's own concerns.

Conclusion

An anonymous blogger's constitutional right of anonymity should give way in a civil suit only when a plaintiff can survive the blogger's motion for summary judgment. This test fairly accommodates competing interests of freedom and accountability. Some suits will fail, as in *Cahill*, others will continue, as in the Yale Law action. The summary judgment test provides the sort of balance that the electronic marketplace of ideas, informed by the truth-seeking value, requires for public credibility. Tests more onerous than summary judgment for identifying bloggers may discourage prospective plaintiffs from seeking relief, and counter-speech may not be practical given the threat of liability.

Bloggers who seek prior restraint to protect their anonymity may offer forceful arguments, especially when, like the *Night Jack* blogger and Major Andrew, their communications contribute to public understanding of serious issues. But prior restraint should remain as it is: almost entirely off-limits in US courts. The truth-seeking value is better aligned with opposing prior restraint – even of false or tortious speech – than with seeking it. In the long term, the public is better served by a legal culture that preserves the dichotomy between prior restraint and subsequent punishment, furthering the Millian project of experiment, proof and disproof in the search for social fact.

Notes

1 *Reno v ACLU*, 521 US 844 (1997).
2 *McIntyre v Ohio Elections Commission*, 514 US 334 (1995).
3 See, e.g., Lyrissa B. Lidsky and Thomas F. Cotter, 'Authorship, Audiences, and Anonymous Speech' (2007) 82 *Notre Dame Law Review* 1537; Nathaniel Gleicher, Note, 'John Doe Subpoenas: Toward a Consistent Legal Standard' (2008) 118 *Yale Law Journal* 320.
4 Cf. Megan Richardson and Julian Thomas, '"Privacy" of Social Networking Texts', below (discussing web speakers as amateurs in the sense of lacking expertise and experience 'in the matter of establishing and maintaining their anonymous and pseudonymous character').
5 [2009] EWHC 1358 (QB) ('*NightJack*').
6 The speech values of self-realisation, democratic self-governance, truth-seeking and adaptability to change are discussed in Thomas I. Emerson, 'Toward a General Theory of the First Amendment' (1963) 72 *Yale Law Journal* 877. President Lee C. Bollinger of Columbia University has written, 'In today's discourse about free speech, the dominant value associated with speech is its role in getting to the truth, or the advancement of knowledge.' Lee C. Bollinger, *The Tolerant Society*, New York: Oxford University Press, Oxford: Clarendon Press, 1986, p. 45.
7 Scott Rosenberg, *Say Anything: How Blogging Began, What It's Becoming, and Why It Matters*, New York: Three Rivers Press, 2009, p. 7.
8 Ibid.
9 Ibid.
10 Ibid., p. 73.
11 Eric Boehlert, *Bloggers on the Bus: How the Internet Changed Politics and the Press*, New York: Free Press, 2007.
12 Ibid., p. 5.
13 Ibid., p. 51.
14 Ibid., pp. 107–9.
15 Ibid., pp. 168–69.
16 Ibid., pp. 102–3 (quoting Rachel Maddow).
17 See, e.g., *Doe v Cahill*, 884 A 2d 451 (Del, 2005) (city councilman suing anonymous political critic); *Greenbaum v Google Inc*, 18 Misc 3d 185 (NY Sup Ct, 2007) (school board member suing anonymous commentators for postings about member's policy positions).
18 See, e.g., *Doe I & Doe II v Individuals*, 561 F Supp 2d 249 (D Conn, 2008) (female law students suing anonymous posters for sexual and other comments on website); *Cohen v Google Inc*, 25 Misc 3d 945 (NY Sup Ct, 2009) (professional model suing anonymous poster for sexual and other comments on website).
19 See, e.g., *Dendrite International Inc v Doe*, 775 A 2d 756 (NJ, 2001) ('*Dendrite*') (corporation suing anonymous commentators who responded to quarterly report by posting unflattering assertions about the business's performance and practices); *Krinsky v Doe 6*, 159 Cal App 4th 1154 (Cal Ct App, 2008) (corporate officer suing anonymous contributor to

message board); *Independent Newspapers Inc v Brodie*, 966 A 2d 432 (Md, 2009) (business owner suing anonymous posters of critical comments on newspaper's internet discussion forum); *Solers Inc v Doe*, 977 A 2d 941 (DC Ct App, 2009) (privately held company suing anonymous user of a trade association's 'website reporting form' through which user accused company of illegalities).

20 See, e.g., *Chang v The Regents of the University of California* (Superior Court of California, 2009–00033484-CU-OE, 9 September 2009) slip op (in employment action brought by police officer discharged from university, trial judge denies blogger's motion to quash subpoena seeking identities of persons whose postings on blog indicated knowledge of facts relevant to employment action).

21 See, e.g., *Lefkoe v Jos A Bank Clothiers Inc*, 577 F 3d 240 (4th Cir, 2009) (defendant corporation in securities fraud litigation seeking identity of anonymous individual who hired law firm to relay to corporation allegations concerning corporation's financial reporting; when corporation delayed earnings report in order to investigate, stock price fell).

22 Michael S. Vogel, 'Unmasking "John Doe" Defendants: The Case Against Excessive Hand-Wringing over Legal Standards' (2004) 83 *Oregon Law Review* 795, 799.

23 Lidsky and Cotter, 'Authorship, Audiences, and Anonymous Speech', p. 1600, n. 281.

24 25 Misc 3d 945 (NY Sup Ct, 2009)

25 Ibid.

26 884 A 2d 451 (Del, 2005).

27 Ibid., 454.

28 Ibid., 462.

29 Ibid., 463.

30 Ibid., 460 (citing *Dendrite*, 775 A 2d 756, 760–61 (NJ, 2001).

31 Ibid., 461.

32 Ibid., 467.

33 Jonathan D. Jones, 'Cybersmears and John Doe: How Far Should First Amendment Protection of Anonymous Internet Speakers Extend?' (2009) 7 *First Amendment Law Review* 421, 429.

34 Lidsky and Cotter, 'Authorship, Audiences, and Anonymous Speech', p. 1602.

35 See Judge Tatel's concurrence in *In Re Grand Jury Subpoena, Judith Miller*, 438 F 3d 1141, 1174–75 (DC Cir, 2006), and Judge Sack's dissent in *New York Times Co v Gonzales*, 459 F 3d 160, 185–86 (2nd Cir, 2006).

36 See *Free Flow of Information Act of 2009* S 448, 111th Congress (2009) (including provision under which court compelling reporter's testimony would be required to make a finding, *inter alia*, that 'nondisclosure of the information would be contrary to the public interest, taking into account both the public interest in compelling disclosure and the public interest in gathering news and maintaining the free flow of information').

37 497 US 1 (1990) ('*Milkovich*').

38 *In Matter of Ottinger v Non-Party the Journal News* (Sup Ct Westchester County, NY, No 08–03892, 27 June 2008) slip op, a New York trial judge purported to balance as provided in *Dendrite*, but its analysis consisted of a single sentence: 'Applying the fourth prong of *Dendrite*, the court finds that the balance in this case weighs in favor of the petitioners.' The lack of analysis arguably is a function of the fourth prong's lack of criteria.

39 Compare Justice Marshall's cautionary remarks in *Rosenbloom v Metromedia*, where he doubted that judges possess the 'extraordinary prescience' to 'somehow pass on the legitimacy of interest in a particular event or subject', and to determine 'what information is relevant to self-government': 403 US 29, 79 (1971) (Marshall J, dissenting, joined by Stewart J). A majority echoed Marshall's concerns in *Gertz v Robert Welch*, 418 US 323 (1974), where Powell J, writing for the Court, noted that 'we doubt the wisdom of committing the task [of labelling as public or private the subject matter of press stories] to the conscience of judges': ibid, 346. Later, in *Dun & Bradstreet Inc v Greenmoss Builders Inc*, 472 US 749 (1985), a plurality thought better of it and took up the task of characterizing news stories in libel actions as implicating private or public concern. Even so, neither the Supreme

Court nor the lower federal courts have shown any eagerness to take on this task beyond the rudimentary distinctions made in confidential source cases. *Dendrite* invites judges to expand their function dramatically by declaring news value in advance of trial and without standards.

40 *Thornhill v State of Alabama*, 310 US 88, 102 (1940). The truth-seeking value, one scholar has noted, concerns the 'open-ended pursuit of knowledge' through speech – the exploration of all ideas 'relevant to our understanding of the world, whether or not those ideas are political in nature': Robert Post, 'Reconciling Theory and Doctrine in First Amendment Jurisprudence', in Lee C. Bollinger and Geoffrey R. Stone (eds), *Eternally Vigilant: Free Speech in the Modern Era*, Chicago: University of Chicago Press, 2002, p. 153, pp. 161, 163, n. 44.

41 *Abrams v United States*, 250 US 616, 630 (1919) (Holmes J dissenting).

42 *Red Lion Broadcasting Co v F.C.C.*, 395 US 367, 390 (1969).

43 *Dennis v United States*, 341 US 494 (1951).

44 Keith Werhan, *Freedom of Speech: A Reference Guide to the United States Constitution*, Westport, CT: Praeger, 2004, p. 33.

45 Richard Reeves, *John Stuart Mill: Victorian Firebrand*, London: Atlantic Books, 2007, pp. 165–66.

46 Ibid., p. 278 (quoting Alan Ryan, *The Philosophy of John Stuart Mill*, Basingstoke: Macmillan, 1988, 255).

47 *Zeran v America Online Inc*, 129 F 3d 327, 330 (4th Cir, 1997) (quoting 'specific statutory findings' of the *Communications Decency Act of 1996* 47 USC § 230(a)(3)).

48 Jane B. Singer, 'Contested Autonomy: Professional and Popular Claims on Journalistic Norms' (2007) 8 *Journalism Studies* 79, 85.

49 Ibid.

50 E.g. Jones, 'Cybersmears and John Doe', p. 443 (claim brought by Yale Law women is 'suspect at best', and *Dendrite* balancing is needed to prevent chill).

51 561 F Supp 2d 249 (D Conn, 2008) ('*Does I and II*').

52 David Margolick, 'Slimed Online', *Portfolio* (online), 11 February 2009: www.portfolio.com/news-markets/national-news/portfolio/2009/02/11/Two-Lawyers-Fight-Cyber-Bullying.

53 *Does I and* II, 561 F Supp 2d 249, 256 n 7 (recounting Doe's argument).

54 Ibid.

55 Jones, 'Cybersmears and John Doe', p. 443.

56 Ashley I. Kissinger and Katharine Larsen, 'Shielding Jane and John: Can the Media Protect Anonymous Online Speech?' (2009) 26(3) *Communications Lawyer* 4, 6.

57 Likely scenarios would be cases such as *Public Relations Society of America v Road Runner High Speed Online*, 8 Misc 3d 820 (Sup Ct NY, 2005), where a speaker made factual assertions in anonymous emails about a manager's performance, or *Butler University v Doe* (lawsuit filed Marion County Superior Court, Minn, No. 49D020901PL0011164, 08 Jan 2009); see David Moltz, *University Sues Student Blogger* (16 October 2009) Inside Higher Ed www.insidehighered.com/news/2009/10/16/butler, where an anonymous blogger asserted that specific university administrators 'lied' about a personnel decision.

58 172 Cal App 4th 1125 (Cal Ct App, 2009) ('*Moreno*').

59 See Cynthia Moreno, *Coalinga Record*, 'Ode to Coalinga', full date not ascertainable, p. 4, available at: http://media.fresnobee.com/smedia/2010/09/15/11/OdeToCoalinga.source.prod_affiliate.8.pdf (reprinting Moreno's ode as letter to editor with signature and response).

60 John Ellis, 'Coalinga Grad Loses MySpace Rant Lawsuit', *The Fresno Bee* (Fresno, CA) 20 September 2010, available at http://0166244.blogspot.com/2010/09/heres-your.html.

61 *Foretich v Capital Cities/ABC Inc*, 37 F 3d 1541, 1559 (4th Cir, 1994) ('*Foretich*').

62 *Restatement (Second) of Torts* (1977) § 594 cmt (k).

63 *Foretich*, 37 F3d 1541, 1560 (quoting *New York Times Co v Sullivan*, 376 US 254, 270 (1964)).

64 Ibid., at 1562 (citing Prosser & Keeton on the Law of Torts, § 115, at 825 (5th edn 1984)).

65 *Novecon Ltd v Bulgarian-American Enterprise Fund*, 190 F 3d 556, 569 (DC Cir, 1999).

66 37 F 3d 1541, 1559.

67 Ibid., 1560.
68 Ibid., 1562.
69 Ibid.
70 Daniel J. Solove, *The Future of Reputation: Gossip, Rumor, and Privacy on the Internet*, New Haven, CT: Yale University Press, 2007, p. 177.
71 Ibid., p. 181 (noting that online posting 'transforms gossip into a widespread and permanent stain on people's reputations', and that even postings on 'an obscure blog' can appear 'in a google search under a person's name').
72 American Law Institute, *Restatement (Second) of Torts* (1977) § 652G.
73 *State v Eighth Judicial District Court*, 42 P 3d 233 (Nev, 2002).
74 Neil M. Richards and Daniel J. Solove, 'Privacy's Other Path: Recovering the Law of Confidentiality' (2007) 96 *Georgetown Law Journal* 123.
75 One commentator considered three doctrinal models: first, a 'general duty' of nondisclosure arising 'whenever personal information is received from another in confidence;' second, a duty of nondisclosure attaching only to fiduciary relationships; and third, a duty situated between the other two, attaching to 'nonpersonal relationships customarily understood to carry an obligation of confidence': Alan B. Vickery, Note, 'Breach of Confidence: An Emerging Tort', (1982) 82 *Columbia Law Review* 1426, 1456–62.
76 As noted, US cases are few. In one noted federal case, a student sued her professor for breaching confidentiality by widely circulating written charges of sexual harassment that the student had lodged against the professor. The court found that the interest in confidentiality of student complaints was a legitimate consideration in the university's decision to suspend the professor, despite his invocation of the First Amendment right of academic freedom. *Bonnell v Lorenzo*, 241 F 3d 800 (6th Cir, 2001).
77 Vickery, 'Breach of Confidence: An Emerging Tort', p. 1465.
78 [2009] EWHC 1358 (QB).
79 Claimant's Skeleton Argument for Hearing 4 June 2009, [3.1](b), on file with the author.
80 Ibid., [9].
81 Defendant's Skeleton Argument for Hearing 4 June 2009, at [7], [8], [9], on file with the author. Subsequently it was revealed that information had been obtained by email hacking, but this was not disclosed at the time of the case: see David Leigh and Lisa O'Carroll. '*Times* email-hacking evidence withheld from High Court, Leveson told', *Guardian*, Tuesday 7 February 2012 (available at.www.guardian.co.uk/media/2012/feb/07/)
82 Judgment, supra note 89, at [7].
83 Ibid., [9].
84 Ibid., [33].
85 Ibid., [11].
86 Ibid., [33].
87 Ibid., [32].
88 283 US 697 (1932).
89 *New York Times Co v US*, 403 US 713 (1971) (per curiam).
90 820 F 2d 1342 (1st Cir, 1986), modified on rehearing, 820 F 2d 1354 (1st Cir, 1986).
91 820 F 2d 1342, 1350.
92 John C. Jeffries, Jr., 'Rethinking Prior Restraint', (1983) 92 *Yale Law Journal* 409, 433.
93 94 P 3d 624 (Colo, 2004) ('*Bryant*')
94 Ibid., 635–37.
95 561 F 3d 261 (4th Cir, 2009).
96 Ibid., 272 (Wilkinson J concurring).
97 Ibid., 273.
98 Ibid.
99 Ibid.

17 The privacy interest in anonymous blogging

Lisa Austin

'It's a dangerous business, Frodo, going out of your door,' he used to say. 'You step onto the Road, and if you don't keep your feet, there is no knowing where you might be swept off to.'

–J. R. R. Tolkien, *The Lord of the Rings*

Introduction

In the evolving legal landscape regarding anonymous speech on the internet, much turns on the choice of metaphor, analogy and framework. For example, anonymity evokes powerful analogies within the framework of free speech. As Chief Justice Steele stated in *Doe v Cahill*, '[a]nonymous internet speech in blogs or chat rooms in some instances can become the modern equivalent of political pamphleteering',[1] which itself has been described as an 'honorable tradition of advocacy and dissent'.[2] But if we frame anonymous online speech as a privacy issue, then available legal metaphors and analogies seem to cut the other way. As Justice Eady recently stated in *The Author of a Blog v Times Newspapers Limited*, 'blogging is essentially a public rather than a private activity' and therefore there is no reasonable expectation of anonymity.[3] Implicit in such statements is a geographical metaphor in which walking out your front door takes you from a private and domestic sphere into the public realm. In this comment, I want to defend the position that understanding the privacy dimension of anonymous speech on the internet requires the abandonment of this simple language of public and private spheres in favour of an approach that focuses on audience segregation. While this does not, on its own, solve the legal questions regarding anonymous speech, I argue that it at least gets privacy interests on the table rather than dismissed out of hand.

I offer these comments in support of – and hopefully in the spirit of – Murchison's rich analysis of the speech interests in relation to anonymous internet speech. The strength of many of his arguments lies in his sensitivity to the ways in which speech on the internet is unlike speech in other contexts. I think that his examples of the importance of accountability and trust in creating an effective on-line marketplace of ideas, his concerns regarding 'more speech' as a self-help response to defamation, and his cautions against the usefulness of the analogy with confidential journalist sources are all extremely helpful. Similarly, Richardson and Thomas outline some of the important speech-related values that are furthered by anonymous and pseudonymous speech. In this comment I will outline the privacy interest in anonymous internet speech and use this to re-examine two cases that Murchison discusses: *Moreno v Hanford Sentinel Inc*[4] and the *Night Jack* case.[5] My argument is that the privacy analysis offered in both cases is deeply problematic because it is rooted in a geographic metaphor of a private realm that the blogger exited through a public speech act. An approach focusing on the question of audience and audience segregation is much more helpful for determining the privacy interests at stake.

Privacy, anonymity and audience segregation

Anonymity has long been viewed by many privacy scholars as an example of privacy in 'public'. For example, in his influential book *Privacy and Freedom*, Westin describes anonymity as one of the four basic states of individual privacy, a state that 'occurs when the individual is in public places or performing public acts but still seeks, and finds, freedom from identification and surveillance'.[6] Although an individual expects to be observed in public, Westin argues that unless a person 'is a well-known celebrity, he does not expect to be personally identified and held to the full rules of behavior and role that would operate if he were known to those observing him'.[7] He also notes:

> Anonymous relations give rise to what Georg Simmel called the 'phenomenon of the stranger,' the person who 'often received the most surprising openness – confidences which sometimes have the character of a confessional and which would be carefully withheld from a more closely related person.' In this aspect of anonymity the individual can express himself freely because he knows the stranger will not continue in his life and that, although the stranger may give an objective response to the questions put to him, he is able to exert no authority or restraint over the individual.[8]

In this way, freedom from being identified provides individuals with freedom from social expectations associated with that identity. This connects anonymity to what Schoeman described as one of the chief functions of privacy – the insulation of the individual from inappropriate forms of social pressure.[9] Many others have also pointed to privacy's role in protecting individuals from the inhibiting effect of exposure, whether actual or anticipated.[10] Through anonymity, one can 'hide' in plain sight, as it were, free of such social reactions. In this way, anonymity functions in the same way as privacy norms that are more explicitly tied to ideas of social withdrawal. It also indicates why anonymous speech can sometimes have such an intimate and confessional nature.

These insights into the privacy function of anonymity can be further refined in light of contemporary critiques of the public/private dichotomy. Many scholars have joined in critiquing the inability of such a simple dichotomy to address the variety of contexts and social roles that constitute the rich and complex matrix of contemporary lives.[11] Several scholars, including myself, have turned to Erving Goffman's concept of self-presentation as a helpful way of framing the relationship between privacy norms and social interaction in a manner that does not rely upon a simple dichotomy between public and private spheres.[12] The basic idea that I have tried to defend is that privacy norms protect an individual's identity, understood in terms of self-presentation. What is important for the discussion of anonymity is that we present ourselves to others and the particular audience of our self-disclosure matters. Instead of framing privacy in terms of the demarcation of a private sphere, we should instead think in terms of maintaining the integrity of one's audience. On this view, one of the central functions of privacy norms and conventions is the segregation of audiences.

Tied to the importance of audience segregation is the idea that audience reaction matters. Different audiences demand different things from us. Sometimes this is because of the specific identities of the people in our audience. For example, an individual might treat a status update on Facebook differently if read only by classmates than if her mother is also included as a 'friend' and therefore an audience member.[13] But the norms of the specific social setting within which an audience is situated can also matter. An off-the-cuff remark to close friends might be entirely appropriate but the same remark in the context of a public lecture might be entirely inappropriate. Social norms regarding how one is to comport oneself within different social contexts are at least partly responsible for giving content to this sense of the appropriateness of a particular disclosure.[14]

Nissenbaum's work on contextual integrity is helpful to show how a change in the nature of one's audience can be understood to be a violation of privacy without needing to invoke the idea of a private sphere. A privacy violation occurs when a disclosure that is appropriate to one social context crosses its contextual boundary and is disclosed within a very different social context – such as, for example, when a friend relays my off-the-cuff remark in a public forum. My disclosure is then judged according to a different set of social norms, ones that I did not anticipate (because I made the disclosure within a different social context) and likely do not welcome (either because according to such norms my disclosure is inappropriate or because the 'who' of my audience has changed to include people I do not wish to disclose this information to).

These two aspects of privacy understood in terms of self-presentation, centring on the ideas of intended audience and audience reaction, shed important light on the nature of anonymity. From the perspective of one's intended audience, the value of anonymity might seem opaque since anonymity is something that characterises the individual who is disclosing information rather than the audience who receives that information. However, the fact that I am willing to tell you something is sometimes intrinsically tied to the fact that I am also unwilling to tell certain others the same thing. If I tell you something and you do not know my 'real' identity then the likelihood of this information crossing the boundary of its social context and reaching my unintended audience is minimal. In this way, anonymity helps secure audience segregation. Moreover, audience segregation ensures that we are insulated from the unwanted reactions of our unintended audiences. Identification changes the context of our self-presentation, creating different expectations in our audience as well as potentially changing our audience.

Blogging and the courts

I want to show how a focus on audience segregation rather than public/private spheres is a more helpful framework for analysing the privacy interest in anonymous speech on the internet by examining the cases of *Moreno* and *Night Jack*.

Cynthia Moreno was a college student who posted 'An Ode to Coalinga', a disparaging description of her hometown of Coalinga, on her online journal on myspace.com. Although she removed it after six days, her former high-school principal sent it to the local newspaper where it was published in the Letters to the Editor section, along with Moreno's full name. The community reaction was extremely negative for Cynthia's family, who still lived in Coalinga: 'Appellants received death threats and a shot was fired at the family home, forcing the family to move out of Coalinga.'[15] Moreno claimed that her privacy had been invaded.[16]

Moreno tried to bring her claim under the public disclosure of private facts branch of the US tort of invasion of privacy. The court held that because Moreno posted her Ode on a 'hugely popular internet site' she made it 'available to any person with a computer and thus opened it to the public eye'.[17] Moreno's identity as the author of the Ode was also not a 'private fact'. Moreno's MySpace page only used her first name and a photo of herself but since this was enough for the former high-school principal to identify her without access to further private or confidential information then her full identity was already 'public' information.[18] The newspaper's publication of the Ode alongside Moreno's full name was simply giving further publicity to what was already public.

What is lost in this categorisation of private and public is the sense of audience: who did Moreno think she was speaking to and was it reasonable to keep this audience segregated from the very different audience of her hometown newspaper readers? It is at least arguable that Moreno thought that she was posting her Ode to a very particular audience – those who knew her by her first name on her MySpace site. Moreover, for many users the context of such online postings is more like the intimate and informal chatting with friends in a pub than the deliberate and formal writing of a letter to the editor. In other words, both the type of communication Moreno thought she was making and the audience she thought she was making this to were quite different than the newspaper publication she complained about. While this does not necessarily answer all of the questions regarding legal liability, it does show that characterising the newspaper disclosure as merely giving further publicity to what was already public ignores these important aspects of online communication. We have many different audiences and – especially in the online world – the various forms of anonymity and pseudonymity employed by individuals can help us to keep these audiences and their norms of communication segregated from one another.[19]

The *Night Jack* case concerned a police blog – 'Night Jack' (or 'NightJack' as it is sometimes called) – written by someone who was a detective constable. The blog was widely read and meant to be.[20] Prior to its nomination for the Orwell Prize, the blog had a readership of 1500 a day and after winning the prize this number increased to 60,000 a day.[21] This brought Night Jack increased media attention and eventually led the author to seek an injunction to restrain the publication of his identity by *The Times* Newspapers Ltd. The injunction was argued for on the grounds of confidentiality, including its expanded version of improper disclosure of private facts.[22]

Unlike the *Moreno* case, in which the mode of Cynthia Moreno's identification changed both the nature of the communication made (online journal to letter to the editor) and the nature of the audience, here the issue with identifying the author of Night Jack was solely about the nature of the audience. Night Jack was concerned about repercussions from his employer. However, similarly to Moreno, the court relied upon a simple view of privacy that is largely unhelpful.

In dismissing the privacy argument, Justice Eady accepted the case of *Mahmood v Galloway* as 'closely analogous' and 'entirely persuasive'.[23] But they are not 'closely' analogous if we pay more careful attention to the function that anonymity plays in the two cases. Mazher Mahmood was not a blogger but an investigative journalist who used a variety of 'undercover' identities in order to conduct covert interviews with individuals suspected of crimes and get them to reveal things to him that they would not if they knew he was an investigative journalist.[24] He was not using the cloak of anonymity to segregate his audience, but to trick his interlocutor into mistaking the nature of his own role as audience. None of this is illuminated by the reasoning in *Mahmood*, which framed the question of identification in terms of whether the identifying information at issue – in the *Mahmood* case, two photographs – is private rather than public. For example, in relation to the first photo, a passport photograph, Justice Mitting stated: 'it was not obtained for any purpose that could possibly be considered private or domestic'.[25] Neither was it a photo of Mahmood engaged in activities that could be described as domestic or private: 'it is simply a photograph of his face'.[26] This of course ignores the point of publishing the photos, which was to identify Mahmood rather than to provide information about him. And we cannot understand what is at stake in identifying Mahmood and how this is different from identifying Night Jack unless we have a more granular understanding of the function of anonymity. That the court in *Night Jack* viewed *Mahmood* as essentially the same case shows the poverty of its privacy analysis concerning anonymity.

Conclusion

In this brief comment, I have tried to show how trying to apply geographic metaphors regarding private and public spheres to internet communication is misguided. Such an approach too easily leads to the view that the internet is a public place and that speaking up is like leaving your private sphere of domesticity and taking your risks in the greater world. But if we see it as a sphere in which different people seek to reach different audiences with different types of communications then the picture is a great deal more complicated – but also more accurate. Privacy understood in terms of audience segregation can help to isolate the privacy interests at stake. Doing so does not answer the question of when it would be wrongful to identify someone engaged in anonymous speech, or when the courts should order such identification – for there may be many different and competing interests at stake. But it at least ensures that privacy enters the legal discussion.

Notes

1 *Doe v Cahill*, 884 A 2d 451 (Del, 2005).
2 Ibid., citing *McIntyre v Ohio Elections Commission*, 514 US 334, 357 (1995).
3 [2009] EWHC 1358 (QB) (the *'NightJack'* case). The anonymous blogger in this case framed his argument in terms of breach of confidentiality, including the 'improper disclosure of private facts' version that developed out of *Campbell v MGN Ltd* [2004] 2 AC 457 and *McKennit v Ash* [2008] QB 73: see [2009] EWHC 1358 (QB) at [2].
4 172 Cal App 4th 1125 (Cal Ct App, 2009) (*'Moreno'*).
5 [2009] EWHC 1358 (QB).
6 Alan F. Westin, *Privacy and Freedom*, New York: Atheneum, 1967, p. 31.
7 Ibid.
8 At pp. 31–32, citing Kurt Wolff (trans. and ed.) *The Sociology of Georg Simmel*, Glencoe, IL: Free Press, 1950, pp. 402–8.
9 Ferdinand D. Schoeman, *Privacy and Social Freedom*, Cambridge: Cambridge University Press, 1992.
10 Ruth Gavison, 'Privacy and the Limits of Law', (1980) 89 *Yale Law Journal* 421; Thomas Nagel, 'Concealment and Exposure' (1998) 27 *Philosophy & Public Affairs* 3 (discussing the inhibiting effect of the 'public gaze'); Beate Rössler, *The Value of Privacy*, Cambridge: Polity Press, 2005 (discussing the way in which known observation interferes with authenticity).
11 The best recent work to do so is Helen Nissenbaum's account of privacy as 'contextual integrity': Helen Nissenbaum, *Privacy in Context: Technology, Policy and the Integrity of Social Life*, Stanford, CA: Stanford University Press, 2010. See also Valerie Steeves, 'Reclaiming the Social Value of Privacy' in Ian Kerr, Valerie Steeves and Carole Lucock (eds), *Lessons From the Identity Trail: Anonymity, Privacy and Identity in a Networked Society*, Oxford: Oxford University Press, 2009, p. 191.
12 Lisa M. Austin, 'Privacy and the Private Law: The Dilemma of Justification' (2010) *McGill Law Journal* 165.
13 See Danah Boyd, 'Dear Voyeur, meet Flâneur ... Sincerely, Social Media' (2011) 8 *Surveillance & Society* 505.

14 I say 'partly' because there is also the separate set of considerations, as indicated earlier, regarding third-party interests in information. These interests may be part of these social norms or may be separate from them.

15 172 Cal App 4th 1125, 1129 (Cal Ct App, 2009).

16 There was also a claim that the family's privacy had been violated. The court held that even if there had been an invasion of Cynthia Moreno's privacy, her family members would not have standing. Ibid., 1131.

17 Ibid., 1130.

18 Ibid.

19 For an interesting discussion of audience segregation in relation to the design of social network sites see: Bibi van den Berg and Ronald E. Leenes, 'Audience Segregation in Social Network Sites' (paper presented at Second IEEE International Conference on Social Computing/Second IEEE International Conference on Privacy, Security, Risk and Trust, Minneapolis, Minnesota, 9 November 2010, available at http://ssrn.com/abstract=1706298 (accessed 24 June 2011)).

20 An archive is available here: http://nightjackarchive.blogspot.com/.

21 Sam Jones, 'A Fair Cop: Policeman's "Perfect" Blog Wins Orwell Prize', *Guardian* (online) 24 April 2009 at www.guardian.co.uk/books/2009/apr/24/orwell-prize-jack-night-winner-blog (accessed 24 June 2011); Richard Horton, 'NightJack: My Everyman Posts Seemed to Strike a Chord', *The Times* (online) 17 June 2009 at http://technology.timesonline.co.uk/tol/news/tech_and_web/article6515061.ece (accessed 24 June 2011).

22 [2009] EWHC 1358 (QB).

23 Ibid., [10].

24 *Mahmood v Galloway* [2006] EMLR 26 ('*Mahmood*').

25 Ibid., [16].

26 Ibid., [19].

18 'Privacy' of social networking texts

Megan Richardson and Julian Thomas

Introduction

The cases discussed in Brian Murchison's chapter show the risks of engaging in social networking, especially for amateurs – who in this context may be surprised to learn they are not the experts they thought they were when it comes to securing their privacy in the internet's bewilderingly complex social and technological environment. The Murchison chapter focuses on examples from the US and UK, but local Australian examples can be found as well. For instance, the furore over the firing, in 2010, of Melbourne *Age* journalist Catherine Deveny for her tweeting about the Logies (the Australian television industry awards) provides another salutary reminder of the uneasy scope of privacy available to those who choose to use social networking sites as their medium of discourse. One of Deveny's defences in the face of the heated public reaction to her found-offensive comments about local celebrities Bindi Irwin and Belinda Emmett was that tweeting was just like 'passing notes in class', suggesting she had not expected such a large public readership for her private asides,[1] in response to which David Penberthy commented in *The Weekend Australian*: 'It's a rubbish excuse; Twitter is just another form of publishing. It's a wholly public domain, one used by more than 50 million people worldwide.'[2] Such statements leads us to ask the question whether comments made on social networking sites are necessarily public, subject to effective steps taken to secure their protection by the author of the comments, or whether a degree of privacy can remain.

As the Murchison chapter shows, the courts to date seem intent on backing Penberthy's position. Thus we have the decision of Eady J in the English *Night Jack* case that 'blogging is a public activity' and therefore the author Richard Horton could not rely on privacy law to prevent *The Times* from exposing his identity as the Night Jack blogger.[3] Much the same was said by the California Court of Appeal in *Moreno v Hanford Sentinel* where it was held that Cynthia Moreno could reasonably expect no privacy when she published her 'Ode to Coalinga' on her 'Cynthia' MySpace page, later to find it reproduced in the *Coalinga Record* (through the agency of the headmaster of her former school) under her full name.[4] Murchison, a free-speech scholar, argues that these decisions were right in giving priority to public expression. But many social commentators thought *The Times* acted badly in revealing Horton's identity, his efforts to secure it notwithstanding.[5] For these commentators, the seriousness of the author's engagement with his project of exposing the life of a policeman on the beat and the quality of his blog – which received the Orwell Prize for online journalism – were reasons why Horton's privacy should have been respected, notwithstanding he breached his employer's code of conduct. On the other hand, the public reaction to *Moreno* was more along the lines that the claimant had only herself to blame for failing to use the MySpace privacy settings – and it was considered irrelevant that she had used only part of her name and had taken down her Ode from her MySpace page six days after putting it up in an effort to protect her and family's privacy.[6] The expressive and critical character of Moreno's Ode (and even the fact of her copyright which supposedly secured to her the sole and exclusive right to reproduce the text, although copyright was not actually relied on in the case) were treated as insufficient in these commentaries to the question of privacy. And in the actual decisions in the cases themselves the legal 'issues' were treated in an even less nuanced way. The courts treated expressions in cyber-space as if made to the public at large, including even those elements that the authors themselves preferred were kept from public knowledge, but had not taken steps to secure. In both cases, courts reached the same conclusion, viz that these authors who lack the skills and expertise to secure their privacy (i.e. in this setting were amateurs) could not expect the law to step in and protect their 'privacy' on the internet.

The decisions may be more important in normative than in factual terms. As Lisa Austin notes in her comment on Murchison's chapter, it may be questioned whether the internet is as automatically public as the decisions on their face may appear to suggest. Rather, we suggest, the *Night Jack* and *Moreno* decisions mark out the standards for future authoring behaviour on the internet in some very specific ways. How should those who engage in social networking respond to these decisions? For some the answer will be simple – as Pemberthy puts it, don't tweet to the world at large if you only want your (true) friends to see what you say. But there are many cases where the message is such that the widest possible audience is desired. In these cases, for all their weaknesses, anonymity or pseudonymity may still be the preferred technique of authors looking to publish their ideas.

Some historical comparisons and insights

History shows that identity-covering techniques have been integral to the development of our political and social literature, notwithstanding the public curiosity the practices aroused, the numerous exposés and the limited support given by courts (in a very few cases, most of those exposed never thinking of bringing legal action after the event). From 'Isaac Bickerstaff' and 'Mr Spectator' in *The Tatler* and *The Spectator* to the dignified anonymity of the essays in *The*

Quarterly Review and *Edinburgh Review*, much of the eighteenth- and early-nineteenth-century periodical literature was published without identification of authorship, although identification may have come later.[7] The major newspapers continued to employ anonymity into the twentieth century and some, such as *The Economist*, go on to this day. Poetry might have quite often been signed, at least by their more respectable authors, by the early years of the nineteenth century. But the newer form of the novel was more often anonymously published. According to one survey, approximately 80 per cent of new titles published in England in 1820 were without attribution of authorship.[8] The pattern only began to change after the first instalments of *Pickwick Papers* began to appear under Charles Dickens's name in the 1830s. Even then there were plenty of authors still who preferred not to be so identified.

Trollope argued against the practice of anonymity in the influential *Fortnightly Review* in 1865,[9] considering it an irresponsible act of publication for an author not to be publicly accountable for his or her own work. Nevertheless, he suggested that it was especially preferred by women as well as tolerated more on their behalf. Others have suggested it was used especially when a piece was seen as particularly revealing of the author's private personality – so that even when Charlotte Brontë's intensely intimate novels were the talk of London in the 1840s she was, according to her biographer Elizabeth Gaskell, insisting that her identity be preserved.[10] When the *Bradford Observer* announced in February 1850 that 'the only daughter of the Rev P. Brontë, incumbent of Haworth' was 'the authoress of *Jane Eyre* and *Shirley*, two of the most popular novels of the day, which have appeared under the name of "Currer Bell"',[11] Brontë's identity as the author of her books was a matter of wide public knowledge. Even then, her books continued to be published as Currer Bell's, although reviewers universally referred to the author as 'she' and some even used her name.

These authors must have known that they were vulnerable to exposure when they adopted their artificial authorial personas, or identified themselves obscurely as 'the author' (or 'the author of', as Jane Austen signed off *Pride and Prejudice* – another kind of pseudonym perhaps), or simply used no name at all to identify their authorship. Usually, there would be some who knew the secret of their true identity or could work it out. As William Cowper wrote in the sprightly magazine *The Connoisseur* in 1756, the chances of one's friends and confidants keeping secrets when the world wants to know them are slim indeed:[12]

> There is no mark of our confidence taken more kindly by a friend, than the entrusting him with a Secret; nor any that he is so likely to abuse. Confidantes in general are like crazy fire-locks, which are no sooner charged and cocked, than the spring gives way and the report immediately follows. Happy to have been thought worthy the confidence of one friend, they are impatient to manifest their importance to another; till between them and their friend, and their friend's friend, the whole matter

is presently known ... The secret catches on as it were by contact, and like electrical matter breaks forth from every link in the chain, almost at the same instant.

For those who thought that the law would protect them, it was plain that this was a risky assumption after the case of *Southey v Sherwood* in 1817.[13] Poet Laureate and conservative essayist Robert Southey sought ineffectively to prevent unauthorised publication of his allegedly seditious play *Wat Tyler* which he had written in his radical youth as a sometime-student at Oxford University and entrusted to a friend with a view to possible publication 20 years earlier (never to enquire since), complete with his identifying name. Lord Eldon refused the injunction, on the basis that Southey had not established he kept his property in the play and also intimating that a possibly seditious play would not be protected by a court of equity in any event. In the aftermath of the case, some 60,000 pamphlets of *Wat Tyler* were reportedly published and circulated throughout Britain and the colonies, gleefully attributed to Southey. In an article in the *Quarterly Review* soon after the case, it was remarked that *Southey v Sherwood* was one of the most notorious cases in literary circles.[14] Yet, even after *Wat Tyler*, Southey continued his practice of writing anonymously in the *Quarterly Review* for many further years. And Cowper's insight about the risks of secret revelation did not prevent his using the pseudonym 'Mr Town, Critic and Censor-General' for his essays in *The Connoisseur*.

Given the risk of exposure, we wonder whether there are good reasons why anonymity and pseudonymity may be employed by authors who (in general) may be said to be rational and experienced in decision-making as well as fully aware of their limited capacity to protect their identity through other means – again using history as a guide. We tentatively posit two scenarios where authors may reasonably seek out one or other of these forms of authorship, and where the law may also reasonably be called upon to support them if a case came to court.

The first scenario is one of valuable public expression which places the author at risk if his or her identity is uncovered. Here, we suggest, authors might reasonably choose anonymity or pseudonymity as the premise of their expression. Further, the law might reasonably support authors in protecting their identity on the basis that otherwise free speech may be chilled, subject to any overriding public policy consideration that may justify exposure. Trollope argued that literary expression requires an author to take responsibility by identifying himself or herself, suggesting that anonymity was not only questionably realistic but undesirable in the large majority of cases. Yet Brontë in the same society felt that her ability to speak truthfully in her fictional writings was easier behind a mask and went to great lengths to preserve this even when her books were successful. Might there be more modern cases where valuable expression is found easier behind a mask and if expression is desired the mask is worth supporting – for instance, the Iranian protestors blogging about the 2009 presidential election? *Night Jack* is another example (although it may still be argued that the fact of Horton's breach of the police code of conduct could be seen as outweighing the value of his speech – something that Eady J also pointed out in giving judgment in the case). Against these examples, however, there are cases in which expression seems the opposite of socially valuable, being directed more by personal animas or destructiveness: in these cases, viewed from a public policy perspective the case for anonymity or pseudonymity seems rather weaker.[15] In the middle are the difficult cases in which social value is possible but is harder to assess and may be offset by social costs – here a balancing of interests may be the only feasible approach.

Second, a fictional identity may serve a creative and/or business purpose, this being something again that both individual authors and the law might reasonably support, at least in some cases. Interestingly, Trollope thought that newspapers such as *The Times* were entitled to insist that their authors write anonymously on matters of news and politics since readers are looking to the newspaper's beacon as a source of opinion not its individual authors. In other words, he appreciated that the fictional identity of the newspaper might be its most effective brand.[16] However, generally he considered that individual authors do better to use their own name, especially when they have become successful and thus have a reputation of their own.[17] And he conducted a small experiment in anonymous publishing to show that it was indeed the case that his books had a better market when published under his own name.[18] We might wonder whether Trollope was right in surmising that a successful author's own name is always the best signifier. The persona of the elderly gentlemen Isaac Bickerstaff and Mr Spectator and their coterie of friends observing on public behaviour and manners entertained the audiences of *The Tatler* and *Spectator* for many years (although Steele's identity at least was guessed at by 'the cognoscenti of London').[19] 'Currer Bell' seemed to be sufficient to sell Bronte's books. In the same way, *Sketches by Boz* may have been published as if authored by 'Boz' but this did not reduce the public's enjoyment, even after Dickens was known to be the author. Dickens may have used his own name on his later stories and essays. But whether this was necessary or whether an authorial persona – as with the American 'Mark Twain', the English 'George Orwell' and the Australian 'Banjo' Paterson, whose pseudonyms were adopted and used for reasons that had little to do with privacy[20] and continued to be used long after their authors' true identities were known – would have been as effective a brand and more entertaining for the audience is something we can only speculate about.

This brings us to a final observation. For all the genuine privacy concerns behind the *Night Jack* and *Moreno* cases, is there perhaps more of interest to the particular choices of authorial disguise here than we have hitherto supposed? For instance, was the evocative 'Night Jack' a better label than 'Richard Horton' for a policeman blogging about the beat? That the blog quickly captured a wide audience and won the Orwell Prize for online journalism is no mean feat. In the same way, might the mysterious name of 'Cynthia' be a more alluring device than the more obvious name of 'Cynthia Moreno' to write about one's home town? These authors may have intended privacy but in choosing to write under a *non de plume* they engaged in a practice that has long been used for various purposes and over time has developed multiple functions for its audience.

Acknowledgements

With thanks to James Parker, Marc Trabsky and Thomas Vranken for helpful advice.

Notes

1 Thomas Hunter, '"Taken out of context": Deveny Defends Twitter Comments on Logies Night', *The Age* (online), 4 May 2010: www.theage.com.au/entertainment/tv-and-radio/taken-out-of-context-deveny-defends-twitter-comments-on-logies-night-20100504-u50y.html.

2 David Penberthy, 'Tweet Nothings Lack Good Taste and Substance', *Weekend Australian* (Sydney), 8–9 May 2010, Inquirer, p 7.

3 *Author of a Blog v Times Newspapers Ltd* [2009] EWHC 1358 (QB) ('*Night Jack*' or, as it is sometimes called, '*NightJack*').

4 *Moreno v Hanford Sentinel Inc*, 172 Cal App 4th 1125 (Cal Ct App, 2009). The court refused to strike out an alternative claim for intentional infliction of emotional distress and noted but did not determine the potential issue of copyright infringement, considering that a matter for a Federal Court.

5 For round-ups see Judith Townend, 'Right of a Blogger's Anonymity: A Selection of Views' on journalism.co.uk (17 June 2009): http://blogs.journalism.co.uk/editors/2009/06/17/right-of-a-bloggers-anonymity-a-selection-of-views/; Paul Bradshaw, 'The Complicated Case of the (Now Not) Anonymous Police Blogger, *The Times*, and "Public Interest"' on *Online Journalism Blog* (16 June 2009): http://onlinejournalismblog.com/2009/06/16/the-complicated-case-of-the-now-not-anonymous-police-blogger-the-times-and-public-interest/ and Gaurav Mishra, 'The Curious Case of Night Jack Richard Horton: What Does it Mean for Blogger Anonymity?' on *Gauravonomics Blog* (28 June 2009) at www.gauravonomics.com/blog/the-curious-case-of-nightjack-richard-horton-what-does-it-mean-for-blogger-anonymity/.

6 See, for instance, Eric Goldman, 'Republishing MySpace Post in Local Paper Might Be Intentional Infliction of Emotional Distress: *Moreno v. Hanford Sentinel*' on *Technology & Marketing Law Blog* (4 April 2009) at http://blog.ericgoldman.org/archives/2009/04/republishing_my.htm. For a more sympathetic treatment see, however, Julie Hilden, *Is It a Violation of Privacy Law to Reproduce a MySpace Posting in a Context Where the Very People It Targets Will See It?* (27 April 2009) Findlaw.com at http://writ.news.findlaw.com/hilden/20090427.html.

7 See John Mullan, *Anonymity: A Secret History of English Literature*, London: Faber & Faber, 2007, Ch. 6.

8 See James Raven, 'Anonymous Novels in Britain and Ireland' in Robert Griffin (ed.), *The Faces of Anonymity: Anonymous and Pseudonymous Publication from the Sixteenth to the Twentieth Century*, New York: Palgrave Macmillan, 2003, p. 141 at 143.

9 Anthony Trollope, 'On Anonymous Literature', *Fortnightly Review*, Vol. 1, 1865, 491.

10 Elizabeth Gaskell, *The Life of Charlotte Brontë*, London: Smith Elder & Co, 1857, Ch. 19.

11 See Mullan, *Anonymity: A Secret History of English Literature*, pp. 97–98.

12 William Cowper, 'On Keeping a Secret', *The Connoisseur* No. 119, 6 May 1756. And see Denise Gigante, *The Great Age of the English Essay: An Anthology*, New Haven, CT: Yale University Press, 2008, Ch. 6, where the essay is reproduced at pp. 188–92.

13 *Southey v Sherwood*, 2 Mer 434 (1817). The case and its aftermath are discussed in Frank Hoadley, 'The Controversy Over Southey's "Wat Tyler"' (1941) 38 *Studies in Philology* 81.

14 Cases of *Walcot v Walker; Southey v Sherwood; Murray v Benbow*, and *Lawrence v Smith, Quarterly Review*, Vol. 27, 1822, 123.

15 Thus Trollope concluded that only 'bad criticism – the criticism which is in fact unsigned, and which is useless both to the artist and public – would perish under the practice which I recommend, to the great benefit of all survivors': 'On Anonymous Literature' at 497–98.

16 'The newspaper is not a lamp lighted by a single hand, but a sun placed in the heaven by an invisible creator': per Trollope, ibid., 495.

17 Ibid., 491 (books) and 495–96 (magazine articles).

18 See, for an intriguing account, Judith Knelman, 'Trollope's Experiment with Anonymity' (1981) 14 *Victorian Periodicals Review* 21.

19 Richmond Bond, *The Tatler: The Making of a Literary Journal*, Cambridge, MA: Harvard University Press, 1971, p 20.

20 See Charles Neider (ed.), *The Autobiography of Mark Twain*, New York and London: Harper Row, 1917, p. 105 ('Mark Twain', based on a Mississippi leadsman's warning call, adopted to 'save [the] time' of those given to criticising Clement's articles); Alok Rai, *Orwell and the Politics of Despair*, Cambridge: Cambridge University Press, 1988, p. 43 ('Orwell developed, in time, the perfect myth ... [and the] fact that the "transformation" of Blair into Orwell ... was an event or process of some significance has been widely recognised by Orwell critics'); and A. B. ('Banjo') Paterson, 'Giants of the Paddle, Pen and Pencil' *Sydney Morning Herald*, 11 February 1939, p 21 (Paterson recollecting that he used 'Banjo' for poems submitted to *The Bulletin* to avoid being associated with the failure of his pamphlet 'Australia for Australians').

Select bibliography

Compiled by Alex Heller-Nicholas and Oscar O'Bryan

Books and reports

Andrejevic, Mark, *Reality TV: The Work of Being Watched*, Lanham, MD: Rowman & Littlefield, 2004.

Atton, Chris and James F. Hamilton, *Alternative Journalism*. London: Sage, 2008.

Bailey, Olga G., Bart Cammaerts and Nino Carpentier, *Understanding Alternative Media*, Maidenhead: Open University Press, 2007.

Banks, Mark, *The Politics of Cultural Work*, Basingstoke: Palgrave, 2007.

Baudrillard, Jean, *Simulacra and Simulations* (trans. Sheila Faria Glaser) Ann Arbor: University of Michigan Press, 1994.

Beahm, George, *Fact, Fiction and Folklore in Harry Potter's World*, San Francisco, Hampton Roads Publishing, 2005.

Benkler, Yochai, *The Wealth of Networks: How Social Production Transforms Markets and Freedom*, New Haven, CT: Yale University Press, 2006.

Boehlert, Eric, *Bloggers on the Bus: How the Internet Changed Politics and the Press*, New York: Free Press, 2007.

Bonham-Carter, Victor, *Authors By Profession*, London: Society of Authors, 1978.

Bouchard, Donald F. (ed.), *Michel Foucault: Language, Counter-Memory, Practice*, Oxford: Basil Blackwell 1977.

Bruns, Alex, *Blogs, Wikipedia, Second Life and Beyond*, New York: Peter Lang, 2008.

Burgess, Jean and Joshua Green, *YouTube: Online Video and Participatory Culture*, Cambridge: Polity Press, 2009.

Corfield, Penelope, *Power and the Professions in Britain, 1700-1850*, London and New York: Routledge, 1995.

Coyer, Kate, Tony Dowmunt and Alan Fountain (eds), *The Alternative Media Handbook*, London: Routledge, 2007.

Downing, John, *Radical Media: The Political Experience of Alternative Communication*, Boston, MA: South End Press, 1984.

Ezell, Margaret J.M., *Social Authorship and the Advent of Print*, Baltimore, MD: Johns Hopkins University Press, 1999.

Garber, Marjorie, *Academic Instincts*, Princeton, NJ: Princeton University Press, 2000.

Hellekson, Karen and Kristina Busse (eds), *Fan Fiction and Fan Communities in the Age of the Internet*, Jefferson, NC: McFarland, 2006.

Helprin, Mark, *Digital Barbarism: A Writer's Manifesto*, New York: HarperCollins, 2009.

Hemmungs Wirtén, Eva, *Cosmopolitan Copyright: Law and Language in the Translation Zone*, Uppsala University, 2011.

Hesmondhalgh, David, *The Cultural Industries*, London: Sage, 2002.

Hesmondhalgh, David and Sarah Baker, *Creative Labour: Media Work in Three Cultural Industries*, Abingdon and New York: Routledge, 2010.

Intellectual Property Office (UK), © *The Way Ahead: A Strategy for Copyright in the Digital Age*, Report (2009).

Jenkins, Henry, *Textual Poachers: Television Fans and Participatory Culture*, New York: Routledge, 1992.

——, *Convergence Culture: Where Old and New Media Collide*, New York: New York University Press, 2006.

——, *Fans, Bloggers and Gamers: Exploring Participatory Culture*, New York: New York University Press, 2006.

Jenkins, Henry et al., *Confronting the Challenges of Participatory Culture: Media Education for the 21st Century* (Report, John D. and Catherine T. MacArthur Foundation, 2009). http://mit-press.mit.edu/books/full_pdfs/Confronting_the_Challenges.pdf

Keen, Andrew, *The Cult of the Amateur: How Blogs, MySpace, YouTube, and the Rest of Today's User-Generated Media are Destroying our Economy, our Culture, and our Values*, New York: Crown Business, 2008.

Lanier, Jaron, *You Are Not a Gadget: A Manifesto*, New York: Alfred A. Knopf, 2010.

Larson, Magali L., *The Rise of Professionalism: A Sociological Analysis*, Los Angeles: University of California Press, 1977.

Lastowka, Greg, *Virtual Justice: The New Laws of Online Worlds*, New Haven, CT, and London: Yale University Press, 2010.

Leadbeater, Charles and Paul Miller, *The Pro-Am Revolution: How Enthusiasts Are Changing Our Economy and Society*, London: Demos, 2004.

Lessig, Lawrence, *Remix: Making Art and Commerce Thrive in the Hybrid Economy*, New York: Penguin, 2008.

Levy, Steven, *Hackers: Heroes of the Computer Revolution*, Garden City, NY: Anchor Press/Doubleday, 1994.

Lindberg, Ulf, Gestur Gudmundsson, Morten Michelsen and Hans Weisenthaunet, *Rock Criticism From the Beginning: Amusers, Bruisers and Cool-Headed Cruisers*, New York: Peter Lang, 2005.

Lovink, Geert and Sabine Niederer (eds), *Video Vortex Reader: Responses to YouTube*, Amsterdam: Institute of Network Cultures, 2008.

Manuel, Peter, *Cassette Culture: Popular Technology and Music in North Italy*, Chicago and London: University of Chicago Press, 1993.

Napoli, Philip M., *Audience Evolution: New Technologies and the Transformation of Media Audiences*, New York: Columbia University Press, 2011.

Negus, Keith, *Producing Pop: Culture and Conflict in the Popular Music Industry*, London: Arnold, 1992.

OECD, *Participative Web and User-Created Content: Web 2.0, Wikis and Social Networking*, Paris: Organisation for Economic Co-operation and Development, 2008.

Portes, Alejandro, Manuel Castells and Lauren A. Benton (eds), *The Informal Economy: Studies in Advanced and Less Developed Countries*, Baltimore, MD: Johns Hopkins University Press, 1989.

Robbins, Bruce, *Secular Vocations: Intellectuals, Professionalism, Culture*, London and New York: Verso, 1993.

Rosenberg, Scott, *Say Anything: How Blogging Began, What It's Becoming, and Why It Matters*, New York: Three Rivers Press, 2009.

Schwartz Cohen, Ruth, *More Work for Mother: The Ironies of Household Technology From the Open Hearth to the Microwave*, New York: Basic Books, 1985.

Sennett, Richard, *The Craftsman*, London: Allen Lane, 2008.

Sennett, Sean and Simon Groth, *Off the Record: 25 Years of Music Street Press*, St Lucia: University of Queensland Press, 2010.

Shirky, Clay, *Here Comes Everybody: The Power of Organizing Without Organizations*, New York: Penguin Press, 2008.

——, *Cognitive Surplus: Creativity and Generosity in a Connected Age*, New York: Penguin, 2010.

Stebbins, Robert A., *Amateurs: On the Margin Between Work and Leisure*, Beverly Hills, CA: Sage, 1979.

——, Amateurs, Professionals, and Serious Leisure, Montreal: McGill-Queen's University Press, 1992.

Sternberger, Paul S., *Between Amateur and Aesthete: The Legitimization of Photography as Art in America, 1880–1900* (PhD thesis, Columbia University, New York, 1997).

Tapscott, Don and Anthony D. Williams, *Wikinomics: How Mass Collaboration Changes Everything*, New York: Penguin Group, 2010 expanded edition.

Terranova, Tiziana, *Network Cultures*, London: Pluto Press, 2004.

von Hippel, Eric, *Democratizing Innovation*, Cambridge, MA: MIT Press, 2006.

Wahl-Jorgensen, Karin, *Journalists and the Public: Newsroom Culture, Letters to the Editor, and Democracy*, Cresskill, NJ: Hampton Press, 2007.

Waltz, Mitzi, *Alternative and Activist Media*, Edinburgh: Edinburgh University Press, 2005.

Winchester, Simon, *The Meaning of Everything: The Story of the Oxford English Dictionary*, Oxford: Oxford University Press, 2003.

Wolff, Janet, *The Social Production of Art*, Basingstoke: Macmillan, 2nd edn, 1993.

Zittrain, Jonathan, *The Future of the Internet and How to Stop It*, New Haven, CT, and London: Yale University Press, 2008.

Chapters in edited books

Atton, Chris, 'Alternative and Citizen Journalism' in Karin Wahl-Jorgensen and Thomas Hanitzsch (eds), *The Handbook of Journalism Studies*, New York: Routledge, 2009, p. 265.

Burgess, Jean and Joshua Green, 'The Entrepeneurial Vlogger: Participatory Culture Beyond the Pro-Am Divide' in Pelle Snickars and Patrick Vonderau (eds), *The YouTube Reader*, Stockholm: The National Library of Sweden, 2008, p. 89.

Burri-Nenova, Mira, 'User Created Content in Virtual Worlds and Cultural Diversity' in Christoph Beat Graber and Mira Burri-Nenova (eds), *Governance of Digital Game Environments and Cultural Diversity: Transdisciplinary Perspectives*, Cheltenham: Edward Elgar, 2010, p. 74.

Castells, Manuel and Alejandro Portes, 'World Underneath: The Origins, Dynamics, and Effects of the Informal Economy' in Alejandro Portes, Manuel Castells and Lauren A. Benton (eds), *The Informal Economy: Studies in Advanced and Less Developed Countries*, Baltimore, MD: Johns Hopkins University Press, 1989, p. 11.

Centeno, Miguel A. and Alejandro Portes (1989). 'Out of the Shadows' in Alejandro Portes, Manuel Castells and Lauren A. Benton (eds), *The Informal Economy: Studies in Advanced and Less Developed Countries*, Baltimore, MD: Johns Hopkins University Press, 1989, p. 23.

Garber, Marjorie,'The Amateur Professional and the Professional Amateur' in *Academic Instincts*, Princeton, Princeton University Press, 2001, p. 1.

Green, Joshua and Henry Jenkins, 'The Moral Economy of Web 2.0: Audience Research and Convergence Culture' in Jennifer Holt and Alisa Perren (eds), *Media Industries: History, Theory and Method*, New York: Wiley-Blackwell, 2009, p. 213.

Gudmundsson, Gestur, Ulf Lindberg, Morten Michelsen and Hans Weisethaunet, 'Brit Crit: Turning Points in British Rock Criticism, 1960–1990' in Steve Jones (ed.), *Pop Music and the Press*, Philadelphia, PA: Temple University Press, 2002, p. 60.

Hendry, Jennifer and Kay E. Goodall, 'Facebook and the Commercialisation of Personal Information: Some Questions of Provider-to-User Privacy' in Morag Goodwin, Bert-Jaap Koops and Ronald Leenes (eds), *Dimensions of Technological Regulation*, Nijmegen: Wolf Legal Publishers, 2010, p. 107.

Hu, Kelly, 'Chinese Subtitle Groups and the Neoliberal Work Ethic' in Eyal Ben Ari and Nissim Otmazgin (eds), *Popular Culture Collaborations and Coproductions in East and Southeast Asia*, Kyoto: Kyoto University Press, forthcoming.

Hunt, A. J., 'A Brief History of Field Archaeology in the UK: The Academy, the Profession and the Amateur' in Ruth Finnegan (ed.), *Participating in the Knowledge Society: Researchers Beyond the University Walls*, Basingstoke: Palgrave Macmillan, 2005.

Ito, Kenji, 'Possibilities of Non-Commercial Games: The Case of Amateur Role-Playing Game Designers in Japan' in Suzanne de Castell and Jennifer Jenson (eds), *Worlds In Play: International Perspectives on Digital Games Research*, New York: Peter Lang, 2007, p. 129.

Tushnet, Rebecca, 'Copyright Law, Fan Practices, and the Rights of the Author' in Jonathan Gray, Cornel Sandvoss and C. Lee Harrington (eds), *Fandom: Identities and Communities in a Mediated World*, New York: New York University Press, 2007, p. 60.

Journal articles, conference papers

Andrejevic, Mark, 'Watching Television Without Pity: The Productivity of Online Fans' (2008) 9 *Television and New Media* 24.

Arrow, Kenneth, 'Gifts and Exchanges' (1972) 1 *Philosophy and Public Affairs* 343.

Benkler, Yochai, 'A Free Irresponsible Press: WikiLeaks and the Battle over the Soul of the Networked Fourth Estate' (2011) 46 *Harvard Civil Rights – Civil Liberties Law Review* 311.

Berman, Morris, '"Hegemony" and the Amateur Tradition in British Science' (1975) 8 *Journal of Social History* 30.

Bowen Martin, Chase and Mark Deuze, 'The Independent Production of Culture: A Digital Games Case Study' (2009) 4 *Games and Culture* 276.

Bowrey, Kathy, 'The New Intellectual Property: Celebrity, Fans and the Properties of the Entertainment Franchise' (2011) 20(1) *Griffith Law Review* 188.

Brennan, Marc, 'This Place Rocks! The Brisbane Street Press, Local Culture, Identity and Economy', (2007) 21(3) *Continuum: Journal of Media & Cultural Studies* 433.

Bruns, Alex, 'Exploring the Pro-Am Interface Between Production and Produsage' (paper presented at The Internet Turning 40 Conference, Hong Kong, 19 June 2010): http://produsage.org/files/2010/Exploring%20the%20Pro-Am%20Interface%20between%20Production%20and%20Produsage.pdf.

Buckingham, David, Maria Pini and Rebekah Willett, 'Take Back the Tube!: The Discursive Construction of Amateur Film and Video Making' (2007) 8 *Journal of Media Practice* 183.

Chander, Anupam and Madhavi Sunder, 'Everyone's a Superhero: A Cultural Theory of "Mary Sue" Fan Fiction as Fair Use' (2007) 95 *California Law Review* 597.

Chung, Jacqueline Lai, 'Drawing Idea from Expression: Creating a Legal Space for Culturally Appropriated Literary Characters' (2007) 49 *William & Mary Law Review* 903.

Cianci, Christopher C., 'Entertainment Or Exploitation?: Reality Television And The Inadequate Protection Of Child Participants Under The Law' (2009) 18 *Southern California Interdisciplinary Law Journal* 363.

Condry, Ian, 'Dark Energy: What Fansubs Reveal About the Copyright Wars' (2010) 5 *Mechademia* 194.

Coté, Mark and Jennifer Pybus, 'Learning to Immaterial Labour 2.0: MySpace and Social Networks' (2007) 7(1) *Ephemera* 88.

Deery, June, 'Reality TV as Advertainment' (2004) 2(1) *Popular Communication* 1

de Peuter, Greig and Nick Dyer-Witheford 'A Playful Multitude? Mobilising and Counter-Mobilising Immaterial Game Labour' (2005) 5 Fibreculture: www.fibreculture.org/journal/issue5/depeuter_dyerwitheford.html.

de Zwart, Melissa, 'Angel(us) is my Avatar! An Exploration of Avatar Identity in the Guise of the Vampire' (2010) 15 *Media & Arts Law Review* 318.

Duchesne, Scott, 'Stardom/Fandom: Celebrity and Fan Tribute Performance' (2010) 141 *Canadian Theatre Review* 21.

Fore, Steve, 'America, America, This is You!: The Curious Case of America's Funniest Home Videos' (1993) 21 *Journal of Popular Film and Television* 37.

Fox, Broderick, 'Rethinking the Amateur' (2004) 24(1) *Spectator* 4.

Freedman, Alisa, 'Train Man and the Gender Politics of Japanese "Otaku" Culture: The Rise of New Media, Nerd Heroes and Consumer Communities' (2009) 20 *Intersections: Gender and Sexuality in Asia and the Pacific*: http://intersections.anu.edu.au/issue20/freedman.htm.

Freedman, Matthew B., 'Machinima and Copyright Law' (2005) 13 *Journal of Intellectual Property Law* 235.

George, Carlisle and Jackie Scerri, 'Web 2.0 and User-Generated Content: Legal Challenges in the New Frontier' (2007) 2 *Journal of Information, Law & Technology* www2.warwick.ac.uk/fac/soc/law/elj/jilt/2007_2/

Gervais, Daniel, 'The Tangled Web of UGC: Making Copyright Sense of User-Generated Content' (2009) 11 *Vanderbilt Journal of Entertainment and Technology Law* 841.

Haley, William, 'Findings: Amateurism' (1976) Spring American Scholar (available at http://theamericanscholar.org/amateurism/).

Hamilton, James, 'Remaking Media Participation in Early Modern England' (2003) 4 *Journalism* 293.

Hesmondhalgh, David, 'User-Generated Content, Free Labour and the Cultural Industries' (2010) 10 *Ephemera* 278.

Hetcher, Steven, 'User-Generated Content and the Future of Copyright: Part Two - Agreements Between Users and Mega-Sites' (2008) 24 *Santa Clara Computer & High Tech Law Journal* 829.

——, 'Using Social Norms to Regulate Fan Fiction and Remix Culture' (2009) 157 *University of Pennsylvania Law Review* 1869.

Humphreys, Sal, 'Productive Players: Online Computer Games' Challenge to Conventional Media Forms (2005) 2 *Communication and Critical/Cultural Studies* 1.

Hunter, Dan and Greg Lastowka, 'Amateur-to-Amateur' (2004) 46 *William & Mary Law Review* 951.

Hunter, Dan and John Quiggin, 'Money Ruins Everything' (2008) 30 *Hastings Communications & Entertainment Law Journal* 203.

Jahn-Sudmann, Andreas, 'Innovation Not Opposition: The Logic of Distinction of Independent Games' (2008) 2 *Eludamos. Journal for Computer Game Culture* 5.

Jann, Rosemary, 'From Amateur to Professional: The Case of the Oxbridge Historians' (1983) 22 *Journal of British Studies* 122.

Jenkins, Henry, 'The Cultural Logic of Media Convergence' (2004) 7(1) *International Journal of Cultural Studies* 33.

Jetto, Beatrice, 'Music Blogs, Music Scenes, Sub-Cultural Capital: Emerging Practices in Music Blogs' (paper presented at *Cybercultures: Exploring Critical Issues*, Salzburg, Austria, 13 March 2010).

Johnson, Brian, 'Someone Call Karl Marx: The Means of Production is in the Hands of the Masses and a Revolution is Under Way' (2005) 118(51) *Maclean's* 56.

Jones, Jonathan D., 'Cybersmears and John Doe: How Far Should First Amendment Protection of Anonymous Internet Speakers Extend?' (2009) 7 First Amendment Law Review 421.

Katyal, Sonia K., 'Performance, Property, and the Slashing of Gender in Fan Fiction' (2006) 14 *Journal of Gender, Social Policy and the Law* 461.

——, 'Semiotic Disobedience' (2006) 84 *Washington University Law Review* 489.

Kinsella, Sharon, 'Japanese Subculture in the 1990s: Otaku and the Amateur Manga Movement' (1998) 24 *Journal of Japanese Studies* 289.

Kissinger, Ashley I., and Katharine Larsen, 'Shielding Jane and John: Can the Media Protect Anonymous Online Speech?' (2009) 26(3) *Communications Lawyer* 4.

Kustritz, Anne, 'Slashing the Romance Narrative' (2003) 26 *Journal of American Culture* 371.

Lastowka, Greg, 'User Generated Content & Virtual Worlds' (2008) 10 *Vanderbilt Journal of Entertainment and Technology Law* 893.

Lerner, Josh and Jean Tirole, 'Some Simple Economics of Open Source' (2002) 50 *Journal of Industrial Economics* 197.

Lessig, Lawrence, 'Innovating Copyright' (2002) 20 *Cardozo Arts & Entertainment Law Journal* 611.

Levenson, Jacob, 'Why John Lennon Matters: The Case for Professional Pop-Music Critics in an Amateur Age' (2009) July/August *Columbia Journalism Review* 54.

Lobato, Ramon, Julian Thomas and Dan Hunter, 'Histories of User-Generated Content: Between Formal and Informal Media Economies' (2011) 5 International *Journal of Communication* 899.

McLelland, Mark, 'No Climax, No Point, No Meaning? Japanese Women's Boy-Love Sites on the Internet' (2000) 24(3) *Journal of Communication Inquiry* 274.

——, 'The World of Yaoi: The Internet, Censorship and the Global "Boy's Love" Fandom' (2005) 23 *Australian Feminist Law Journal* 61.

Melican, Jay and Susan Faulkner, 'Getting Noticed, Showing-Off, Being Over-Heard: Amateurs, Authors and Artists Inventing and Reinventing Themselves in Online Communities' (paper presented at EPIC 2007 Conference, Keystone, Colorado, 3–6 October 2007): http://citeseerx. ist.psu.edu/viewdoc/download?doi=10.1.1.87.3505&rep=rep1&type=pdf#page=55 p. 46.

Mensel, Robert E., '"Kodakers Lying in Wait": Amateur Photography and the Right of Privacy in New York, 1885–1915' (1991) 43 *American Quarterly* 24.

Milner, Ryan M., 'Working for the Text: Fan Labor and the New Organization' (2009) *International Journal of Cultural Studies* 491.

Moe, Hallvard, 'Everyone a Pamphleteer? Reconsidering Comparisons of Mediated Public Participation in the Print Age and the Digital Era' (2010) 34 *Media, Culture & Society* 691.

Moor, Elizabeth, 'Branded Spaces: The Scope of "New Marketing"' (2003) 3 *Journal of Consumer Culture* 39.

Muniz, Albert M. and Hope Jensen Schau, 'Vigilante Marketing and Consumer-Generated Communications' (2007) 36(3) *Journal of Advertising* 35.

Negus, Keith, 'The Work of Cultural Intermediaries and the Enduring Distance between Production and Consumption' (2002) 16(4) *Cultural Studies* 501.

Nicholson, Judith A., 'FCJ-030 Flash! Mobs in the Age of Mobile Connectivity' (2005) 6 *Fibreculture Journal* http://six.fibreculturejournal.org.

Noda, Nathaniel T., 'Copyright Retold: How Interpretive Rights Foster Creativity and Justify Fan-Based Activities' (2010) 57 *Journal of the Copyright Society of the USA* 987.

Norris, Craig and Jason Bainbridge, 'Selling Otaku? Mapping the Relationship between Industry and Fandom in the Australian Cosplay Scene' (2009) 20 *Intersections: Gender and Sexuality in Asia and the Pacific* 1.

Nov, Oded, 'What Motivates Wikipedians?' (2007) 50 *Communications of the ACM* 60.

Oakley, Kate, 'Include Us Out: Economic Development and Social Policy in the Creative Industries' (2006) 15(4) *Cultural Trends* 255.

Ortega, Felipe, Jesus M. Gonzalez-Barahona, and Gregorio Robles, 'On the Inequality of Contributions to Wikipedia' (paper presented at the 41st *Annual Hawaii International Conference on System Sciences*, Waikoloa, Hawaii, 2008) 304.

Ouellette, Laurie, 'Camcorder Dos and Don'ts: Popular Discourses on Amateur Video and Participatory Television' (1995) 36 *Velvet Light Trap* 33.

Paasonen, Susanna, 'Labors of Love: Netporn, Web 2.0, and the Meanings of Amateurism' (2010) 20(10) *New Media & Society* 1.

Peluchette, Joy and Katherine Karl, 'Examining Students' Intended Image on Facebook: "What Were They Thinking?!"' (2010) 85 *Journal of Education for Business* 30.

Postigo, Hector, 'Video Game Appropriation through Modifications' (2008) 14. *Convergence: International Journal of Research Into New Media Technologies* 59.

Quilter, Harry, 'The Amateur' (1886) 49 *Contemporary Review* 383.

Rauch, Eron, and Christopher Bolton, 'A Cosplay Photography Sampler' (2010) 5 *Mechademia* 176.

Raymond, Eric, 'Homesteading the Noosphere' (1998) 3(10-5) *First Monday* www.firstmonday. org/htbin/cgiwrap/bin/ojs/index.php/fm/article/view/621/542

Reuveni, Erez, 'Authorship in the Age of the Conducer' (2007) 54 *Journal of the Copyright Society of the USA* 285.

Ribstein, Larry E., 'From Bricks to Pajamas: The Law and Economics of Amateur Journalism' (2006) 48 *William and Mary Law Review* 185.

Richardson, Megan and David Tan, 'The Art of Retelling: Harry Potter and Copyright in a Fan-Literature Era' (2009) 14 *Media & Arts Law Review* 31.

Ritzer, George and Nathan Jurgenson, 'Production, Consumption, Prosumption: The Nature of Capitalism in the Age of the Digital "Prosumer"' (2010) 10 *Journal of Consumer Culture* 13.

Rushkoff, Douglas, 'There's More to Being a Journalist than Hitting the "Publish" Button' (2010) 64(2) *Neilman Reports* 39.

Russo, Julie L., 'User-Penetrated Content: Fan Video in the Age of Convergence' (2009) 48 *Cinema Journal* 125.

Salvato, Nick, 'Out of Hand: YouTube Amateurs and Professionals' (2009) 53 *TDR: The Drama Review* 67.

Schwabach, Aaron, 'The Harry Potter Lexicon and the World of Fandom: Fan Fiction, Outsider Works, and Copyright' (2009) 70 *University of Pittsburgh Law Review* 387.

Shao, Guosong, 'Understanding the Appeal of User-Generated Media: A Uses and Gratification Perspective' (2009) 19 *Internet Research* 7.

Simon, Jane, 'Recycling Home Movies' (2006) 20 *Continuum: Journal of Media and Cultural Studies* 189.

Singer, Jane B., 'Contested Autonomy: Professional and Popular Claims on Journalistic Norms' (2007) 8 *Journalism Studies* 79.

Sotamaa, Olli, 'Who's Game is This Anyway? Creative User-centred Design Practices among Gaming Cultures' (paper presented at The Good, the Bad and the Irrelevant: The User and the Future of Information and Communication Technologies, Uiah, Helsinki, 1–3 September 2003), pp. 257–259.

Stebbins, Robert A., 'The Amateur: Two Sociological Perspectives' (1997) 20 *Sociological Review* 582.

Stroude, Rachel L., 'Complimentary Creation: Protecting Fan Fiction as Fair Use' (2010) 14 *Marquette Intellectual Property Law Review* 191.

Tarrant, Patrick, 'Camera Movies: Awesome, I Fuckin' Shot Them' (2009) 10 *Journal of Media Practice* 149.

Taylor, Brian, 'Professionals and the Knowledge of Archaeology' (1995) 46 *British Journal of Sociology* 499.

Taylor, T. L., 'Whose Game Is This Anyway? Negotiating Corporate Ownership in a Virtual World' (paper presented at *Computer Games and Digital Cultures*, Tampere, Finland, 6–8 June 2002) 227.

Terranova, Tiziana, 'Free Labor: Producing Culture for the Digital Economy' (2000) 18(2) *Social Text* 33.

Tushnet, Rebecca, 'Legal Fictions: Copyright, Fan Fiction, and a New Common Law,' (1997) 17 *Loyola of Los Angeles Entertainment Law Journal* 651.

——, 'User-Generated Discontent: Transformation in Practice' (2008) 31 *Columbia Journal of Law & Arts* 497.

Ursell, Gillian, 'Television Production: Issues of Exploitation, Commodification and Subjectivity in UK Television Labour Markets' (2000) 22 *Media, Culture & Society* 805.

van den Berg, Bibi, and Ronald E. Leenes, 'Audience Segregation in Social Network Sites' (paper presented at Second IEEE International Conference on Social Computing/Second IEEE International Conference on Privacy, Security, Risk and Trust, Minneapolis, MN, 9 November 2010) available at http://ssrn.com/abstract=1706298.

van Dijck, José, 'Users Like You? Theorizing Agency in User-Generated Content' (2009) 31 *Media, Culture & Society* 41.

Von Lohmann, Fred, 'Unintended Consequences: Twelve Years Under the DMCA' (Report, Electronic Frontier Foundation, February 2010) www.eff.org/files/eff-unintended-consequences-12-years.pdf.

Walker, Rebecca A., 'Badgering Big Brother: Spectacle, Surveillance, and Politics in the Flash Mob' (2011) 7(2) *Liminalities: A Journal of Performance Studies* 1.

Winge, Theresa, 'Costuming the Imagination: Origins of Anime and Manga Cosplay' (2006) 1 *Mechademia* 65.

Wittel, Andreas, 'Toward a Network Sociality' (2001) 18 *Theory, Culture and Society* 51.

Zimmerman, Patricia R., 'Hollywood, Home Movies and Common Sense: Amateur Film as Aesthetic Dissemination and Social Control, 1950–1962' (1988) 27(4) *Cinema Journal* 23.

Zwick, Detlev, Samuel K. Bonsu and Aron Darmody, 'Putting Consumers to Work: "Co-creation" and New Marketing Govern-mentality' (2008) 8 *Journal of Consumer Culture* 163.

Media reportage and internet materials

Bradshaw, Paul, 'The Complicated Case of the (Now Not) Anonymous Police Blogger, *The Times*, and 'Public Interest' on *Online Journalism Blog* (16 June 2009): http://onlinejournalismblog.com/2009/06/16/the-complicated-case-of-the-now-not-anonymous-police-blogger-the-times-and-public-interest/.

Bronstad, Amanda, 'Viacom v. YouTube' Appeal May Decide Future of Web (14 December 2010) *National Law Journal*: :www.law.com/jsp/nlj/PubArticleNLJ.jsp?id=1202476144090.

Cohen, Noam, 'Use My photo? Not Without Permission', *New York Times* (online) 1 October 2007: www.nytimes.com/2007/10/01/technology/01link.html.

Elliott, Tim, 'Junior MasterChef Contract Indigestible', *Sydney Morning Herald* (online), 2 July 2011: www.smh.com.au/entertainment/junior-masterchef-contract-indigestible-20110701-1gvbl.html.

Ellis, John, 'Coalinga Grad Loses MySpace Rant Lawsuit', The Fresno Bee (Fresno, CA) 20 September 2010, available at http://0166244.blogspot.com/2010/09/heres-your.html.

Fletcher, Dan, 'How Facebook is Redefining Privacy' (20 May 2010) *Time Magazine* (online): www.time.com/time/magazine/article/0,9171,1990798,00.html.

Garfield, Bob, 'Listenomics' (10 Oct. 2005) *Advertising Age* 76(41), 1

Goldman, Eric, 'Republishing MySpace Post in Local Paper Might Be Intentional Infliction of Emotional Distress: Moreno v. Hanford Sentinel' on *Technology & Marketing Law Blog* (4 April 2009) at http://blog.ericgoldman.org/archives/2009/04/republishing_my.htm.

Grossman, Lev, 'Person of the Year 2010: Mark Zuckerberg' (15 December 2010) *Time Magazine* (online): www.time.com/time/specials/packages/article/0,28804,2036683_2037183_2037185,00.html.

Hilden, Julie, 'Is It a Violation of Privacy Law to Reproduce a MySpace Posting in a Context Where the Very People It Targets Will See It?' (27 April 2009) *Findlaw.com* at http://writ.news.findlaw.com/hilden/20090427.html.

Horton, Richard, 'NightJack: My Everyman Posts Seemed to Strike a Chord', *The Times* (online) 17 June 2009: http://technology.timesonline.co.uk/tol/news/tech_and_web/article6515061.ece.

Hunter, Thomas, '"Taken out of Context": Deveny Defends Twitter Comments on Logies Night', *The Age* (online), 4 May 2010: www.theage.com.au/entertainment/tv-and-radio/taken-out-of-context-deveny-defends-twitter-comments-on-logies-night-20100504-u50y.html.

Interactive Advertising Bureau, User Generated Content, Social Media and Advertising- An Overview (April 2008): www.iab.net/media/file/2008_ugc_platform.pdf.

Jones, Sam, 'A Fair Cop: Policeman's "Perfect" Blog Wins Orwell Prize', *Guardian* (online) 24 April 2009: www.guardian.co.uk/books/2009/apr/24/orwell-prize-jack-night-winner-blog.

Kakutani, Michiko, 'Books of the Times: The Cult of the Amateur', *New York Times* (online), 29 June 2007: www.nytimes.com/2007/06/29/books/29book.html.

——, 'A Rebel in Cyberspace, Fighting Collectivism', *New York Times* (online) 14 January 2010: www.nytimes.com/2010/01/15/books/15book.html.

Lanier, Jaron, 'One-Half of a Manifesto', *Wired* (online), December 2000: www.wired.com/wired/archive/8.12/lanier.html.

Lessig, Lawrence, 'Keen's "The Cult of the Amateur": BRILLIANT!' on *Lessig 2.0* (31 May 2007): http://lessig.org/blog/2007/05/keens_the_cult_of_the_amateur.html.

lifesforsharing, The T-Mobile Dance (16 January 2009) YouTube: www.youtube.com/watch?v=VQ3d3KigPQM.

McCool, Grant, 'Appeals Court Zeroes in on Viacom-YouTube Dispute', Reuters (online) 18 October 2011: www.reuters.com/article/2011/10/18/us-viacom-google-idUSTRE79H8EK20111018.

Mishra, Gaurav, 'The Curious Case of Night Jack Richard Horton: What Does It Mean for Blogger Anonymity?' on *Gauravonomics Blog* (28 June 2009) at www.gauravonomics.com/blog/the-curious-case-of-nightjack-richard-horton-what-does-it-mean-for-blogger-anonymity/.

Moltz, David, 'University Sues Student Blogger' (16 October 2009) Inside Higher Ed: www.insidehighered.com/news/2009/10/16/butler.

Moreno, Cynthia, *Coalinga Record*, 'Ode to Coalinga', full date not ascertainable, p. 4, available at http://media.fresnobee.com/smedia/2010/09/15/11/OdeToCoalinga.source.prod_affiliate.8.pdf.

Penberthy, David, 'Tweet nothings lack good taste and substance', *Weekend Australian* (Sydney), 8–9 May 2010, Inquirer, p. 7.

Reality Raver, 'Junior Masterchef—Would You Sign the Contract?' on Reality Ravings (1 July 2011): www.realityravings.com/2011/07/01/junior-masterchef-would-you-sign-the-contract/.

RockCritics.com, 'Everyone's a Rock Critic: The Lost Lester Bangs Interview' (1980). http://rockcriticsarchives.com/interviews/lesterbangs/lesterbangs.html.

Tassi, Paul, 'Minecraft's Notch: "Piracy is Not Theft"', *Forbes* (online) 4 March 2011: www.forbes.com/sites/insertcoin/2011/03/04/minecrafts-notch-piracy-is-not-theft/.

Townend, Judith, 'Right of a Blogger's Anonymity: A Selection of Views' on journalism.co.uk (17 June 2009): http://blogs.journalism.co.uk/editors/2009/06/17/right-of-a-bloggers-anonymity-a-selection-of-views/.

Index

Note: the reference 67n6 refers to note 6 on page 67.